Employees, Careers, and Job Creation

Employees, Careers, and Job Creation

Developing Growth-Oriented Human Resource Strategies and Programs

Manuel London, *Editor*

Foreword by Manuel London

Jossey-Bass Publishers • San Francisco

Substantial discounts on bulk quantities of Jossey-Bass books are available to corporations, professional associations, and other organizations. For details and discount information, contact the special sales department at Jossey-Bass Inc., Publishers.

(415) 433–1740; Fax (800) 605–2665.

For sales outside the United States, please contact your local Paramount Publishing International Office.

 Manufactured in the United States of America on Lyons Falls Pathfinder Tradebook. This paper is acid-free and 100 percent totally chlorine-free.

Library of Congress Cataloging-in-Publication Data

Employees, careers, and job creation : developing growth-oriented
  human resource strategies and programs / Manuel London, editor ;
  foreword by Manuel London. — 1st ed.
     p. cm. — (A joint publication in the Jossey-Bass management
series and the Jossey-Bass social and behavioral science series)
    Includes bibliographical references and index.
    ISBN 0–7879–0125–3 (alk. paper)
    1. Career development. 2. Displaced workers. 3. Job creation.
4. Occupational retraining. I. London, Manuel. II. Series: Jossey-
Bass management series. III. Series: Jossey-Bass social and
behavioral science series.
HF5549.5.C35E47 1995
331.25'92—dc20   95–9390

FIRST EDITION
HB Printing 10 9 8 7 6 5 4 3 2 1

A *joint publication in*
The Jossey-Bass Management Series
and
The Jossey-Bass Social and Behavioral Science Series

Society for Industrial and Organizational Psychology
Professional Practice Series

To Douglas W. Bray

Contents

Foreword

Employees, Careers, and Job Creation is part of the Professional Practice Series sponsored by the Society for Industrial and Organizational Psychology. The books in the series address contemporary ideas and problems, focus on how to get things done, and provide state-of-the-art technology based on theory and research from industrial and organizational psychology. We try to satisfy the needs of practitioners and those being trained for practice.

Douglas W. Bray, to whom the current volume is dedicated, served ably as the first series editor and edited the first volume, *Working with Organizations and Their People* (1991). This book examines the role of industrial and organizational psychologists as practitioners involved in evaluation, training, and organization development.

The second book, *Diversity in the Workplace* (1992), edited by Susan E. Jackson, offers cases and methods for creating and assessing a diverse workplace, managing workplace diversity through personal growth and team development, and strategic initiatives to manage workplace diversity.

Abraham K. Korman's *Human Dilemmas in Work Organizations: Strategies for Resolution* (1994) considers the expanding world of the human resource practitioner. Chapters describe programs for employee assistance, stress management, marginal performers, reorganizations, employee ethics, and elder care.

Ann Howard's book *Diagnosis for Organizational Change* (1994) focuses on organizational diagnosis for design and development. The contributors examine the assessment of human talent for staffing and training. They also provide an overview of the high-involvement workplace with a consideration of organization cultures, reward systems, and work teams.

These books were originally published by Guilford Press under the watchful and concerned guidance of Seymour Weingarten, senior editor. Beginning with this volume, all future books in this series will be published and distributed by Jossey-Bass Publishers. William Hicks, senior editor at Jossey-Bass, has provided expert oversight for this series and the Frontiers of Industrial and Organizational Psychology Series, also sponsored by the Society for Industrial and Organizational Psychology.

I am grateful to a valuable editorial board: Warner Burke, Pat Dyer, Nita French, Ann Howard, Allen Kraut, Walter Tornow, and Victor Vroom contributed many helpful ideas in the evolution of the current volume and others planned for the series. Future books are planned on employee attitude surveys, individual assessment, ethics, and employee loyalty and citizenship.

May 1995   Manuel London
                                                 State University of New York
                                                 Series Editor

Preface

This book examines ways human resource development programs contribute to an organization's viability and growth in tough economic times. It shows how industrial and organizational psychologists help to solve organizational and societal problems associated with corporate restructuring and redeployment. The programs described are alternatives to employee displacement and organizational downsizing, or they promote economic growth after layoffs have occurred. Some of these programs are internal to the organization as responses to shifting job requirements in relation to new organizational objectives. Other programs are external in that they focus on the retraining and redeployment of individuals who are already displaced. Still other programs demonstrate organizational initiatives that help employees create new ventures and career opportunities within or outside the organization.

Audience

Employees, Careers, and Job Creation is for industrial and organizational psychologists and other human resource professionals who contribute to establishing effective organizational strategies. It is also for human resource professionals who are consultants in such fields as outplacement, career counseling, training, and organization design. The book will help these professionals, and students preparing for these professions, evaluate the current economic and organizational scene, consider future trends, and understand the contribution of human resource development in changing organizations.

In addition, the book is for federal, state, and local government agencies, for instance, departments of labor and economic development and associated private industry councils charged with facilitating retraining and redeployment of displaced workers.

The book presents many suggestions for the design and enhancement of such programs in response to organizational downsizings and defense plant and military base closings. The ideas about how people cope with the psychological aspects of job displacement and about training methods for individuals in mid and late career should be useful to counselors and to continuing education departments in universities and community colleges that develop and deliver these programs.

Overview of the Contents

The authors explain processes for designing and implementing employee development programs that enhance organizational growth and career opportunities. Thus, the chapters not only describe innovative programs, they also show how to make them successful. The chapters are problem centered and practice oriented. They cover problems faced by human resource professionals and present ideas for overcoming barriers and increasing chances for individual and organizational success.

The book offers a diversity of perspectives based on research and practice. Authors focus on career management within organizations for current employees and on esteem building, internships, and community action for displaced employees. The chapters have implications for both organizational and public policies supporting retraining, redeployment, and economic development.

Employees, Careers, and Job Creation shows how career development programs prompt individual and organizational initiatives for job creation and economic growth. Career-development initiatives should reflect opportunities created by environmental and organizational changes (Campbell, 1991; Hall, 1986; London & Stumpf, 1986). Within organizations, changes in career opportunities for current employees occur as new ventures are established and existing areas of business decline. Employees who lose their jobs as a result of these changes need opportunities for development and redeployment. Reemployment in an economic climate of limited job vacancies must go beyond traditional outplacement strategies such as counseling, resume preparation, interview training, and networking to the creation of new ventures that expand employment opportunities.

This book emphasizes that individuals and organizations need to change their mindset about career development. We are experiencing major organizational transitions in response to changing technologies, competition, and the international economic and geopolitical scene. Career planning and counseling are insufficient responses to these sea changes, and individuals are finding they must shoulder the burden of ensuring their own employment security. While employees may be used to thinking about, and planning, their career in relation to their needs, desires, interests, and capabilities, they are finding that self-reflection and searching for a job match just don't work in many cases. They must be proactive in creating opportunities. Sometimes this involves new employment relationships or redefinition of existing ones, resulting in such arrangements as contracting, temporary employment, job sharing, and part-time positions. Employees are finding that they must continuously assess the changing environment and determine what they need to learn to be in demand. They have to understand how they add value to an enterprise and that their employment depends on continuously demonstrating their value.

The contributors to this book consider individuals' and organizations' roles in the creation of new opportunities for current employees within their own organizations and for displaced workers within other organizations or new ventures. Career development requires that current and displaced employees recognize organization changes and participate in their evolution as a means of enhancing the likelihood of continued employment. They should understand how organizational growth creates new opportunities and new determinants for career advancement. They should know how to add value and, in the process, create jobs for themselves and others. Moreover, they should understand, and be able to cope with, the frustrations of the job-creation and job-search process.

Organizations increasingly demand more from employees, sometimes taking harsh action in an effort to improve efficiency and increase profitability. However, they must learn to use their current employees to maximum advantage. The continued viability of the organization depends on the competence of employees to meet today's job demands and be ready for organizational changes. Organizations must support the continuous learning of their employees and be willing to give employees a chance to experiment with new ventures. Thus, organizations need ways to assess employees' skills, direct them into fruitful training programs, expand their experience base by placing them in different jobs, and allow them to show new ways they can add value to the firm. When layoffs are necessary, the organization can support job creation and business start-ups, thereby supporting the economy of the surrounding community.

Human resource professionals educate employees about these new responsibilities and the tools that help them. They show organizations how employee development can contribute to organizational change and growth. Moreover, they find ways to encourage individuals and organizations to create new career opportunities. The authors of this book show how human resource professionals can affect the strategies of the organization. They suggest that current human resource talent can be used to build new enterprises within the firm. They demonstrate the strategic role of human resources to the survival and enhancement of the organization. Also, they show how human resource professionals, as in-house staff members or outside consultants, help carry out organizational restructuring and outplacement in ways that create new ventures and job opportunities.

This book is divided into three parts. Part One considers career development programs in changing organizations, demonstrating how industrial and organizational psychology contributes to economic development and organizational growth. Part Two examines emerging patterns of employment, such as contingent and part-time work and entrepreneurship as a second career. Part Three gives examples of methods for career revitalization. It describes innovative programs for the retraining and redeployment of displaced workers. Emphasis is placed on processes for the effective design and implementation of such programs.

Acknowledgments

Together with the contributors, I dedicate this book to Douglas W. Bray. Doug optimizes the role of the human resource practitioner. His research and practice have been a model of how industrial and organizational psychology contributes to strategic organizational change and individual development. As the first editor of this Professional Practice Series, he set the stage for a focus on how to apply industrial and organizational psychology to key societal and organizational problems. This tradition continues with the present volume's focus on human resource strategies for employee development and job creation.

Stony Brook, New York   Manuel London
May 1995

References

Campbell, R. J. (1991). Human resource development strategies. In K. N. Wexley (Ed.), *Developing human resources* (pp. 1–34). Washington: Bureau of National Affairs.

Hall, D. T. (1986). An overview of current career development theory, research, and practice. In D. T. Hall and Associates (Eds.), *Career development in organizations* (pp. 1–20). San Francisco: Jossey-Bass.

London, M., & Stumpf, S. A. (1986). Individual and organizational career development in changing times. In D. T. Hall and Assoc. (Eds.), *Career development in organizations* (pp. 21–49). San Francisco: Jossey-Bass.

The Authors

Melissa A. Bilger is an organization development consultant in AT&T's finance department. In her more than thirteen years with this firm, she has served as operations manager, training manager, and human resource manager. She has developed technical, professional, and management training, as well as performance management, programs. She holds an MBA degree from the University of Pennsylvania's Wharton School.

Joel Brockner is professor of management in the Graduate School of Business, Columbia University. He received his Ph.D. degree (1977) in social/personality psychology from Tufts University. His research interests include the effects of organizational change (layoffs in particular) on employees' productivity and morale, self-processes in organizations, and decision making in response to "sunk costs." Brockner's articles have appeared in the leading journals in management and psychology. He also consults regularly to organizations on such issues as managing change, leadership, motivation, and decision making.

Jeff Casey is associate professor of management and policy at the State University of New York, Stony Brook, where he also holds a joint appointment in the Department of Political Science. He received his Ph.D. degree (1986) in psychology from the University of Wisconsin, Madison, and has held positions as research scientist at the Laboratory for Information and Decision Systems at the Massachusetts Institute of Technology and as visiting assistant professor at the Graduate School of Business, University of Chicago. His primary research interests are behavioral decision making (including judgment and decision making under risk and uncertainty, and psychological models of economic behavior) and human resource management (including retraining programs for professional career change and job performance feedback systems). During 1993 he co-directed the retraining program described in Chapter Eleven.

Joseph F. Coates is president of Coates & Jarratt, Inc., Washington D.C. (formerly J. F. Coates, Inc.), a policy research organization specializing in the study of the future. Probing the future carries Joe into activities all over the world. He has worked as a futurist in business, industry, and government for over thirty years. He is adjunct professor at the George Washington University as well as coauthor of *Future Work: Seven Critical Forces Reshaping Work and the Work Force in North America* (with J. Jarratt and J. B. Mahaffie, 1990). He writes columns for *Technological Forecasting and Social Change* and *Research and Technology Management.*

David V. Day is assistant professor of psychology at Pennsylvania State University. He received his Ph.D. degree (1989) in industrial and organizational psychology from the University of Akron. His primary research interests include leadership, performance appraisal, and personality influences in organizations, especially with regard to person-environment fit. Day serves on the editorial board of *Leadership Quarterly* and as a reviewer for numerous professional journals.

John H. Eggers is program manager, lead researcher, and designer of the Center for Creative Leadership's Entrepreneurial Leadership Programs (in Greensboro, North Carolina). He is author of numerous articles on the topic of entrepreneurship. The American Society for Training and Development has acknowledged his work as "the first to demonstrate a clear link between leadership and entrepreneurship" (*Training and Development,* August 1994). He is also the co-designer and coauthor of all three of the center's entrepreneurial leadership and organizational culture assessment instruments. Prior to joining the center, John started, owned, and operated several successful small companies. One of the most viable was Sport Dynamics, Inc., the original distribution and marketing company for Oakley sunglasses and goggles worldwide. Eggers received his Ph.D. degree in industrial/organizational psychology from the California School of Professional Psychology in San Diego, California.

Daniel C. Feldman is professor of management and Distinguished Business Partnership Foundation Fellow at the University of South Carolina. He received his Ph.D. degree from Yale University. He is author of over seventy articles and five books on career development and organizational behavior, including *Managing Careers in Organizations* (1988). He has served as chair of the careers division of the Academy of Management and on the editorial boards of the *Academy of Management Journal,* the *Journal of Management,* and *Human Resource Management.* Feldman has won numerous undergraduate and graduate teaching awards and was recently named Eli Lilly Senior Teaching Fellow at the University of South Carolina.

Amy E. Hurley is assistant professor of human resource management at the Catholic University for Leadership and Career Studies at Emory University. She received her Ph.D. degree in business management from the Stern School of Business at New York University. She has published in the *Journal of Applied Psychology* and has presented papers at numerous conferences. Hurley is a member of the Academy of Management and the Society for Industrial and Organizational Psychology. Her research interests include the application of behavioral decision theory to strategic aspects of career mobility and executive succession. She has recently examined the managerial promotion process within large companies and the accuracy of employee perceptions of factors contributing to promotion.

Jennifer Jarratt is vice president of Coates & Jarratt, Inc. She received her M.S. degree in studies of the future from the University of Houston, Clear Lake, where she taught in 1990–91 as a visiting instructor in the future studies program. She is coauthor of *Future Work: Seven Critical Forces Reshaping Work and the Work Force in North America* (with J. F. Coates and J. B. Mahaffie, 1990). She has also been responsible for several projects on the future of work and other topics, including a forthcoming book with the American Society of Association Executives titled *Managing Your Future as an Association: Thinking About Trends and Working with Their Consequences, 1994–2020.*

Harold G. Kaufman is professor of management and director of the organizational behavior program at Polytechnic University in Brooklyn, New York, where he has taught since 1970. He specializes in the study of the utilization, obsolescence, and development of professionals, with a focus on technical careers. He has reported his research in over sixty publications, including three books. His first book, *Obsolescence and Professional Career Development* (1974), was cited by the Harvard Business School as advancing the state of knowledge in the personnel field and is now considered a classic. He has presented the results of his studies to industry as well as government organizations in the United States and abroad. He received his Ph.D. degree (1970) in industrial psychology from New York University.

Larry R. Last is associate program director for the Center for Commercial Competitiveness and was instrumental in the start-up activities for the first entrepreneurial training program. He received his M.S. degree in electrical engineering from the University of Cincinnati. Prior to his retirement from the General Electric Company in 1993, he was a technical/program management executive, with thirty years of accomplishments in the area of new-product development (aerospace, military, and commercial), production, marketing, and business development.

Carrie R. Leana is associate professor of business administration and of international and public affairs at the University of Pittsburgh, where she also serves as coordinator of the organizational behavior and human resources faculty. She has published widely on the topics of employee participation programs, authority structures at work, and the effects of plant closings and business restructuring on individuals and organizations. Her recent book, *Coping with Job Loss: How Individuals, Organizations, and Communities Respond to Layoffs,* was a finalist for the Academy of Management's Best Book Award for 1993. She also serves as a consultant for a variety of for-profit and not-for-profit organizations and has received numerous awards for her public service activities.

Robert J. Lee is president of the Center for Creative Leadership in Greensboro, North Carolina. Previously he has been co-chairman of Lee Hect Harrison, a major career services and outplacement counseling firm. He is founder and past president of the Association of Outplacement Firms International and is a charter fellow of the Outplacement Institute. He received his Ph.D. degree in industrial and organizational psychology from Case Western Reserve University.

Manuel London is professor of management at the State University of New York, Stony Brook, and director of the university's Center for Human Resource Studies in the Harriman School for Management and Policy. Prior to coming to Stony Brook in 1989, London spent twelve years at AT&T in a series of human resources and training positions as a manager and researcher. Before that he taught in the business school at the University of Illinois, Champaign, for three years. His recent books include *Developing Managers, Change Agents: New Roles and Innovation Strategies for Human Resource Professionals* (winner of the 1989 Book Award given by the American Society for Personnel Administration), *Managing the Training Enterprise* (1989), and *Career Growth and Human Resource Strategies* (1988). London has served on the editorial boards of *Administrative Science Quarterly,* the *Journal of Applied Psychology, Personnel Psychology,* the *Academy of Management Review,* and the *Academy of Management Journal.* He has served on the board of governors of the Academy of Management and on the executive board of the Society for Industrial and Organizational Psychology. He is a fellow of the American Psychological Association and the American Psychological Society. He is currently editor of the Society for Industrial and Organizational Psychology's Professional Practice Series. He received his Ph.D degree (1974) in industrial and organizational psychology from the Ohio State University. His areas of research and practice are human resource development, career motivation, and appraisal programs with a recent emphasis on upward and 360-degree feedback.

Edward M. Mone is an organization development consultant in AT&T's finance department. In his more than twelve years with this firm, he has served in a variety of positions, developing programs in such areas as management and leadership development, career development, performance management, and strategic human resources planning. He is coauthor of *Career Management and Survival in the Workplace* and is completing his doctoral degree in adult and continuing education at Columbia University.

Robert W. E. Peterson, CFPIM, is program director for the Worker Enterprise Development Program at the Center for Commercial Competitiveness. He received his M.S. degree in industrial engineering from the Stevens Institute of Technology. Peterson's experience includes information systems management, manufacturing management, and college and adult education. He is a fellow in the American Production and Inventory Control Society.

Richard H. Price is professor and chair of the organizational psychology program at the University of Michigan. He is also research scientist and program director in the social environment and health program at the Institute for Social Research, where he serves as the director of the Michigan Prevention Research Center, funded by the National Institute of Mental Health. He is a fellow of the American Psychological Association, the American Psychological Society, and the Society for the Psychological Study of Social Problems. His articles have appeared in the *Academy of Management Journal,* the *Journal of Applied Psychology, Human Resources Management,* the *Journal of Health and Social Behavior,* and the *Psychological Bulletin.* Price has served as a consultant to a variety of corporations, foundations, government agencies, and foreign governments.

Joseph M. Pufahl is a Long Island entrepreneur with twenty-two years of experience in manufacturing and product design. He was co-director of the Jobs Project Retraining Program and director of the Executive Management Center at the University at Stony Brook from 1992 to 1994. Pufahl is now consulting in the rapidly emerging field of computer-based patient records and medical devices for the geriatrics community, and he assists firms in developing strategic alliances. He is president-elect of the Long Island chapter of the American Society for Training and Development and serves on the advisory board for the Institute for Retraining.

Jack Rappaport was the first program executive for the Center for Commercial Competitiveness and retired in June 1993 at the successful conclusion of the first entrepreneurial training program.

He received his M.S. degree in engineering management from Syracuse University. At his retirement from CAE-Link Corporation in 1992, he was senior vice president of operations. Prior to joining CAE-Link, Rappaport spent approximately thirty years in various management and engineering positions in the IBM Federal Systems Division.

James W. Smither is associate professor in the management department at La Salle University in Philadelphia. Previously he was a manager in corporate human resources at AT&T, where he developed and validated procedures for selecting professional and management-level employees. Smither's research on recruiting, personnel selection, and performance appraisal has been published in journals such as the *Journal of Applied Psychology, Personnel Psychology,* and *Organizational Behavior and Human Decision Processes.* He is also a member of the editorial board of *Personnel Psychology* and serves as a reviewer for several other scholarly journals. He received his Ph.D. degree in industrial and organizational psychology from Stevens Institute of Technology.

Jeffrey A. Sonnenfeld is professor of organization and management and the director of the Center for Leadership and Career Studies at Emory Business School. Sonnenfeld was a professor at Harvard Business School for a decade before joining the Emory faculty, where he specializes in human resource management, interpersonal behavior, and career management and executive development. He received his Ph.D. degree from Harvard University. Sonnenfeld has received the Irwin Award for Social Research in Industry, AT&T's Hawthorne Fellowship for Social Research in Industry, and the John P. Whitehead Faculty Fellowship and has twice won Emory's Outstanding Educator Award. Sonnenfeld's book *The Hero's Farewell: What Happens When CEOs Retire* was designated *Business Week's* "standout new management book of the year" in 1988 and earned the executive search community's Golden Baton Award. Sonnenfeld is continuing this line of research on leadership transitions while conducting research on executive development patterns at various levels in the firm.

Robert J. Vance is associate director of the Center for Applied Behavioral Sciences at Pennsylvania State University. He received his

Ph.D. degree (1981) in industrial and organizational psychology from Pennsylvania State University. Prior to joining Penn State in 1990, he served on the psychology faculty at Ohio State University for nine years. His research and teaching interests are in the areas of personnel selection, job performance measurement, work motivation, and organizational development. Vance serves on the editorial board of *Human Performance* and as a reviewer for numerous professional journals.

Amiram D. Vinokur is research scientist at the Institute for Social Research, University of Michigan. He is co-principal investigator of the Michigan Prevention Research Center at the Survey Research Center. His research focuses on determinants and consequences of stress in the areas of health, work, and unemployment and on the roles of social undermining and social support in the stress and coping process.

Carin A. Webb is program director for the Small and Medium Enterprise Information Service Program at the Center for Commercial Competitiveness. She has a B.A. degree in education and experience in both the education and business worlds. Her experience includes general management as CEO of a small business, management and advising positions for several nonprofit agencies' boards of directors, and both elementary and adult education.

Gerrit Wolf has been professor at the Harriman School for Management and Policy and also in the department of psychology at the State University of New York, Stony Brook, since 1985. He received his Ph.D. in social psychology from Cornell University. Wolf has served on the management and psychology faculties of Yale University, Georgia Tech, and the University of Arizona and managed the organizational behavior area at these schools. His present teaching and research interest is entrepreneurship. In 1993, he received a Fulbright Fellowship, serving as the Alexander Hamilton Chair of Entrepreneurship at the SEED Foundation and the Economic Sciences University in Budapest, Hungary.

Employees, Careers, and Job Creation

CHAPTER 1

Employee Development and Job Creation
Trends, Problems, Opportunities

Jennifer Jarratt
Joseph F. Coates

Continuing to produce effectively with a workforce that lives in fear of being laid off is one of many ongoing challenges for the management of large corporations. Besides the threat of a new round of cost cutting, many other factors and trends are reshaping the recruitment, retention, and development of the workforce in the 1990s. The practitioner who can identify these trends and interpret their significance for the future workforce will be able to use that knowledge to inform and direct organizational initiatives.

In this introduction we look at several trends that have important consequences for future employee development. These trends are only a sample. The reader can identify and interpret many more. In each case, we look at what the trend implies for human resources strategies and what it might mean for a person's choice of job or career. The human resources practitioner will find implications here for forecasting and planning the future workforce.

Some of the most important trends for the U.S. workforce are in education, because the health and effectiveness of the educational system determine the quality and capabilities of future entry-level workers. Furthermore, it is becoming increasingly obvious that what people learn in school or college will not be enough to ensure effective performance at work for long. Organizations are discovering that everyone must go on learning if the organization

1

is to survive. Table 1.1 summarizes the trends in this chapter, their economic implications, and their implications for employee development and job creation.

The Collapse of U.S. Public Education

The United States is in the second generation of a decline in the quality of public education. No longer only a matter of short-changing poor, rural, and minority children, the decay in academic performance is hitting the core of middle-class society. By any measure, literacy, understanding the written word, numeracy, geographic knowledge, social science knowledge, and historic knowledge show continuing decline. The U.S. Census Bureau estimated that 13 percent of Americans over fourteen were illiterate in 1982.

The United States is not alone in having a deteriorating educational system. European countries are experiencing a similar decline. In Denmark, a country with an apparent high rate of literacy, college freshmen cannot write a sentence in their own language without making errors (Dr. Christian Jensen Butler, Aarhus University, Denmark, personal communication, 1993).

Fortunately for the future, although education is a difficult, recalcitrant, and obstinate system, it is at last being outflanked by new, non-school-based education and learning. Unfortunately for the near term, it has delivered a generation of poorly educated adults to a workforce that urgently needs more education and skills. Every business should anticipate a workforce that is totally unprepared. At the higher levels, those with a college education, for example, may not know they are underprepared for the demands of work. One consequence for employee development is that young workers do not understand the labor market, how it works, how volatile it will continue to be, and how to present their skills and interests in a marketable way.

The proportion of young people coming out of the educational system with above-average skills and knowledge is narrowing, thus reducing the potential labor pool. Employers must either recruit more widely or realize that those hired will need remedial training. A strategy for tackling this problem is to establish a "university" to teach job skills. Some industries, such as financial services, are joining together to do this. Some corporations, such as

**Table 1.1. Trends Affecting Employee Development
and Job Creation Strategies.**

The Trend	Economic Implications	Implications for Employee Development and Job Creation
The collapse of U.S. public education.	Poorly prepared workforce, fewer with above-average skills. Threat to business competitiveness.	Young workers do not understand the labor market, or know how to present their skills. Remedial education and skill training are needed.
Expanding opportunities for learning outside the schoolhouse.	Large market for lifelong education, formal and informal, will develop.	Organizations can take advantage of new learning opportunities and create easy access for the workforce. People will need to broaden and maintain their skills and knowledge, for emerging job technologies.
Expanding corporate training.	Training and education related to work will become a larger part of the economy.	Training can be everyone's key to continued employability. More people should be given access to learning.
Continuing shift away from manufacturing and into service and information work.	High productivity areas of the U.S. economy, agriculture and manufacturing employ few workers. Productivity issues will arise for services and information-based jobs and workers.	Almost all future jobs will require computer literacy, good communications skills, ability to process information.
The growth of the contingent workforce.	A larger portion of the U.S. workforce will have less job security than	Future issue for contingent workers will be connecting with jobs.

Table 1.1. Trends Affecting Employee Development and Job Creation Strategies, (continued).

The Trend	Economic Implications	Implications for Employee Development and Job Creation
	formerly, thus changing their economic behavior. Some protection for such workers by regulation may become necessary.	Temporary firms today are growing huge, supplying this need. Other issues include how much orientation, training, HR support do contingents require?
The emerging distributed workforce.	Patterns of commuting, shopping, service needs, will change. Increased demands for in-home services are possible. Potential effects on downtown office space as workers distribute themselves.	New approaches to development required for workers who are mostly out of the office. What assurances do they have of being considered for promotion and good assignments? Distributed work will create opportunities for niche businesses and careers based on work at home.
Women's increasing impact on the workforce.	Working parents mean few adults are home during the day. Greater demand for support services likely, as well as for convenience and timeliness.	Many women will gain business experience on the job then leave to start their own enterprise. Promising women must be developed and set on a leadership path before this occurs. HR should take into account that women's goals and workstyles may be different from those of men.

Table 1.1. Trends Affecting Employee Development and Job Creation Strategies, (continued).

The Trend	Economic Implications	Implications for Employee Development and Job Creation
Middle-aging of the workforce.	The large baby boom generation, as it ages, will reshape the economy. Current concern about health care is typical. Work-force costs could be higher, as a result of more experienced and mature workers.	The reinvigoration of mature workers with training, education, and new assignments could be critical for older workforces. Mature workers may need to look at new life choices and careers.
Growing diversity among the entry-level workforce.	The U.S. population is becoming more diverse and this will be reflected in the workforce, region-ally at first. Regulations such as the ADA also increase diversity.	Flexibility is the sensible approach to meeting each person's needs for development. Flexibility in job sharing and contracting should also make more jobs available.
Globalization of the American economy and U.S. business.	International compe-tition will sharpen as all economies globalize.	HR responsibilities for overseas workforces will increase. More U.S. workers will work over-seas and in the U.S. for foreign-owned compa-nies. The ability to man-age cultural differences must be developed.
Information technologies' spreading impacts on business.	Information tech-nologies will continue to shake up business and the economy.	Employees need tech-nical training, and must learn how to operate with discretion in an open information environment. The

**Table 1.1. Trends Affecting Employee Development
and Job Creation Strategies, (continued).**

The Trend	Economic Implications	Implications for Employee Development and Job Creation
		design, building, and support of electronic networks will create new occupations.
The growing imbalance between workers and management.	The turbulence of the transition to an information-driven global economy will continue. Dissatisfied and laid-off workers may call for government or union action.	Few workers will trust the organization to keep its promises of jobs and career development. However, most large organizations have institutionalized job insecurity by preparing people to leave the minute they are hired. Professional and other associations will be looked to for networking and job information.

Motorola, have established their own institutions. In these institutions workers can acquire new skills and find out what career opportunities might be developed.

The business community must pay attention to the effects of the decline in quality of public education. The need for a workforce that can perform effectively and enhance corporate competitiveness is obvious, immediate, and central. On the other hand, an educated customer base is necessary for a healthier and more positive business environment. An educated customer base implies a substantially more informed electorate to shape the future of the nation and hence the future of business.

The states, in their drive to bring in new business and more jobs, are affecting public education. For example, a state educational initiative in South Carolina has turned around the local school systems, particularly in the area around Spartanburg, which has become a center of foreign manufacturing.

Lifelong Learning

By far the most positive trend in U.S. education is the expanding demand for adult and lifelong education. So far, however, our educational system has not met the need for universal, lifelong, completely individualized education.

Note that education for lifelong learning comes in many forms and styles, and currently is more informal, and more customized, than the education offered in school (the primary and secondary educational systems) and college (tertiary education). Methods for lifelong learning include on-the-job training, television, books, magazines, newspapers, museums, conferences, tourist travel, tours, package inserts, backs of cereal boxes and grocery bags, videos, movies, self-help groups, open universities, online communications—almost any medium or source of information that delivers knowledge. Much work-based training and education tends to expand on college-level work or makes up the deficiencies of the formal educational system, but there is no reason why it should do only this. Any forecast of the human resources needs for a corporation must build in assumptions of lifelong education and training. An individual's plans for career development must carry the same assumptions. Some of the industrial unions have realized this; the United Auto Workers agreement with Ford specifically included all kinds of quaternary education, recognizing that its members needed to keep on learning in order to survive in an industry that was employing fewer workers in traditional jobs.

Information technology, workplace training needs, and the tendency of an educated population to regard learning as worthwhile recreation will drive quaternary education for the next decade. To encourage people's desire to learn more, human resources must promote new learning technologies and create easy access to new knowledge at the individual's convenience.

Expanding Corporate Roles

About 20 percent of the U.S. adult population (some 50 million people) has had some college education, and more than 80 percent has at least a high school education. Both groups, if they are part of the workforce, are candidates for alternative forms of college-level education or lifelong learning. At least 75 percent of the workforce—100 million people—will need training or retraining in this decade to meet the new demands of their jobs.

If companies are to invest more in training and education, they must be able to measure their value. Companies will have to make judgments between the relative values of in-house versus contractor-supplied training and between in-house and off-site education.

Training magazine's annual survey of corporate training found that U.S. organizations budgeted $48 billion for training in 1993, almost three quarters of it for training-staff salaries. And 21 percent of all companies doing training sponsor some form of remedial education, 10 percent more than in 1989. As might be expected, the largest companies, those with workforces over 10,000, are more likely to be doing remedial or basic education (36 percent). Reading and math are most often offered, with 48 percent offering English as a second language.

Besides gaps in education and lifelong learning, a continuing need to train comes from changing technologies and changing business practices. A stronger focus on the customer, for example, means that more people in the organization must be trained in how to work effectively with customers. Another driving force will be the growing need for cross-cultural skills, to work with a more diverse U.S. workforce and with the intercultural demands of expanding global business. One problem in the past has been the imbalance of training investment, with most of the education being offered to managers and professionals. In future, human resources practitioners will need to maintain wider access to the corporation's training resources. Lifelong learning is a strategy on the one hand for retaining effective workers, and on the other an insurance for the individual workers that they will remain employable elsewhere should the need arise.

Major trends in work that the human resources planner ought

to be aware of include changes in what workers do, when they work, where they work, and how they get paid.

The Growth of Service and Information-Related Work

In 1920, about 40 percent of the U.S. workforce was on the farm. Today, no more than 2.5 percent work in agriculture. Knowledge replaced people with machinery. In manufacturing, knowledge and smart machines are replacing workers (U.S. Department of Labor, 1994). Figure 1.1 shows that the redistribution of the U.S. workforce between two major sectors, from goods-producing to service-producing, will continue into the next century.

Where are the rest of the workers? In a broad area called service, which is, to a large extent, made up of information workers. This workforce, unlike earlier generations of workers, no longer generally faces physical stress or dangerous conditions at work. It is more sedentary, and most of its safety and health concerns are

Figure 1.1. The Ongoing Redistribution of Jobs in the U.S. Workforce.

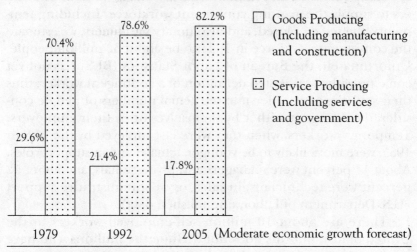

□ Goods Producing (Including manufacturing and construction)

▫ Service Producing (Including services and government)

Source: Franklin, 1993, p. 47.

above the neck. Nor, as we discuss later, does it have a fixed site for work, as manufacturing and agricultural workers do. Its effectiveness depends on its ability to process information, a key factor that human resources planning should keep in mind.

The ability to process information is one factor in the information worker's success; the other, which will need to be developed, is the ability to communicate well in person and electronically. Information technology enables more people to communicate with each other over distance and regardless of time, but it does not ensure that they will be able to do so effectively. Workers may need to learn the skills of working with a team, some of whose members they have never met.

The Growth of the Contingent Workforce

The large corporation today wants to be more like a small company, able to shift its people quickly to new tasks. With this goes a desire to shift the administrative and financial burden of a large permanent workforce onto other, external organizations like Manpower, Inc., that can then contract to supply people and skills. Often the contractor will be an individual worker who contracts to supply his services and makes his own arrangements about how and where to do the work.

Manpower, Inc. and similar firms are hiring millions of workers to supply the growing contingent workforce. Including temporary, the self-employed, and involuntary part-timers, we estimate the contingent workforce in 1994 to be about 32 million people. Unfortunately, the Bureau of Labor Statistics (BLS) has not yet come up with an accepted definition of a contingent worker; thus their statistics may understate the actual numbers of people considered contingent, either by themselves or by their employers. Temporary workers, when they were last surveyed by the BLS in 1985, were more likely to be younger, female, and in support roles. About 11 percent were managers and professionals, and about 52 percent were technicians, in sales, or in administrative support (U.S. Department of Labor, unpublished data).

There are about 10 million self-employed workers in the United States, but this does not include the millions who have small businesses that they have incorporated, who are therefore counted as salaried workers. These 10 million plus are the core of the U.S. army of contract workers. Figure 1.2 shows that self-employment is increasing overall except in agriculture.

The part-time workforce is more than 20 million people. Many people in this workforce today work part time because they cannot find full-time work. They are also less likely to receive benefits (see Table 1.2), more likely to be female (13.6 million in 1992, compared with 6.9 million men), young, and in sales, administrative support, and services. Outsourcing of the recruiting and hiring functions (that is, purchasing these services from other firms) will further erode the loyalty of the worker to the company, creating new issues in commitment and reliability.

Workers' drive for more security and stability at work than can be gained in temporary and contingent jobs will gather momentum

Figure 1.2. Trends in Self-Employment, 1968–1992.

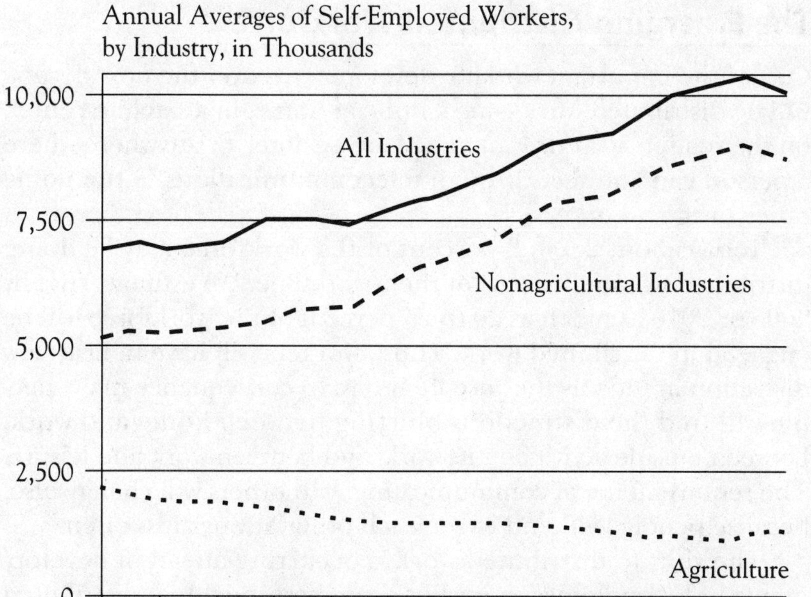

Annual Averages of Self-Employed Workers, by Industry, in Thousands

Source: U.S. Department of Labor, 1988.

Table 1.2. Workers Receiving Benefits from Their Employers.

	Part time	Full time
Health insurance	15.4	72.0
Sick leave	18.2	63.7
Disability insurance	9.2	43.5

in the next decade, leading to new workplace and benefits policies and new government policy and regulation. In the meantime, human resources managers must evaluate their approach to the contingent workforce. How much training do contingent workers need to perform effectively, for example? How much do they actually get? Senior management will look to human resources planners to forecast the relative size of the permanent core workforce and how large its backup of contingent or contract workers needs to be to meet business goals.

The Emerging Distributed Workforce

One of the important worklife developments over the next decade will be distributed work—work done at home, in a satellite center, on the road in a car or van, in a plane or hotel, or anywhere where a person can connect through telecommunications to the home office or to co-workers.

Today about 2.5 to 3 percent of the workforce may be doing distributed work all or part of their worktime. We estimate that by 2005 or 2010 as much as 20 to 25 percent of the workforce will be engaged in distributed work. Those workers will have radical new discretion in the way they use their day. In consequence many people will find the distinctions blurring between home and work, between outside activities and work, and between work and leisure. The requirements of communicating with others will change also, because people will tend to see each other at work less often.

The shift to distributed work is occurring ahead of developments in technologies that will become essential to a distributed workforce. These include effective, high-speed digital telecommunications, widespread, low-cost videoconferencing, and extensive computer networking. Distributed workers will include telecommuters for whom the computer is an essential business aid, but also other kinds of workers, such as those in sales, consulting, maintenance and repair, and services. For these workers, computers will be important tools but not central to their jobs.

Telecommuters today are likely to be between thirty-five and thirty-seven years old. Three-quarters of them are part of a dual-income household with a median income of $40,000. About half have children under eighteen, and about a quarter have children under six (U.S. Department of Transportation, 1993). This indicates that one of the important drivers of distributed work is the pressured working parent who needs flexibility. From the corporate point of view, distributed work potentially saves office overhead. The Clean Air Act requires companies with more than two hundred employees in metropolitan areas to reduce their workforce's commuting mileage 25 percent by 1996, creating another driver for distributed work. About 50 percent of distributed workers today work from one to three days a week out of the office, then work the remainder in the office or at another work site. Few work entirely at home. About 25 percent consider themselves telecommuters but work less than eight hours a week at home (U.S. Department of Transportation, 1993).

This varied pattern is likely to continue for the next five to ten years as companies and people explore the possibilities of distributed work. It has been easier for smaller organizations to experiment with distributed work, particularly informal telecommuting. However, the use of distributed work is now growing most rapidly among large companies, those with more than a thousand employees.

Communication with the distant worker will be more electronic than face to face. As distributed work becomes more widespread, the dominant mode of communication within and outside the organization will be electronic. Whole organizations will shift to doing business by phone, network, e-mail, voice mail, and video-conferencing. Managers and workers will need training and practice in achieving and maintaining effective relationships with co-workers through electronic communications. One of the barriers to be overcome could be managers' resistance to dispersing the workforce beyond their line of sight.

As this trend develops, new issues could arise in maintaining commitment to the organization's goals among people who have never seen or met most of the people they work with or for. New developments in personal video technology may help. If it is important for two people working together to see each other, then an image in the corner of the computer screen could increase personal contact.

Distributed work may open many career opportunities to people who were limited by their reluctance or inability to move for the sake of a job, just as it expands the recruitment and retention options for employers.

Impact of Women on the Workforce

The increasing commitment of women to education and to full-time work is creating revolutionary change in the workplace. The presence of women at work is changing the workplace for everyone. Their absence from the home is influencing family life, education, family eating habits, recreation, entertainment, and indeed every aspect of the U.S. economy.

Four key issues relate to women in the workplace. The first is pay equity. Women earn, on average, only 71 cents for every dollar men earn. This gap varies by field, education, experience, and by country. Also, highly educated young women may be paid more than young men on entering the workforce, but by the time they reach senior status, they could be earning much less. According to surveys, women executives are losing ground. In 1982, they earned about 68 percent of male executives' pay. By 1992, their average pay had fallen to 57 percent of the men's (Kim, 1994).

The second issue is pressure on time and concerns for children and family. Working mothers are demanding but not always being given the flexibility that will enable them to integrate work with home life. Child care, family care, and often elder care are still considered women's responsibilities, and their needs to have these responsibilities taken into account at work will eventually change the workplace for everybody, making it more flexible and more responsive to family and personal needs.

Children today are found in smaller numbers per family, and as a result, their psychological value will increase. This leads to guilt about whether all their needs are being met, and that guilt is primarily carried by working women. Their guilt is not enough to drive them out of the workforce, but it is enough to be a dominant factor in their worklives and thus also the worklives of those around them.

The monster issue on the horizon is elder care. One of our clients with 45,000 employees canvassed the workers and found that 5 percent had a current elder care problem and 50 percent anticipated a problem in the next decade. Why is this a problem? Because you cannot treat a sentient, alive, educated, informed seventy-year-old the way you treat a seven-year-old. You can warehouse a seven-year-old in day care, but you cannot do that with an adult. Elder care calls for innovations in management. To try to handle older people the way we handle children will break both the family bank and the corporate bank.

The third issue for corporations is the rise of the two-income household. The average married couple with two incomes takes home 153 percent of the single-earner income. And many couples today earn 200 to 250 percent of a single-earner income. Millions of households for the first time have enough money to put six or twelve months of income equivalent in the bank. As a result, an epidemic of independence is sweeping across the workplace. Anybody with six months' pay in her savings can leave a job that becomes unsatisfactory. The best and the brightest, the ones most important to the future of the organization, are the best-educated, married to a worker who has an equally high income, have the broadest view of the world, and have the widest range of options.

The balance of power in the dual-earning couple's relationship is also changing, especially in situations where women are out-earning their partners. This may lead couples to evaluate career moves, relocations, and job changes based on the economic potential of either partner. Decisions on career options will be made among at least three people: the employer, the worker, and the worker's partner. Human resources managers will do well to acknowledge this.

The fourth issue, the feminizing of the workplace, will occur as more women become managers and leaders in their fields. Their needs, interests, and particular approaches will begin to influence everyone's worklife. The rise of sexual harassment lawsuits over the past decade is an example of women seeking a solution to a troublesome problem they encounter at work. The outcomes are change in how people at work treat one another and a reevaluation of what workplace behavior is and is not acceptable. Women are not now well represented as either managers or executives. But the pressure from below ensures they will move into the executive suite early in the next century. If change at the top is made too difficult, outstanding women in the corporation have the option to move on. To retain top talent, businesses should acknowledge the difficulties of bringing them into the mainstream leadership and develop a career strategy with promising female (and minority) candidates well before they are likely to leave. Even with the best will in the world, however, practitioners should be aware that this strategy will not always succeed. The best career opportunities now for women with business and management experience are in breaking away and starting their own enterprises. According to the National Association of Women Business Owners, more people today are employed in women-owned businesses in the United States than in all the Fortune 500 companies combined (*Reading Across Boundaries,* 1994).

More women in the leadership of organizations will have impacts on international business, as women become managers and executives in the company's operations outside the country. The achievements of U.S. women executives may open opportunities for women in cultures where women now have fewer opportunities. As women achieve political power, they will bring up and deal with neglected or dormant business issues, such as pay inequity.

Middle-Aging of the Workforce

The baby boom, whose entry-level numbers kept the workforce young in the 1970s, now leads the middle-aging of that workforce into the twenty-first century. The median age of the workforce, which had dropped to 34.5 in 1979, will rise to 38.9 by 2000. The end of the 1990s will see the completion of a shift to a workforce and a society dominated by middle-aging boomers. Their behavior, wants, needs, and ideas will set the standard for the workplace, the government, and the media. As the leading edge of the baby boom encounters each new concern of middle-aging—career plateauing, weight gain, the need for elder care, retirement planning—it will attempt to redefine society's goals to meet its needs. Employers could face rising costs associated with a maturing workforce—in pay, benefits, pensions, and health care—and with the need for professional development and retraining to keep people's skills current.

Dealing with potential problems arising from a maturing workforce may require automating some routine operations. Other work could be done part time, at home, or on more relaxed schedules. Wellness and fitness programs could be seen as an investment in maintaining energy and commitment. Planning a strategy to recruit young staff now is another alternative.

Other demographically driven workplace issues, beside those of the baby boom, will compete for time and attention: legal and illegal immigration and the health, education, and welfare of immigrant families, to mention a few. It will be important for human resources forecasters to keep a close eye on the internal demography of their workforce and to maintain a desired balance in age, gender, ethnicity, and background.

Some organizations today, particularly older corporations with static technology and hiring freezes, are experiencing rapid aging of their workforces. A conscious effort to bring in younger workers could be critical to the company's well-being and survival in the twenty-first century. The reinvigoration of older workers with new training, education, and opportunities for new assignments will be necessary too.

Early retirement has been one way for companies to encourage mature workers to leave but this may be less attractive for today's workers, who may have less financial stability and will not have generous pension and health care benefits to look forward to. Lifelong learning, therefore, becomes an important strategy for companies and individuals alike.

Growing Diversity Among the Entry-Level Workforce

The American workforce is growing more diverse as more women and minorities enter it. By 2005, for example, the 150 million U.S. workforce will be 73 percent white, 12 percent black, 11.2 percent Hispanic, and 4.3 percent Asian and other minorities. Figure 1.3 shows in more detail the changes over the next ten years.

Figure 1.3. The Changing Composition of the U.S. Workforce, 1990 and 2005.

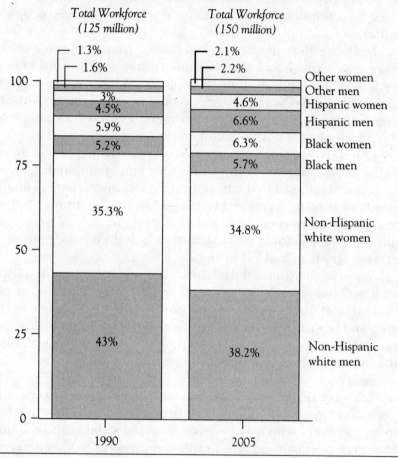

Source: U.S. Department of Labor, 1994.

White women's share of the workforce will shrink slightly, to 34.8 percent; black women will increase their share to 6.3 percent and Hispanic women to 4.6 percent. Regional demographic trends ensure that the level of racial and ethnic diversity in the workforce will vary by city and by region.

Another important source of diversity is the growth in numbers of working parents. The family with a male breadwinner and female homemaker has represented a shrinking share of family participation in the workforce since about 1955. In 1992, that share was less than 20 percent. The dual-worker family now represents more than 40 percent of all families with members in the workforce. Single mothers represent more than 10 percent of working parents.

Besides demographics and family change, many of the factors already discussed will contribute to greater diversity in tomorrow's workforce: more variety in employment arrangements, including contingent workers, contractors, temporary workers, and so on.

This greater variety in worklife will quickly become the norm. Management's most sensible response to the needs generated by greater diversity is to be flexible, but managers should be aware that each flexible response will create greater diversity and generate higher expectations that needs for flexibility can be met. Managers will be continually challenged to make diversity and flexibility productive and effective. Everyone in the workforce will "own" some aspect of diversity—female, Asian, dual career, job sharer, hearing impaired, and so on—and thus will have an interest in having his or her own difference integrated into the organization's policies and practices. Since few managers will be able to keep in mind all the diversities, a few general principles should be useful: fairness, speaking up when necessary, tolerance, allowing for differences, and willingness to explore misunderstandings.

Using diversity for competitive advantage will be the biggest challenge. Supporting diversity, however, is one way in which people can be encouraged to shape their own abilities and characteristics and to use them effectively on the job. In many businesses, employees with particular ethnic or cultural backgrounds are using their special cultural knowledge to bring in new customers and develop business in new communities.

Globalization of the American Economy

American business faces increased global competition at home and abroad. The wave of privatization in Europe and the formerly communist countries will create new competitors for the United States, as well as new overseas opportunities in alliances and joint ventures. In some parts of the world, notably Asia, joint ventures are almost the only way of gaining entry into new markets. Some of these new arrangements will be in partnership with government.

More and more, human resources managers will be expected to anticipate the impacts on the workforce of working with foreign-owned companies. In the case of Japanese-owned firms in the United States, front-line workers gain more responsibility while executives tend to lose some of their autonomy.

Human resources planners will be expected to assess other companies for cultural differences in ways of doing business that might affect potential alliances. The breakup in 1994 of the alliance between Corning (U.S.) and Vitro (Mexico) is described by both parties as an inability to integrate their different cultures.

Alliances, joint ventures, and an expansion of U.S. business into global markets all add to the likelihood that more U.S. human resources practitioners will be planning for and working with international workforces.

The Spreading Impacts of Information Technologies

Information technology provides new tools and capabilities for the organization to improve itself. In effect, information technologies are reshaping business. As a result, these changes will create new social and organizational issues. All organizations will be information entities, with the technology providing the capabilities and people contributing to the flow of information. Information technology can replace some jobs and enhance others, remake how people think and learn, intensify the use of images, and modify business relationships.

One important impact on the organization will be the tearing down of walls and borders, leaving the corporation as a glass house. A glass house is transparent to insiders and outsiders alike, with profound impacts on secrecy, the confidentiality of information, and the ability of insiders to go outside for information and contacts. The Internal Revenue Service has already found this to be true, as hundreds of employees were recently found to be tapping into its Integrated Data Retrieval System to snoop on the salary, incomes, and tax payments of their friends and neighbors (Barr, 1994). To prevent more such situations occurring, practitioners should plan now how to develop the workforce's respect for confidentiality and discretion in the use of information in an open operating environment. It would be useful to gather a group of the most technologically savvy people in the organization to work on this problem.

The Growing Imbalance Between Workers and Management

In their struggle for survival, corporations have undermined the employment contract that, either written or understood, most had with their permanent workforce. An urgent need of the next decade is to rebalance the growing imbalance between labor and management. Even as corporations plan and work for a better-run, more efficient, and more enthusiastic workforce, their success is threatened by the growth of a large and disaffected class of workers, many of whom will never fully trust an employer again. Figure 1.4 is our impression of some of the forces influencing the balance between management and labor.

The alienation of those workers will, however, play itself out in many ways over the next five to fifteen years, with effects on corporations, the workplace, and the economy.

When blue-collar jobs were eliminated in the 1970s and early 1980s, middle managers felt themselves to be protected by their long-term employment relationships, their identification with and commitment to the company. But now many of the middle-class, middle-aged, white-collar managers have lost their jobs and will never recover the income or status they once had or the security they felt.

No imbalance in power can persist forever. The imbalance will be redressed. And as that imbalance is redressed, what will happen? Workers will do what aggrieved workers have always done. They will organize, sue, strike, seek legislative relief, sabotage, and resort to all legitimate tools appropriate to rebalancing a painfully imbalanced situation.

The core population most likely to turn against the corporation, to politicize the abuse, to campaign for new legislation, is the middle-class, middle-aged middle manager. One of the most striking of their grievances is not just the dismissal of millions of workers but

Figure 1.4. The Labor-Management Imbalance.

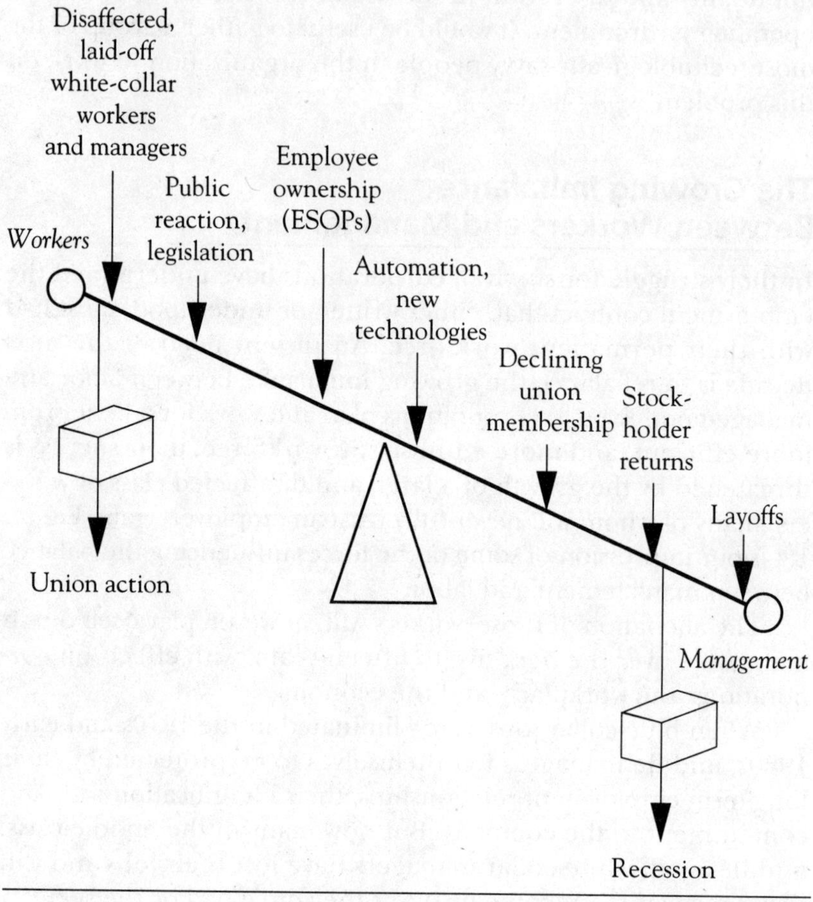

the fact that they are being replaced by machines, by outsourcing, and other cost-saving tactics.

Since the mid-1980s, corporations have laid off at least 3.5 million workers, in a prolonged downsizing that is still going on (Lesly & Light, 1992). About two million middle management jobs have been eliminated. In the early days, about 90 percent of laid-off managers were able to find other jobs at the same pay or better. Now fewer can do so; in 1992, only about 25 percent ("Downward mobility," 1992).

It is possible that the labor-management imbalance will continue tottering on the edge of crisis until better business conditions or the growth of new businesses absorbs the disaffected workforce. But it is unlikely that much of the workforce will recover their trust in large corporate employers in this century.

The democratization of the workforce, with the growth of empowerment and self-managed teams, will continue, but is unlikely to have much effect soon on the payroll cutting of most organizations. The next decade will see new mechanisms to balance power in the workplace. These could be piecemeal, and might include everything from written employment contracts to government restrictions on layoffs and firings. Quality programs and empowerment efforts will be less effective if managers believe these plans will be abandoned for another round of payroll cuts.

The plight of the millions of managers and workers who, as a result of being laid off, have no or fewer health care benefits will be a driver of health care reform.

Managers and professionals are likely to become more loyal to their profession or their field, particularly as a source of new job and career opportunities. Professional associations should see a surge in new members and greater demand for networking and job-finding services.

Layoffs have created many age discrimination issues and will create more as the workforce ages. There may also be more regulation. It is reasonably evident that, if it were not for age discrimination legislation, many payroll cuts would have swept almost all the higher-paid, more senior people from the company. One effect of so much downsizing has been to change the way new people are brought into the company; a second is that the downsizing process has been institutionalized. New people are encouraged not to give up their marketability, assured that the company will help them improve it against the day when their job ends. And when it does, outplacement counseling and job finding resources are already in place.

The middle class cannot be solely an economic category. Middle-class values also reflect an acceptance of society's structures and procedures and a willingness to use them to accomplish ends. An educated and prosperous middle class questions older notions of authority. The priest, doctor, lawyer, school principal, and boss are no longer unquestioned sources of information and direction.

With more information available, authorities inside or outside the organization must earn people's trust with the quality and reliability of the knowledge and information they can supply. Those companies or people who are widely recognized as authorities of the twenty-first century will have a firm information profile, will present themselves in a compelling, reliable way, and will be receptive to ideas and suggestions as well as willing to give advice. The middle-class workforce of the 1990s and the twenty-first century will in some sense be less responsive to control by management fiat, but may be much more responsive to strategies that call on their willingness to learn and to accept new responsibilities for their own work.

The middle-class focus on quality and reliability, including in customer services, will shape many business practices. Peripheral values will persist, however, and must be taken into account. Immigrant groups will maintain the values of their home culture, at least in the first generation. The young may hold more optimistic values that are otherwise similar to those of their parents. The aging may hold on to an older set, or hold a higher value for security and stability than younger people do.

These are significant issues for human resources practitioners, issues that will have serious management and organizational consequences if they are not addressed. Human resources professionals cannot solve these problems alone. But they can bring them to the attention of their organizations and build some accounting of their significance into planning and practice. Human resources practitioners must become as strongly information and knowledge oriented as the workforce will be. Human resources departments must deliver customized services on time and when needed. They are the important link between senior management's business goals and workforce performance, so they must develop their strategic abilities to anticipate emerging needs for programs and initiatives.

References

Barr, S. (1994, July 19). 1,300 IRS workers accused of snooping at tax returns. *Washington Post*, p. 1.

Downward mobility: Corporate castoffs are struggling just to stay in the middle class. (1992, March 23). *Business Week,* p. 58.

Franklin, J. C. (1993, November). Industry output and employment. *Monthly Labor Review,* p. 47.

Kim, J. (1994, January). The executive wage gap: Where women stand. *Working Woman.*

Lesly, E., & Light, L. (1992, March 23). When layoffs alone don't turn the tide. *Business Week,* p. 58.

Reading across boundaries. (1994, July). (Newsletter published by International Orientation Resources, Northbrook, Ill.), p. 2.

U.S. Department of Labor, Bureau of Labor Statistics (1988, May). *Current population survey.*

U.S. Department of Labor, Bureau of Labor Statistics, Current Labor Statistics. (1994, June). Labor market indicators, table 1. *Monthly Labor Review,* p. 70.

U.S. Department of Transportation. (1993, April). *Transportation implications of telecommuting.* Washington, DC: U.S. Government Printing Office.

PART 1

Career Development Programs in Changing Organizations

The first part of the book describes career development programs in changing organizations. The chapters in this section consider how organizational changes affect opportunities for advancement and development, how organizations can enhance self-affirmation of survivors of downsizing, and how human resource programs can be integrated to form a performance system targeted to organizational objectives.

The book began with an examination of trends affecting opportunities for employee development. The authors of Chapter One, Jennifer Jarratt and Joseph Coates, are futurists. They reviewed economic, demographic, technological, political, and organizational trends on workforce requirements and opportunities for development. The trends are the collapse of U.S. public education, expanding opportunities for learning outside the schoolhouse, expanding corporate training, the continuing shift away from manufacturing and into service-information work, the growth of the contingent workforce, the emerging distributed workforce, increasing women's impacts on the workforce, the middle-aging of the workforce, the growing diversity among the entry-level workforce, the globalization of the American economy and U. S. business, the spreading effects of information technologies on business, and the growing imbalance between workers and management.

These trends have implications for human resource practitioners as well as for employees. Jarrett and Coates concluded that human resource practitioners must become as strongly information and knowledge oriented as the workforce will be and that human resources departments must deliver customized services on time and when needed. Thus, human resource practitioners contribute to economic development by linking workforce performance to senior management's business goals.

Chapter Two investigates promotional trends within an organization experiencing periods of growth. A critical element both to career planning, from the individual's standpoint, and career management, from the organization's standpoint, is information about changing career opportunities in the organization. However, theories and models of careers often do not take into account organizational changes. They treat the organization as stable and unchanging (Rosenbaum, 1984; Rosenfeld, 1992). In fact, organizations are continually facing periods of growth, stability, and decline. Organizational expansion leads to more mobility opportunities, but this affects different groups in different ways (Baron, 1984). For instance, Skvoretz (1984) found that women benefited more from growth within an organization than men.

The authors of Chapter Two examine a large U.S.–based international company that has experienced easily demarcated periods of growth during the last forty-five years. They followed 26,198 managers throughout their careers in the firm to see how they benefited from periods of change and to determine if there was a differential effect by group (such as women and minorities) and job function. Moreover, they considered whether determinants of career advancement vary during these growth periods. As such, they show how career opportunities and requirements to take advantage of these opportunities within a firm's internal labor market vary as the organization expands in new directions. Their retrospective investigation has implications for advising and redirecting employees as new opportunities are created in the future.

Chapter Three applies self-affirmation theory to the practice of career development of employees in downsizing organizations. Recognizing that layoffs and other large-scale organizational changes won't go away, the authors demonstrate the value of reinforcing people's sense of identity, esteem, and control in the design of human resource practices and policies. They describe career development innovations that deal with changes in position, work design, job challenge, rewards for learning, and work-life balance. Their goal is to show how these programs can facilitate individual and organizational adjustment to rapidly changing work environments.

Chapter Four describes how human resource programs can be integrated to support the organization's mission and initiatives. Behavioral dimensions critical to the organization can be built into recruitment, goal setting, development, feedback and recognition, appraisal, compensation, career planning, and outplacement. The authors outline a career development module of a human performance system aimed at enhancing the quality of an organization. The module includes communication of organizational goals and expectations; assessment of skills and motivation, including self-analysis and input from others; identification and selection of career goals and development plans; and methods to support the role of the supervisor as coach and developer. Supporting materials include a trends analysis that explains emerging job requirements and career alternatives; a performance management process to aid supervisors in managing marginal performers; guidelines for on-the-job development; and self-assessment procedures for evaluating one's values, interests, and goals. Thus, the chapter outlines a comprehensive, integrated program that supports employees' development planning in light of changing organizational needs. The chapter also discusses ways to overcome such barriers to change as questionable sponsorship, short-term perspectives, management's desire for easy answers, and employees' resistance to learning.

References

Baron, J. N. (1984). Organizational perspectives on stratification. In R. H. Turner (Ed.), *Annual review of sociology* (pp. 37–69). Palo Alto, CA: Annual Reviews, Inc.

Rosenbaum, J. E. (1984). *Career mobility in a corporate hierarchy.* San Diego, CA: Academic Press.

Rosenfeld, R. A. (1992). Job mobility and career process. *Annual Review of Sociology,* Palo Alto, CA: Annual Reviews, pp. 39–61.

Skvoretz, J. (1984). The logic of opportunity and mobility. *Social Forces, 63,* 72–97.

CHAPTER 2

Organizational Growth and Employee Advancement
Tracking the Opportunities

Amy E. Hurley
Jeffrey A. Sonnenfeld

A critical element both to career planning, from the individual's standpoint, and career management, from the organization's standpoint, is information about changing career opportunities in the organization. However, theories and models of careers often do not take into account organizational changes. The organization is treated as stable and unchanging (Rosenbaum, 1984; Rosenfeld, 1992; Sharpe, 1994). In fact, organizations are continually facing periods of growth, stability, or decline. This chapter investigates promotional trends within an organization experiencing periods of growth.

Careers need to be investigated in terms of both individual attributes and organizational growth rates. It has been established that promotion opportunities are heavily dependent on organizational growth rates (Stewman & Konda, 1983). The idea that organizational growth creates greater opportunities for employees is

Note: The study described in this chapter was supported by the Center for Leadership and Career Studies at Goizueta Business School, Emory University. An earlier version of this chapter was presented at the annual conference of the Society for Industrial and Organizational Psychology, Nashville, Tennessee, April 1994.

also widely accepted (Keyfitz, 1973). The study described in this chapter is interested in exploring how organizational growth affects different groups in the organizations.

We would like to believe that growth in an organization helps all employees equitably or perhaps even helps less favored groups more than the favored groups. Companies with low promotion rates for some groups of employees may feel this problem would be alleviated if their organization were to experience a growth period. Research has found that organizational expansion leads to different mobility opportunities for different groups (Baron, 1984). Currently the results from studies trying to identify the effects of organizational growth on different groups is not conclusive.

There is some evidence to support the idea that organizational growth helps the less favored groups. Rosenbaum (1984) found that the most favored group in his study did not benefit from organizational growth but other, less favored groups did. He labeled these "spillover" groups because they had realized a spillover effect from growth. Interestingly, when the growth stopped and the firm returned to a stable period, these spillover groups again received fewer promotions and the favored groups maintained their superior positions in terms of promotability.

Di Prete and Soule (1988) believed that growth would force managers to turn to a pool of employees who had been passed over for promotion earlier. These employees had lost the tournament round, however because of the necessity to promote more people, they would get a second chance. They found that growth did seem to help women and minorities because they made up most of the lower ranks where the promotees had to be chosen from. However, it did not help them gain status promotions that would lead to higher career positions. Those status positions continued to go to men and whites.

It is often thought that in a firm with a hierarchical structure in the shape of a pyramid, employees at lower levels would have more promotion chances than those at higher levels, where there are fewer positions above theirs. Stewman and Konda (1983) investigated this and found it was not true. The different levels in the organizations did have different promotion rates but it was not always true that the higher levels had lower rates than the lower levels. Their study also found that organizational growth was not the great equalizer it is often believed to be. Actually, they found organizational growth to accentuate the existing inequalities. In effect, the growth did help everyone but helped the groups with initial higher promotion rates more than those with lower initial rates. After periods of growth, the differences in promotion rates between groups became greater. The favored groups were helped more in periods of organizational growth than the other groups.

Groups Studied

This chapter's study will investigate the promotion rates of different groups during periods of growth and stability in a large U.S.–based international company. The study follows managers throughout their careers in one firm to see how they benefit from these periods of change and to determine if there is a differential effect by group. The groups that will be examined are functional area, hierarchical level, gender, and race.

Functional Area and Hierarchical Level

Groups at different hierarchical levels may be affected differently by growth. Research has found that promotions at the top of the organization are less affected by growth than promotions at the middle level, and with growth a greater proportion of selections are made from lower hierarchical levels (Stewman & Konda, 1983). This would suggest that those at lower hierarchical levels would benefit more from growth than those at higher hierarchical levels.

Network theories suggest that those with restricted network access will have lower promotion chances than those with more network access. Network access give people increased knowledge of what is going on in the organization and enables them to ensure they are in positions with high promotion probabilities (Ibarra, 1993). Network access may be related to an employee's centrality in the firm. Factors associated with centrality are hierarchical level (Lincoln & Miller, 1979; Roberts & O'Reilly, 1979; Miller, 1986), and functional area (Ibarra, 1992). Those in certain functional areas and at higher hierarchical levels will have greater centrality and therefore greater promotion opportunities. Limited network access produces multiple disadvantages, including restricted knowledge of what is going on in the organization (Ibarra, 1993).

Those with restricted network access will have less awareness of the determinants of career attainment in their firm. Those at higher hierarchical levels may be more aware of the actual career attainment determinants in their firms. High-status individuals have more extensive network connections (Lincoln & Miller, 1979; Miller, 1986) and therefore have more access to more information on career attainment determinants.

Functional area may also play an important role in employees' perceptions of career attainment determinants. Some functional areas are associated with greater centrality in a firm's networks, therefore leading to greater availability of information about the firm. In many firms the functional area leading to greatest centrality is the line department. Functional area has often been investigated in terms of line versus staff departments. Research has found that gaining line experience early in one's career enhances career success and is necessary to move into upper management levels (Cox & Harquail, 1990; Kanter, 1977; Larwood & Gattiker, 1987). From Rosenbaum's (1984) findings we would expect to find that those without line experience will benefit more in periods of growth than those with line experience but less in stable periods.

Gender and Race

Gender and race may be used by managers as signals when making promotion decisions (Martin, Harrison & Dinitto, 1983). It has been found that male executives prefer to promote other men to leadership positions because they prefer peers who are similar to themselves (Hellwig, 1985). Women and minorities may have lower promotion rates because of their restricted network access.

Gender is often highly correlated with organizational positions (Ibarra, 1992). Empirical evidence reveals low representation of women in management (Auster, 1988; Hartmann, 1987; Kanter, 1977). Within management, representation of women tends to be far lower in the upper echelons of organizations than in lower management (Shenhav, 1992; Brenner, Tomkiewicz & Schein, 1989; Kesner, 1988). Men have been found to dominate the managerial and supervisory levels in organizations (Wolfe & Fligstein, 1979). Selective advancement patterns based on gender have been demonstrated in the literature (Acker & Van Houten, 1976; Baron, Davis-Blake & Bielby, 1986). Previous research has suggested that organizational promotion policies favor men over women (Baron, 1984; Cannings, 1988; Kanter, 1977).

Women's lack of advancement to high levels of management often results from their not having access to inside information they need to get ahead (Bartol, 1978; Kanter, 1977). Networks within organizations are often theorized to explain women's low representation in upper-level management (Brass, 1984, 1985). The networks formed by women are largely ineffective because they are not well integrated into the organization's dominant coalition. Women have been found to be less connected to the networks associated with further promotions and the interaction network of the dominant coalition (Brass, 1985). This leads to women and minority members having lower career attainment than their cohorts. Brass (1984) found network contacts with an organization's dominant coalition was an important correlate of perceived power and future promotion.

The signaling effect of early functional area may also be affected by race and gender. Women often find it difficult to gain line experience (Larwood & Gattiker, 1987). Baron, Davis-Blake & Bielby (1986) found that jobs are segregated by gender and that jobs mainly held by women were significantly less likely to exist in job ladders that lead to higher managerial levels. This limits the career mobility of women.

Race is also often highly correlated with organizational positions (Ibarra, 1992). Empirical evidence reveals low representation of blacks in management (Davis & Watson, 1982; Killingsworth & Reimers, 1983). Representation of women and blacks tend to be far lower in the upper echelons of organizations than in lower management (Shenhav, 1992; Kesner, 1988). Black managers have been found to experience restricted advancement opportunities (Irons & Moore, 1985; Nixon, 1985).

Research has found that racial minorities are not given the same opportunities in organizations as other employees (Ilgen & Youtz, 1986). It may be that minority employees are not started in the functional departments that lead to career attainment in the firm or they may not be given the early promotions that others, who were placed in more demanding jobs, were (Kanter, 1979). Greenhaus, Parasuraman, and Wormley (1990) found that blacks received lower promotability assessments from their supervisors than whites. Minority members have also been found to not be involved in the networks in the organization that lead to promotions (Ilgen & Youtz, 1986). Again, we would expect women and minorities to benefit more from growth than men and whites.

Method

Data Site

The research site is a large U.S.–based international service company with more than 200,000 employees. The firm utilizes an internal labor market; all employees enter the firm at a low level and are promoted from within. The firm has a very low turnover rate, less than 4 percent.

Sample

Studies on careers have the option of studying individuals cross sectionally or following cohorts of employees. A cross-sectional analysis would involve investigating all employees with a firm at a specific point in time. However, this requires the assumption that all cohorts have faced the same opportunities throughout their tenure with the firm. Therefore individuals are compared to others in different situations and not with similar others (Ragin & Bradshaw, 1991). The different opportunity prospects of individual cohorts may affect their promotion probabilities (Skvoretz, 1984). The size and exit rates of individual cohorts may also affect their promotion chances (Stewman & Konda, 1983).

Studying individual cohorts in an organization allows us to assume the employees have faced the same opportunities and situations throughout their tenure with the firm (Di Prete & Soule, 1986). Our study investigates the promotion probabilities of two managerial cohorts: individuals entering the firm in 1974 and 1981. Information on these employees was obtained from the firm's computerized record system. The longitudinal records are continuous, representing the ongoing operations of the organization and its internal labor markets. The system contained every employee's complete job history. Table 2.1 provides descriptive information on the characteristics of the managers.

Table 2.1. Sample Characteristics.

Variable	1974 Cohort		1981 Cohort	
	Mean	S.D.	Mean	S.D.
Gender	.10		.12	
Race	.15		.15	
Current Age	41.69	4.34	35.70	4.91
Entering Age	22.69	4.34	23.70	4.91
Entering Operations	.51		.58	
Level	4.79	.85	4.39	.61
Current Operations	.34		.42	

There are two periods of growth easily demarcated in this firm. The three-year periods of 1977–1979 and 1985–1987 showed enormous growth in terms of both sales and employees. The promotion probabilities for different groups of the 1974 and 1981 cohorts will be calculated for these time periods. The 1974 cohort will be examined in both growth periods, allowing the possibility of tenure in the organization affecting promotion chances to be investigated. These growth periods will be compared to two periods of relative stability: 1974–1976 and 1982–1984.

Groups

Hierarchical Level
There are ten career levels in the firm; levels four to ten are managerial levels. These levels will be used to indicate an employee's level of career attainment. Table 2.2 illustrates the number of people currently at each managerial level. This table shows that the largest number of managers is at the lowest managerial level and the smallest number at the highest managerial level.

Functional Area
A dichotomous variable will indicate whether the employee entered through the operations department (indicated by a value of one) or not. The operations department in this firm is the line department of the firm; all others are staff departments. The oper-

Table 2.2. Present Level in Organization.

Level	1974 Cohort	1981 Cohort
4	266	644
5	233	272
6	82	34
7	21	11
8	4	0
9	0	0
10	0	0
	606	961

ations department provides the fundamental service of the firm. Interviews in the firm confirm the importance of the operations department. Another dichotomous variable will indicate whether the employee is currently in the operations department (indicated with a value of one) or not.

Race

A dichotomous variable for race was included in the model. It has a value of zero assigned to white, coded one if black, American Indian, Asian-American, or Hispanic.

Gender

Gender is a dichotomous variable with a value of one assigned to female.

Results

1974 Cohort

1977–1979 Growth

The probability of promotion of the various groups is shown in Table 2.3. The probability of promotion for the entire cohort during the growth period of 1977–1979 increased from 38 to 46 percent. However, the results indicate some groups were helped by this growth more than others. The probability of promotion for women actually went down slightly from 10 to 8 percent, while the promotion probability of men increased by 2 percent. The pro-

Table 2.3. Probability of Promotion.

| | 1974 Cohort | | | | 1981 Cohort | |
| | Stable | Growth | Stable | Growth | Stable | Growth |
Variable	74–76	77–79	82–84	85–87	82–84	85–87
Total	.38	.46	.29	.30	.65	.44
Women	.10	.08	.10	.08	.10	.12
Men	.90	.92	.90	.92	.90	.88
Whites	.84	.86	.90	.87	.86	.89
Minorities	.16	.14	.10	.13	.14	.11
Enter Operations	.48	.56	.56	.55	.56	.59
Enter Non-Operations	.52	.44	.44	.45	.44	.41
Level 2	.23	.45	.29	.13	.72	.40
Level 3	.90	.60	.25	.33	.90	.59
Level 4	.52	.41	.20	.19	.63	.41
Level 5	.44	.69	.46	.42	.77	.67
Level 6	.30	.98	.62	.55	.00	.57
Current Operations	.48	.54	.50	.46	.51	.52
Current Non-Operations	.52	.46	.50	.54	.49	.48

motion probability for minorities also decreased by 2 percent while whites gained 2 percent. During the stable period of 1974–1976 the promotion probabilities for men and whites were much higher than those for women and minorities. Therefore, the growth period seems to have helped those groups who were already favored for promotion before the growth.

This period of growth seems to have had a large effect on functional area. Those who entered in the operations department had an increase in promotion probability from 48 to 56 percent. Therefore, the probability of promotion for those who did not enter in the operations department decreased by 8 percent during this period of growth.

The results for those who were currently in the operations department corresponds to the results of those entering it: their promotion probability increased by 6 percent during this growth phase. During the stable period of 1974–1976 managers who had entered in the operations department or who were currently in it had much lower promotion probabilities than managers who had not entered in operations or who were currently not in operations. For functional area, the growth period seems to have helped the less favored group. The increase in the promotion probabilities of those entering or currently in the operations department actually changes these two groups to the more favored group status. They now have higher promotion probabilities than those who did not enter or who are not currently in the operations department.

Hierarchical level appears also to be greatly affected by the growth period. Levels two, five, and six have very large increases in their promotion probabilities while the probabilities for levels three and four have decreased. These changes are very large in magnitude.

1985–1987 Growth

The effect of the growth period 1985–1987 was not very large on the total 1974 cohort. There was only a 1 percent increase in the promotion probability for the cohort as a whole. However, the growth does seem to have affected which groups have higher promotion rates. The promotion rate for gender was identical to the results for the period 1977–1979; men increased their probability by 2 percent while the rate for women decreased by 2 percent. Minorities did seem to be helped slightly by this growth period as they had not been with the earlier period of growth. While the rate of promotion for whites still remained much higher (87 percent) than minorities (13 percent), there was a 3 percent increase in the promotion rates for minorities. Minority group members did seem to be helped by this period of growth.

Entering in operations did not seem to be affected by this growth phase. There was only a 1 percent change in the promotion rates of those who entered in the operations department versus those who did not. Those currently in operations were again greatly affected by the growth in the firm, as they were in the earlier growth period—but in the opposite direction. During this period of growth those who were currently in operations had their probability of promotion decreased by 4 percent. Again, for functional area, the growth period seems to have helped the less favored group. The decrease in the promotion probabilities of those currently in the operations department actually changes this group to less favored group status. They now have lower promotion probabilities than those who are not currently in the operations department.

There was a decrease in the promotion probabilities for all hierarchical levels except level three. Even with this increase for level three, the promotion probabilities for all levels decreased to less than they had been during the growth period of 1977–1979.

1981 Cohort

1985–1987 Growth

The total promotion rate for the 1981 cohort during the growth period 1985–1987 decreased greatly from the promotion rate in the earlier stable period of 1982–1984. Overall, the growth period does seem to have lowered the promotion probabilities for most groups, with a few exceptions.

The promotion rate for women actually increased by 2 percent. This is the first time period where women are shown to have benefited from the period of growth. However, at the same time, the promotion rate of minorities decreased by 3 percent.

Those who entered in operations and were currently in operations showed a slight increase in their promotion probabilities. Both of these groups were the original favored groups and were helped by the growth of the firm.

The promotion probabilities for all hierarchical levels decreased during this period of growth. Comparing the promotion probabilities for all levels during this time period with the 1974 cohort indicates that the 1981 cohorts have higher promotion rates than the 1974 cohort at all hierarchical levels.

Discussion of Study Findings

The results from this study indicate mixed support for the idea that periods of growth will help the less favored groups in the organization to gain promotions. Interestingly, the growth in 1985–1987 did not seem to help the cohorts as a whole with their promotion chances and actually the promotion probabilities for the 1981 cohort during this time period decreased. This decrease would not be expected and further research should explore its cause. It may be that other changes in the company during 1982–1987 affected the promotion chances of managers in the firm.

Konda and Stewman (1980) suggest that different promotion rates for cohorts may be due to differences in the pool of talent of the cohort. It may be that this effect only occurred for the 1981 cohort. Analysis of additional cohorts in this firm could investigate this possibility. In general the cohorts appeared to have higher rates of promotion closer to their entering year. The 1974 cohort almost always had lower promotion chances than the 1981 cohort regardless of the time period. However, all groups were affected in some manner by the periods of growth in the firm.

It was not until the most recent period of growth that women were helped by the growth. Even during this time period, only the 1981 cohort was helped; the women hired in 1974 were hurt by the growth in terms of their chances for promotion. Minorities were also helped only during this recent period of growth but only the 1974 cohort: the recently hired cohort of 1981 saw their promotion chances decrease. Overall, women and minorities did not seem to gain great advantages from the growth in the organization. This is in contrast to the findings of Di Prete and Soule (1988) that women and minorities were helped by growth in the organization. The promotion rates of men and whites remained much greater than those for women and minorities. Growth in the organization does not appear to be greatly helping to erase this disparity.

Growth had very interesting effects on functional area. For the 1974 cohort, growth did appear to be helping to equalize the disparity between the favored and less favored groups. This is consistent with Rosenbaum's (1984) research. During the growth period of 1977–1979 the growth helped the less favored groups (entered operations and currently operations). The results of this growth period left these two groups as the more favored groups. The growth in 1985–1987 then affected these two groups negatively so they again became the less favored group. This change regarding the functional area of operations does seem to indicate that growth acts as an equalizer for the less favored party, helping whichever groups had lower promotion rates.

The effect on entering operations was much greater when the cohort had recently joined the organization. During the period of 1985–1987 the 1974 cohort had been with the firm for fourteen years. There was not a very large impact on entering operations as there was in the earlier period of growth and for the 1981 cohort during the 1985–1987 period of growth. This may indicate something about the effect of entering a functional area. Research has suggested that the entering functional area may play a great role in managerial career attainment. However, these results indicate the effect of entering functional area may decrease as the manager's tenure in the firm increases. Perhaps there is no effect on entering operations; as we get further from the time when the cohort entered the firm, entering position has a lesser effect than current position.

Hierarchical level was also affected by the periods of growth in the firm. There seemed to be a trend for the promotion chances of most managerial levels to decrease during the periods of growth. This may be an illustration of the effect of tenure rather than growth in the organization. The decrease in promotion probabilities for all hierarchical levels may occur as a manager's tenure with the firm increases.

It is also interesting that the higher hierarchical levels do not always have the lowest promotion probabilities. This is consistent with the findings of Stewman and Konda (1983) that it is not always true that the higher levels had lower promotion rates than the lower levels. It appears that those managers who have moved up in the organization still have very high chances of being promoted to higher levels. Those who have not been promoted upward in the organization have lower probabilities of still being promoted. For example, a manager in the 1974 cohort who remained at level four in the 1985–1987 time period had only a 19 percent chance of being promoted, while a 1974 cohort manager who was at level five during this time period had a 46 percent chance of promotion.

This is consistent with the research findings that the probability of promotions eventually declines with tenure because managers will have passed the optimum point in their careers for promotion (Di Prete & Soule, 1988). This is true for the managers who have not moved up in the organization; those who have moved up do not see their probability of promotion decline as greatly.

Previous research had suggested that promotion at the top of the organization would be less affected by growth than promotions at the middle levels and that with growth lower levels would achieve higher promotion rates (Stewman & Konda, 1983). This was not true in this organization. Promotions at all levels were affected by the periods of growth in the firm. There was not a large difference between the effects for middle levels and those for higher levels. Also, higher levels often had higher promotion rates during periods of growth than lower managerial levels.

Implications for Career Planning

There is a great need for human resource practitioners to obtain information about the promotion opportunities within their firm, from both historical and current records. The promotion opportunities within the firm need to be analyzed for systematic patterns and also for any changes within these patterns. A detailed study of an organization's personnel records, similar to the one described in this chapter, would allow human resource practitioners to understand how the careers of employees in their firm are affected by organizational changes such as organizational growth.

Human resource practitioners faced with the task of ensuring women and minorities are receiving equitable promotion opportunities within the firm should also analyze the patterns of promotion opportunities. Perhaps women and minority employees need to be placed strategically within the firm, allowing organizational growth to help them. For example, in our study, functional area appeared to be an area where women and minorities would be helped by organizational growth.

Continuous monitoring of promotion opportunities is necessary to help high-potential employees, and they need to be placed in areas where they will be helped by organizational growth. This monitoring is important regardless of whether a company is growing. If an organization is in a period of stability or even downsizing, human resource practitioners will be able to identify areas where they can place employees to enhance their promotion opportunities. They will also be able to identify areas that may lead to plateauing or layoffs.

Human resource practitioners need to have information about the promotion opportunities in their firm during periods of growth. Practitioners would then be able to use these periods of growth to their advantage in trying to establish equitable promotion policies. Without careful attention to avoid discrimination, minorities may be precluded from the opportunities generated by organizational growth. Human resource practitioners must be sensitive to the effects of promotion opportunities on minorities, women, and other protected classes and guide the organization to ensure that their promotion practices do take full advantage of available talent. By knowing where opportunities are arising during periods of growth, human resource practitioners may be able to help employees who deserve promotion to be in the right place at the right time.

Job seekers will also find it useful to investigate organizational growth rate. Organizations with different growth rates may be expected to have extremely large differences in promotion chances. If it is not possible to find out the organizational growth rate, job seekers should at the least find out the growth rate for the industry they may wish to work in. However, whether this growth rate will help individual groups requires further analysis.

Organizations cannot expect growth to help solve their problems. Differences in promotion rates for different groups in organizations will not disappear with organizational growth. Firms need to investigate these different rates of promotion and deal with them directly.

References

Acker, J. A., & Van Houten, D. R. (1976). Differential recruitment and control: The sex structuring of organizations. *Administrative Science Quarterly, 19,* 152–163.

Auster, E. R. (1988). Behind closed doors: Sex bias at professional and managerial levels. *Employee Responsibilities and Rights Journal, 1,* 129–144.

Baron, J. N. (1984). Organizational perspectives on stratification. In R. H. Turner (Ed.), *Annual review of sociology* (pp. 37–69). Palo Alto, CA: Annual Reviews, Inc.

Baron, J. N., Davis-Blake, A., & Bielby, W. T. (1986). The structure of opportunity: How promotion ladders vary within and among organizations. *Administrative Science Quarterly, 31,* 248–273.

Bartol, K. M. (1978). The sex structuring of organizations: A search for possible causes. *Academy of Management Review, 3,* 805–815.

Brass, D. J. (1984). Being in the right place: A structural analysis of individual influence in an organization. *Administrative Science Quarterly, 29,* 518–539.

Brass, D. J. (1985). Men's and women's networks: A study of interaction patterns and influence in an organization. *Academy of Management Journal, 28,* 327–343.

Brenner, O. C., Tomkiewicz, J., & Schein, V. E. (1989). The relationship between sex role stereotypes and requisite management characteristics revisited. *Academy of Management Journal, 32,* 662–669.

Cannings, K. (1988). Managerial promotion: The effects of socialization, specialization, and gender. *Industrial and Labor Relations Review, 42,* 77–88.

Cox, T., Jr., & Harquail, C. V. (1990). *Career paths and career success in the early career stages of male and female MBAs.* Paper presented at the meeting of the Academy of Management, San Francisco.

Davis, G., & Watson, G. (1982). *Black life in corporate America.* New York: Doubleday.

Di Prete, T. A., & Soule, W. T. (1986). The organization of career lines: Equal employment opportunity and status advancement in a federal bureaucracy. *American Sociological Review, 51,* 295–309.

Di Prete, T. A., & Soule, W. T. (1988). Gender and promotions in segmented job ladder systems. *American Sociological Review, 53,* 26–40.

Greenhaus, J. H., Parasuraman, S., & Wormley, W. M. (1990). Effects of race on organizational experiences, job performance evaluations, and career outcomes. *Academy of Management Journal, 33,* 64–86.

Hartmann, H. I. (1987). Internal labor markets and gender. In C. Brown & J. A. Pechman (Eds.), *Gender in the workplace.* Washington, DC: Brookings Institution.

Hellwig, B. (1985, April). The breakthrough generation: 73 women ready to run corporate America. *Working Woman,* p. 99.

Ibarra, H. (1992). Homophily and differential returns: Sex differences in network structure and access in an advertising firm. *Administrative Science Quarterly, 37,* 422–447.

Ibarra, H. (1993). Personal networks of women and minorities in management: A conceptual framework. *Academy of Management Review, 18,* 56–87.

Ilgen, D. R., & Youtz, M. A. (1986). Factors affecting the evaluation and development of minorities in organizations. In K. Rowland & G. Ferris (Eds.), *Research in personnel and human resource management: A research annual* (pp. 307–337). Greenwich, CT: JAI Press.

Irons, E., & Moore, G. W. (1985). *Black managers in the banking industry.* New York: Praeger.

Kanter, R. M. (1977). *Men and women of the corporation.* New York: Basic Books.

Kanter, R. M. (1979). Differential access to opportunity and power. In R. Alvarez (Ed.), *Discrimination in organizations* (pp. 52–68). San Francisco: Jossey-Bass.

Kesner, I. F. (1988). Directors' characteristics and committee membership: An investigation of type, occupation, tenure, and gender. *Academy of Management Journal, 31,* 66–84.

Keyfitz, N. (1973). Individual mobility in a stationary population. *Population Studies, 27,* 335–352.

Killingsworth, M. R., & Reimers, C. W. (1983). Race, ranking, promotions and pay at a federal facility: A logit analysis. *Industrial and Labor Relations Review, 37,* 92–107.

Konda, S. L., & Stewman, S. (1980). An opportunity labor demand model and Markovian labor supply models: Comparative tests in an organization. *American Sociological Review, 45,* 276–301.

Larwood, L., & Gattiker, U. E. (1987). A comparison of the career paths used by successful women and men. In B. A. Gutek & L. Larwood (Eds.), *Women's career development* (pp. 129–156). Newbury Park, CA: Sage.

Lincoln, J. R., & Miller, J. (1979). Work and friendship ties in organizations: A comparative analysis of relational networks. *Administrative Science Quarterly, 24,* 181–189.

Martin, P. Y., Harrison, D., & Dinitto, D. (1983). Advancement for women in hierarchical organizations: A multilevel analysis of problems and prospects. *Journal of Applied Behavioral Science, 19,* 19–33.

Miller, J. (1986). *Pathways in the workplace.* Cambridge: Cambridge University Press.

Nixon, R. (1985). *Climbing the corporate ladder: Some perceptions among black managers.* Washington, DC: National Urban League.

Ragin, C. C., & Bradshaw, Y. W. (1991). Statistical analysis of employment discrimination: A review and critique. *Research in Social Stratification and Mobility, 10,* 199–228.

Roberts, K. H., & O'Reilly, C. A. (1979). Some correlates of communication roles in organizations. *Academy of Management Journal, 22,* 42–57.

Rosenbaum, J. E. (1984). *Career mobility in a corporate hierarchy.* San Diego, CA: Academic Press.

Rosenfeld, R. A. (1992). Job mobility and career processes. *Annual Review of Sociology, 18,* 39–61.

Sharpe, R. (1994, March 29). The waiting game. *Wall Street Journal.*

Shenhav, Y. (1992). Entrance of blacks and women into managerial positions in scientific and engineering occupations: A longitudinal analysis. *Academy of Management Journal, 35,* 889–901.

Skvoretz, J. (1984). The logic of opportunity and mobility. *Social Forces, 63,* 72–97.

Stewman, S., & Konda, S. L. (1983). Careers and organizational labor markets: Demographic models of organizational behavior. *American Journal of Sociology, 88,* 637–685.

Wolfe, W. C., & Fligstein, N. D. (1979). Sexual stratification: Differences in power in the work setting. *Social Forces, 58,* 94–107.

CHAPTER 3

Career Development in Downsizing Organizations
A Self-Affirmation Analysis

Joel Brockner
Robert J. Lee

An important lesson from the past decade is that job layoffs often do not produce the positive organizational effects that they are expected to achieve. In fact, they frequently create significant problems not only for the people who leave but also for the survivors, those who remain with the company (Noer, 1993). The negative effects on survivors' productivity and morale, in turn, are likely to have an adverse impact on the organization's bottom line (Cascio, 1993).

In attempting to meet the multifaceted challenges posed by downsizings, a variety of interest groups have taken action, including:

1. The government, in the forms of the Workers' Adjustment and Retraining Notification (WARN) Act, retraining monies, and so forth.
2. Compensation, pension, and benefits specialists, along with lawyers and union leaders, who have been fine tuning the art of offering incentives for early retirements and voluntary terminations.

Note: We are grateful to Manny London and Batia Wiesenfeld for their useful feedback on a previous version of this chapter.

3. Outplacement firms, who are using more efficient models, such as those based on career centers, group delivery, high technology, and the integration of counseling with reemployment and training services.
4. Work redesign consultants, who have developed reengineering, just-in-time methods of production, workout, total quality management, and other high-participation methods to streamline and improve operations.
5. Organization redesign theorists and practitioners, who have provided new logics for how to do business, such as virtual organizations, cloverleaf designs, alliances, outsourcing, and other flexible approaches.
6. Career development theorists, who have offered better ways to understand our working lives as they play themselves out in society, in organizations, in families, and over time.
7. Organization development specialists, who have been offering new ways for managers to plan and implement major changes.

In spite of all these sources of guidance (and in spite of all the opportunities to try them out), there is still considerable room for improvement in how organizations manage downsizings. Toward that end, we offer a conceptual framework based on sound theory, empirical results, and years of practice in the field. More specifically, by looking at the challenges of managing layoffs and related organizational changes through the lens of self-affirmation theory, we will be better able to diagnose our clients' needs, and therefore view our own roles as practitioners more usefully.

Reframing the Problem

There would be no problem if survivors would just go along happily with the changes imposed on them by management, learn their new jobs, and perform them in a loyal, productive, and energetic way. Instead, managers in downsizing organizations encounter resistance in its various manifestations (employee withdrawal, uncooperativeness, and general reductions in survivors' productivity and morale). As psychologists, we know that during times of change people are eager to know what is in it for themselves. Among the questions they want answers to are "Can it hurt me?" "Can I control it?" "Will it surprise me?" and "Will it make me a bigger/better person?" In short, the raw fact is that organizational changes such as layoffs diminish, confuse, scare, and upset people. Little wonder, then, that downsizings often elicit considerable resistance, even when they are strategically correct.

What is the underlying basis for employees' resistance to significant organizational changes such as layoffs? Although numerous reasons abound in the change-management literature, we believe one to be of critical importance: the threat to the self-concept posed by the change event. Consider, for example, the following reaction of an AT&T employee shortly after divestiture: "I knew the old Bell System, its mission, its operation, its people, its culture. In that knowledge, I had identity and confidence about my company and myself. Now I work for a new company, one fourth its former size. I find myself asking, 'Who are we? Who am I?'"

The notion that threats to the self-concept underlie employees' resistance to change has been advanced by several prominent organizational theorists. Argyris (1985) suggests that the process of strategy implementation often is impeded by "defensive routines." Defensive routines reflect individuals' "governing values," which, in turn, stem from individuals' needs for self-identity. As Argyris noted: "The requirements of everyday life do not normally provide us the needed time . . . to design a particular action. *The need to feel some sense of personal wholeness* requires that there be an underlying consistency across the actions. These needs and actions combine . . . to lead us to hold values that govern the kinds of action strategies we will try to implement" (p. 79, emphasis added).

Commenting on the psychological barriers to organizational change, William Bridges (1988, p. 19) noted: "At bottom, it is a person's identity that he or she has trouble letting go of [during organizational change], and it is that identity that stands in the way of the change producing its desired result."

In his theory of self-affirmation, social psychologist Claude Steele (1988) offers a perspective closely related to the views expressed by Argyris, Bridges, and other organization experts. Steele claims that people strive to see themselves "as adaptively and morally adequate, that is, competent, good, coherent, unitary, stable, capable of free choice, capable of controlling important outcomes and so on" (p. 262).

These self-conceptions may be grouped into three related but different categories: esteem (competent, good), identity (coherent, unitary, stable), and control (capable of free choice, capable of controlling important outcomes). Information contradicting one or more of these self-conceptions is experienced as a threat to self-integrity; in the face of self-integrity threat, people will change their beliefs or behaviors until the threat has been reduced to a manageable level. Moreover—and herein lies one of the most important implications of self-affirmation theory—individuals' attempts to reaffirm do not have to be in the same domain that initially threatened their self-integrity. Reaffirmation efforts need only to restore self-integrity, regardless of whether they redress the objective situation that initially threatened the self.

Implications of Self-Affirmation Theory for Managing Organizational Change

Our central thesis is that self-affirmation theory helps to explain the effects of layoffs on survivors; moreover, the theory provides a source of potentially creative ideas on how to manage downsizings, and related organizational changes, more effectively. Our subsequent remarks are guided by the following propositions:

1. The basis of employee resistance to change is threatened self-integrity; therefore it is best to plan and implement change in ways that minimize that threat.
2. In spite of managers' best intentions, significant organizational changes are likely to be at least somewhat disaffirming. Therefore, the recipients of the change need to take action (behavioral or psychological or both) that promote reaffirmation.
3. The context in which reaffirmation occurs does not have to be related to the one that initially threatened employees' sense of self.

These three propositions provide general guidelines for understanding and managing organizational change. In this chapter the guidelines will be applied, however, to a specific (and prevalent) change event: job layoffs. We will focus attention on the impact of layoffs on survivors' productivity and morale. While a variety of human resource policies and practices may affect survivors' feelings of esteem, identity, and control, we will limit our discussion to the role of career development.

Layoffs: They Just Won't Go Away

Job layoffs pervade the corporate landscape. The American Management Association's "survey of employment practices at 870 companies found that almost half had reduced their workforces from mid-1992 to mid-1993. For two-thirds of those companies, this was at least their second year of downsizing in a row" (Smith, 1994, p. 46).

It is now widely recognized that layoffs affect not only the people whose jobs are lost but also those who remain. Recent theory and research have identified a variety of factors that influence survivors' reactions to job layoffs (Brockner & Greenberg, 1990; Brockner & Wiesenfeld, 1993). Several studies revealed that survivors responded particularly negatively when their sense of self was threatened.

For example, research has shown that survivors' organizational commitment declines when they feel that the layoffs are procedurally or distributively unfair (Brockner et al., 1994). Perceived unfairness may threaten people's self-integrity for two reasons. First, survivors may identify with the downsizing organization. Social identity theory posits that people define and evaluate themselves on the basis of their beliefs about the collective(s) to which they belong (Tajfel & Turner, 1979). If the collective acted badly (for instance, unfairly), then members of the collective are apt to feel that they acted badly. In essence, people may wonder, "What kind of person am *I* that I would be affiliated with a group that behaves unfairly?"

Second, survivors may identify with the victims of an unfair layoff. When a collective treats its members unfairly, it symbolically communicates a lack of respect for the dignity of its members. Through the process of reflected appraisal—in which people come to see themselves as they think they are viewed by significant others (Mead, 1934)—members of the collective may experience reduced self-esteem. If survivors identify with those laid off, moreover, they may experience the unfair treatment *as if* it were directed toward themselves, suffering self-esteem loss in the process.

In fact, studies have shown that the more that layoff survivors identify with the perpetrator (the organization) or the victims (the laid-off individuals) of the unfairness, the more likely they are to show reduced productivity and morale (Brockner, Grover, Reed, De Witt, & O'Malley, 1987; Brockner, Tyler, & Cooper-Schneider, 1992). Because survivors react quite negatively when their self-integrity is threatened by the layoffs, it is important that layoffs be implemented in ways that minimize their negative implications for survivors' sense of self.

The Opportunity to Bounce Back

Perhaps it is inevitable that layoff survivors will feel at least somewhat disaffirmed by the dismissal of their former co-workers. But there is hope. The same human needs that cause survivors to be hurt also may enable them to rebound from the harmful effects of layoffs. Self-affirmation theory posits that layoff survivors who have experienced a threat to their self-integrity should react much more favorably when they have been given an opportunity to reaffirm themselves.

Recent research has tested and found support for this hypothesis (Wiesenfeld, Brockner, & Martin, 1995). For example, in several studies survivors completed surveys measuring their reactions to the layoffs (such as organizational commitment) as a function of factors that should have influenced their experience of disaffirmation. Two potentially disaffirming factors were assessed: perceived unfairness and job insecurity. The self-threatening nature of unfairness has been discussed above. How might job insecurity threaten survivors' sense of self? Ashford, Lee, and Bobko (1989) define job insecurity as the perceived inability to control the negative consequences of the threat of job loss (or the loss of valued features of one's job). Given that job insecurity refers to an assault on individuals' sense of control, its presence may cause people to experience a threat to their self-integrity. It was generally expected that survivors would react more negatively when they believed that the layoffs were handled unfairly and when they felt greater job insecurity.

Two different versions of the surveys were constructed; one was intended to provide survivors with a reaffirmation experience whereas the other was not. After rating the unfairness of the layoff management process and their level of job insecurity, but before indicating their reactions to the layoffs, half of the participants were asked to write a short essay about an incident or situation in the workplace "that enabled you to feel good about yourself as a person or that allowed you to get to know yourself better" (self-affirmation condition). We expected that by writing the essay survivors would relive a presumably self-affirming experience.

One person wrote: "I recently received a voicemail message expressing gratitude and appreciation and asking me to pass it on to my supervisor. This simple gesture meant more to me than a raise or plaque." Another said: "Given a specific task and a very short time frame to accomplish such a complex project, I was given the freedom to select my team, schedule events, deal directly with external companies, and deliver a recommendation. Although 'not funded' the team members actively participated in delivery of a high quality recommendation."

The other half of the participants were not asked to write an essay (control condition). In the control condition, survivors' reactions were strongly related to perceptions of unfairness and job insecurity; as expected, survivors reacted much more negatively when they felt that the layoff was handled unfairly or when it engendered relatively greater job insecurity.

The results in the self-affirmation condition were markedly different; survivors' reactions were unrelated to their perceptions of unfairness and job insecurity. Said differently, among those survivors who presumably were disaffirmed by the experience of unfairness or job insecurity, they reacted much more positively in the self-affirmation than in the control condition. Whether people had an opportunity to write a self-affirming essay had no effect, however, on the people who were less disaffirmed by the layoffs (those who viewed the handling of the layoff as relatively fair or those who felt less job insecurity). It is worth reemphasizing that the self-affirming experience elicited favorable survivor reactions even though it was not necessarily related to issues of unfairness or job insecurity, which initially threatened survivors' self-integrity. These findings have important implications for managers in downsizing organizations. Following layoffs (even those that are disaffirming) it is not too late to provide opportunities for reaffirmation. And here's the best news of all for human resource directors and their consultants: the reaffirmation experience even can be in a domain unrelated to the one in which the damage was done. As long as the reaffirmation activity is meaningful, it can reduce or even eliminate the potentially dysfunctional consequences of the initial self-integrity threat.

Career Development as Self-Affirmation

Career development is one of several human resource activities that is conceptually linked to the process of self-affirmation. Steele's (1988) theory suggests that the restoration of self-integrity could be a powerful antidote to the stresses produced by downsizings and other significant organizational changes. Because some of the traditional, hierarchy-based approaches to career development have limited utility, many contemporary organizations already have been experimenting with creative alternatives. Furthermore, many of the current innovations in career development seem to have positive effects on people's self-esteem, self-identity, and sense of control. Thus, the terrain of career development provides particularly fertile ground in which to apply the insights offered by self-affirmation theory.

The Traditional Paradigm of Career Development Systems

As organizations grapple with how to compete in an increasingly complex business environment they have reevaluated many of their operating assumptions. Gutteridge, Leibowitz, and Shore (1993) described one of the fundamental shifts in management thinking: "'People development' is more closely aligned than ever before with the strategic business needs of organizations. Because technological advances are continuous and ubiquitous, . . . bottom-line margins of success will be gained through human resources-related advantages. . . . While everyone is automating, not everyone has the skills or experience to exploit successfully the advantages that automation confers. Moreover, competencies in the workplace increasingly demand skills that are not related to technology—traits such as effective communication skills, teamwork, critical thinking, and the ability to react to change, all of which tend to come with a well-developed workforce" (p. xviii). Indeed, the very concept of "strategic human resource management" reflects managers' recognition of the need to integrate their human resource management policies with strategic business initiatives (Fombrun, Tichy, & De Vanna, 1984).

Perhaps nowhere are underlying assumptions being reexamined more than in the arena of career development. In the past "career development" referred to a series of upward promotions through the hierarchy, in which individuals attained greater managerial responsibility and financial gain with each promotion. Upon entering the organization, individuals assumed the possibility (and maybe even the probability) of a long-term relationship with their employers. Formal career ladders, through which employees came to expect regular upward mobility based upon merit or even seniority, helped to reinforce the view that "up is the only way" to develop one's career. However, changes in organizations, employees, and the relationship between the two have made the assumptions underlying traditional career development systems far less tenable.

Organizations Have Changed

Many organizations have become flatter in order to increase flexibility and decision-making speed. The removal of scores of positions in the middle of the hierarchy has had important—and possibly unintended—consequences for career development systems. Positions that previously would have represented career development for individuals promoted to them have become far less abundant.

Employees Have Changed

The baby boom generation constitutes a significant portion of the entire workforce. Now firmly ensconced in middle age, many of them are highly motivated to seek promotion through the hierarchical ranks; those in their forties may especially feel that upward mobility is now or never. Thus, even if many middle management positions had not been eliminated, organizations would be under pressure to develop alternative forms of career development because of demography-induced strains on their existing systems.

Furthermore, the values of baby boomers differ from those of their parents' generation. Hall and Richter (1990) reported that baby boomers do not value promotion nearly as much as their forefathers did. This is not to say that baby boomers are unconcerned with the financial rewards of their work. Rather, baby boomers are less inclined to climb the corporate ladder as the method of attaining financial success; in addition, they appear to be less motivated by money *alone*.

Elaborating on the latter possibility, Hall and Richter (1990) identified several distinctive concerns of baby boomers at work, including the need to be able to act on their basic values, the need for psychological growth and fulfillment, and the need for autonomy. These values seem closely related to the self-conceptions assumed by self-affirmation theorists to motivate human behavior: the needs for self-identity, self-esteem, and control (Steele, 1988).

The Relationship Between Employer and Employee Has Changed

In times gone by, people had the expectation of a long-term relationship with their employers. Under the old psychological contract, most workers received job security in exchange for reasonable levels of job performance and organizational commitment. Over the longer term, promotion through the hierarchy was the payoff for their longevity, meritorious performance, or both. Of course, not everyone was promoted; however, many people were motivated by the *possibility* of promotion.

The current psychological contract under which most employees operate is much less likely to include the expectation of a long-term relationship with their employers. Organizational realities are such that people are simply not likely to remain very long with their current employers. When employees do not anticipate a long-term relationship with their employers, the notion of career development through promotion is far less viable.

Changes in the employer-employee relationship have challenged another traditional assumption underlying career development, one pertaining to its process rather than content. Accompanying the long-term perspective that many employees had with their employers was the expectation of corporate paternalism. Not only were organizations expected to offer job security (in exchange for employee loyalty), but also the major responsibility for career development was seen as residing within the firm. In sharp contrast, the new psychological contract mandates that the responsibility for career development be shared by employees and employers.

The movement toward shared responsibility probably represents more of a change for the employees than employers. After all, the latter still need to impress upon their workers the organization's needs and requirements; furthermore, organizations still must provide the resources and structures that support career development. Unlike ever before, however, employees are being asked to do their fair share: to assess themselves, and to create development plans for themselves that make sense both inside and outside of the organization (Gutteridge, Leibowitz, & Shore, 1993).

So What Are Organizations to Do?

The traditional assumptions underlying the content of career development—"up is the only way"—and the process of career development—"it's the organization's responsibility"—are no longer tenable. Thus, organizations need to develop innovative ends and means of career development. As Hall and Richter (1990) have suggested, "While the number of ways of achieving promotional success is finite (and shrinking), . . . the number of ways of achieving *psychological success* is infinite" (p. 7, our emphasis added). Self-affirmation theory (Steele, 1988) helps specify the nature of psychological success: heightened self-esteem, a clarified sense of self-identity, and an enhanced sense of control.

Toward a Taxonomy of Career Development Innovations

Let us now look at some current and possible uses of career development for achieving psychological success. While these career development innovations are generally useful, they are particularly needed in organizations experiencing downsizings and other forms of change that threaten employees' self-integrity.

Content-Based Activities

Content-based innovations refer to work activities that affirm individuals' self-integrity. They may include changes in one or more of the following: position, nature of the work, level of initiative or challenge, rewards for learning, and work-life balance.

Changes in Position

Although it is not the only kind of career development, "moving along" is an obvious and visible kind of career option. Kaye (1993) has described six kinds of career development action steps:

1. Vertical, or traditional moving ahead, which, while less available in flattened organizations, is still present since effective leaders will always be needed.
2. Lateral moves, which do not change a person's hierarchical status but do expand opportunities for learning new skills, and learning about the organization as a system.
3. Enrichment, which means adding new challenges to the responsibilities currently performed by employees.
4. Exploratory moves, which allow employees to test their skills without making large commitments (such as project assignments, temporary roles, covering for others, and so on).
5. Realignment, or starting a new path; this can be a dramatic but necessary step if the person is in a bad fit or dead-end situation.
6. Relocation, a radical change in which employees change employers, fields, or geographic locations in quest of a better fit.

These and other changes can lead to greater insight into one's self, a broader skill base, and a better fit between one's life space and the work environment. Lateral, enrichment, and exploratory moves may help people develop a greater sense of self-esteem. Realignments and relocations are likely to affect individuals' sense of identity and may heighten their sense of control.

Network theory also may account for the self-affirming quality of many of the position changes described above. If the change puts people in a more central location in the social network, then they may feel more self-affirmed. For example, if people move to boundary-spanning roles within the organization (or between the organization and the external environment), they may feel one or more of the following forms of self-affirmation: (1) greater self-esteem, because their heightened centrality connotes that they are more integral members of the organization, (2) a stronger sense of control, in that various others may be more dependent on them, and (3) a clearer sense of their identity, in that they may be better able to define themselves in relation to others in the network.

Changes in the Nature of the Work

At some point a time-limited enrichment activity may turn into a permanent change in the person's work. This may happen when technology encroaches into an area (for example, compare the work of a "librarian" with that of a "database manager"). The person does not move; rather, the field that the person is in does the moving.

A sea change occurs, sweeping lots of people along. Some people do not see such changes as career development opportunities because they represent a threat, much as in the way that a downsizing can. It is easy to feel out of control during a sea change. However, these events can be viewed as developmental windows if employers and employees cooperate in helping the latter maintain a sense of control.

Changes in Level of Initiative or Challenge

A series of studies on career derailment performed at the Center for Creative Leadership (McCall, 1988) found that start-up situations, turnarounds, and other high-risk challenges can be watershed experiences for up-and-coming executives. The key is to provide support to the individuals so that their sense of control is not overwhelmed. A success of this sort does wonders for self-esteem and identity.

Recently, many organizations have tried to encourage "intrapreneurship," in which members take the initiative to create opportunities or address problems in the existing system. The feasibility of intrapreneuring in large organizations is a matter of some controversy. Further complicating the matter is the pace of organizational change; what was once seen as an intrapreneuring opportunity is now as likely to be seen as an activity to be outsourced, or to be tackled through an alliance. In any event, there are possibilities for people to take major initiatives under supportive conditions, and do both themselves and their employers a big favor.

Changes in Rewards for Learning

There are many criteria that can be used to decide how to pay people. Everyone seems to agree that level and seniority are not the only ways. Some alternatives include need, earnings history, performance, comparable worth, and market considerations. An additional alternative is pay for competence, or for acquiring new skills that may be useful to the employer. Indeed, organizations that encourage lateral moves can put their money where their mouths are by offering financial rewards to employees who have expanded their skill base.

Changes in Work-Life Balance

Career development and life development are intimately woven together. A number of potentially self-affirming options are available to organizations, if they accept the legitimacy of the "total person" approach. Such was the case at Arizona Public Service (APS), a utility company. In a recent address to the Academy of Management, CEO Mark De Michele (1994) described the company's efforts to reengineer itself, beginning in the late 1980s, to be in the "top five by '95." A critical component of their efforts was to provide individuals with the opportunity to define, and then act upon, their personal values. As De Michele explained: "One of our goals was to give people a stronger sense of self, of being in control of their lives and their destiny, and of being able to create and capture their dreams. For years, companies have asked people to leave their personal lives and their dreams at the door—to have a work self and a personal self. That's not realistic! . . . We want them to become more integrated, whole persons. Only by doing that can they meet their fullest human potential."

As exemplified by the following remarks (and consistent with self-affirmation theory) De Michele recognized that by helping employees strengthen their sense of self, the organization would find its workforce better equipped to cope with potential threats to their self-integrity. "We are trying, first, to help people reach their own potential and demand more of themselves than they ever thought possible. Second, we're trying to teach people to use that potential to help APS compete at warp speed. . . . For example, we're encouraging people to develop a strategic plan *for their own lives, not just their work.* Because when competition really heats up, we want people focused. We want them thinking, learning and operating at their peak, not worrying about problems at home. I believe these are the kinds of things that will separate the winners from the also-rans" (our emphasis added).

And oh, yes: APS did reach its goal of being in the top five of all public utility companies—two full years ahead of schedule!

Process-Based Activities

Process-based activities refer to *how* people go about positioning themselves for content-based career development experiences. Most of the emphasis in the recent career development literature is on the content component. Our discussions with human resource managers suggest that they are forever wanting to know *what* other companies are doing by way of innovations in career development. While the content of the innovations is quite significant, it is also important not to lose sight of the process of career development. Like the content component, the process may influence employees' sense of esteem, identity, and control.

The fact that employees are now shouldering more responsibility for their own career development lends itself to several potentially self-affirming experiences. For example, one aspect of employee responsibility for career development is greater emphasis on self-assessment, in which individuals define their skills, values, and preferences. Self-assessment requires individuals to be introspective, the result of which could be a clearer sense of self-identity. Moreover, the ultimate responsibility for introspection must rest with individuals themselves; as a result, they may feel a greater sense of control in shaping their own destinies.

When employees assume greater responsibility for their career development, their self-esteem may increase. Anecdotal evidence is provided by the recent experience of AT&T, which developed the Alliance Learning Center (ALC) to enhance the employment security of survivors of the initial layoffs in the mid–1980s. The ALC offers concrete resources (such as tuition for courses taken at local colleges) as well as a variety of educational, training, and counseling services, all designed to help people take greater initiative for their own career development. The success of the ALC is indicated in part by an extremely high level of employee participation. Furthermore, "ALC staff believe that the most important measure is how people feel about themselves and how they have changed—both of which are positive" (Gutteridge, Leibowitz, & Shore, 1993, p. 168).

Having extolled the virtues of greater employee responsibility for their own career development, we should mention a possible downside risk. According to attribution theory (Weiner, 1980), the valence of an outcome has a greater impact on how people feel about themselves when the outcome is attributed to internal rather than external causes. Thus, people will feel better about themselves when they attribute positive outcomes to themselves, but their self-esteem will suffer when they attribute negative outcomes to internal causes. Consequently, the trend toward greater employee responsibility for their career development may raise the psychological stakes associated with how people see their career development. If they think that their career development is progressing nicely, then they will feel especially self-affirmed. If, however, people think their career development reflects negative outcomes, then their perceived role in producing such outcomes may elicit a strong threat to their self-integrity.

Of course, the extent to which the process of career development is self-affirming depends on how well the organization fulfills *its* share of the responsibility. A sure-fire recipe for employee paralysis is for a previously paternalistic organization to shift the responsibility for career development to its workforce without providing a supportive climate. Commenting more generally about the movement toward greater employee participation, Kanter (1983) noted that delegation of decision-making authority does not free organizations of their responsibilities to support their now empowered workforce.

Indeed, several organizations are offering support in ways that should make the process of career development more self-affirming. Consider the career development workshop at Chevron, which consists of three modules (Lewis, 1994). The first module focuses on self-assessment, in which people define their skills, talents, and interests. In the second module people learn about other job opportunities as well as how to find them. Somewhat controversially, these alternative opportunities may be either inside *or* outside Chevron. In the third module former Chevron employees who were laid off one year earlier report to current employees about their experiences. Former employees describe what they did while at Chevron and what they are doing now; perhaps just as important, they discuss the nature of the journey from their former to their current positions.

Lewis reports that many of the workshop participants felt an enhanced sense of control over their future. The second module in the workshop may have contributed to feelings of control by allowing people to see that there is life after their current position at Chevron, even if it were to mean leaving the company. The third module may have reinforced individuals' sense of control by providing vivid examples of models who formerly held positions similar to their own; the models had been laid off, but nevertheless landed on their feet. In his influential theory of self-efficacy, Bandura (1977) identified observational learning as one of the processes that influence people's feelings of competence. Individuals' self-efficacy may be enhanced when they have the opportunity to see similar others successfully execute the target behavior. If the career development workshop at Chevron heightened individuals' sense of control, then exposure to successful role models probably was one of the influential factors.

An increasing number of companies are recognizing the potential value of employee introspection. Indeed, some organizations even are encouraging their employees to be more introspective outside the domain of career development activity. AT&T, PepsiCo, and Aetna, for example, have included introspection training in their management development programs. Managers and academics alike agree that introspection is especially needed to help employees cope with the uncertainties brought on by layoffs (and other significant changes). Joseph Galerneau, head of executive training at AT&T, suggested that "this company is not going to be successful unless we have people who can learn from experience. . . . It takes a certain amount of reflection to do that successfully" (Sherman, 1994, p. 93). John Kotter of Harvard Business School similarly noted, "You grab a challenge, act on it, then honestly reflect on why your action worked or didn't. . . . That continuous process of lifelong learning helps enormously in a rapidly changing economic environment" (Sherman, 1994, p. 93).

Introspection that has already proved helpful to people experiencing various life stresses also may be useful to layoff survivors. In a series of studies, James Pennebaker and his colleagues had participants experiencing a traumatic change take twenty minutes a day for three to five consecutive days to write their deepest thoughts and feelings about the change event. In one study the participants were a group of seasoned professionals (mean age, fifty-four) who had been laid off by their employer five months earlier (Spera, Buhrfeind, & Pennebaker, 1994). All had failed to become reemployed; not surprisingly, most of them were quite hostile and angry at the time of the study. Three groups were studied. One group took part in the expressive-writing exercise described above, a second group wrote about less personal matters (their plans for the day and their job search activities), and a third group did no writing at all. The first group was significantly more likely to gain reemployment within four months than each of the other two groups (whose reemployment rates did not differ).

Expressive-writing exercises or other activities that promote certain forms of introspection may help layoff survivors adjust to the threats of downsizings. According to self-affirmation theory, such activities will be most useful when they help people gain a clearer sense of who they are, when they heighten feelings of self-esteem, and when they enhance their sense of control. The process of career development includes activities (such as self-assessment) that foster introspection. Given the trend toward greater employee responsibility for career development, more needs to be learned about how to make the self-assessment aspect of career development more effective in promoting employees' self-awareness. Activities that increase survivors' self-awareness may be a powerful antidote to the self-integrity threats elicited by layoffs.

Going Beyond the Self

As important as it is to learn about the self, the process of career development would be incomplete if it did not also help make employees more knowledgeable about their work environments.

London (1983) suggested that one of the important components of career motivation is insight, defined as "the extent to which the person has realistic perceptions of him or herself *and the organization* and relates these perceptions to career goals" (p. 621, emphasis added). Employees need information about the structure of the company, which entails knowing more than reporting relationships. To plan their development people need to know how the work flows through the system; such knowledge will help them determine the skills, interests, and talents that will be needed. There also is the need to know about the direction and speed of change in the company and the industry, and their implications for short-term career planning. Perhaps most of all, people need to know where to learn this kind of information. Who are the informed sources, the mentors, the storytellers, insiders, and sages who can give people a sense of control over what may be experienced as an elusive and volatile organization (or industry)?

Employees also need resources. Career development cannot happen without budgets, without time away from one's desk, and without the chance to talk to people. Access to informed sources is itself a resource and should be shared with the people who need it. Some companies have created in-house career centers, especially in the aftermath of downsizings. Forward-thinking organizations already had such services, or at least installed them concurrently with the downsizings. Other companies were loudly told by survivors that they resented all of the career planning resources being spent on people who were no longer going to be with the firm. As in all aspects of career development, the responsibility for making people more aware of their work environments must be shared by employees and employers.

One virtue of organizationwide career planning is that it assigns to certain parties the task of ensuring that appropriate planning materials find their way into the hands of each employee. Such programs also help to establish a companywide norm that it is appropriate to be discussing career planning matters openly. One possible danger of companywide programs is that they may provide individual managers with an excuse for not paying attention to the career development needs of their own staffs. Morgan, Hall, and Martier (1979) found that in effective companywide career programs, responsibility was shared between employee and employer, and much of the success rested with guidance provided by one's immediate boss and the intelligent utilization of the work tasks at hand.

Conclusion

This chapter applies self-affirmation theory to the practice of career development in organizations that have been buffeted by downsizings (and related large-scale changes). The three dimensions of self-integrity—identity, esteem, and control—may be viewed as goals to achieve in the design of human resource practices and policies (career development *and* otherwise) that facilitate adjustment to a rapidly changing work environment.

In reviewing nine themes of successful innovations in career development Gutteridge, Leibowitz, and Shore (1993) suggested that "one of the most striking features of these themes is that they all demonstrate that career development should be considered *a work in progress*" (p. 194, emphasis added). Perhaps career development is a work in progress because the psychological substrates of career development—esteem, identity, and control—are themselves works in progress. As mental health professionals have repeatedly pointed out (for example, Rogers, 1961), the attainment of a healthy self-image is not a finite end product but rather is an ongoing, lifelong process.

References
Argyris, C. (1985). *Strategy, change, and defensive routines*. Marshfield, MA: Pitman.

Ashford, S. J., Lee, C., & Bobko, P. (1989). Content, causes, and consequences of job security: A theory-based measure and substantive test. *Academy of Management Journal, 32*, 803–829.

Bandura, A. (1977). Self-efficacy: Toward a unifying theory of behavior change. *Psychological Review, 84*, 191–215.

Bridges, W. (1988). *Surviving corporate transition: Rational management in a world of mergers, layoffs, start-ups, takeovers, divestitures, deregulations, and new technologies*. New York: Doubleday.

Brockner, J., & Greenberg, J. (1990). The impact of layoffs on survivors: An organizational justice perspective. In J. S. Carroll (Ed.), *Applied social psychology and organizational settings* (pp. 45–75). Hillsdale, NJ: Erlbaum.

Brockner, J., Grover, S., Reed, T., De Witt, R. L., & O'Malley, M. (1987). Survivors' reactions to layoffs: We get by with a little help from our friends. *Administrative Science Quarterly, 32,* 526–541.

Brockner, J., Konovsky, M., Cooper-Schneider, R., Folger, R., Martin, C., & Bies, R. J. (1994). The interactive effects of procedural justice and outcome negativity on the victims and survivors of job loss. *Academy of Management Journal, 37,* 397–409.

Brockner, J., Tyler, T. R., & Cooper-Schneider, R. (1992). The influence of prior commitment to an institution on reactions to perceived unfairness: The higher they are, the harder they fall. *Administrative Science Quarterly, 37,* 241–261.

Brockner, J., & Wiesenfeld, B. M. (1993). Living on the edge (of social and organizational psychology): The effects of job layoffs on those who remain. In J. K. Murnighan (Ed.), *Social psychology in organizations: Advances in theory and research* (pp. 119–140). Englewood Cliffs, NJ: Prentice Hall.

Cascio, W. (1993). Downsizing: What do we know? What have we learned? *Academy of Management Executive, 7,* 95–104.

De Michele, M. (1994). *Overcoming barriers with a change-ready culture.* Paper presented at the Academy of Management Convention, Dallas.

Fombrun, C. J., Tichy, N. M., & De Vanna, M. A. (1984). *Strategic human resource development.* New York: Wiley.

Gutteridge, T. G., Leibowitz, Z. B., & Shore, J. E. (1993). *Organizational career development: Benchmarks for building a world-class workforce.* San Francisco: Jossey-Bass.

Hall, D. T., & Richter, J. (1990). Career gridlock: Baby boomers hit the wall. *Academy of Management Executive, 4,* 7–22.

Kanter, R. M. (1983). *The change masters.* New York: Simon & Schuster.

Lewis, K. J. (1994). *Implications of career development on employee trust and empowerment at Chevron.* Paper presented at the Academy of Management Conference, Dallas.

London, M. (1983). Toward a theory of career motivation. *Academy of Management Review, 8,* 620–630

McCall, M. W. (1988). *The lessons of experience.* New York: Macmillan.

Mead, G. H. (1934). *Mind, self, and society.* Chicago: University of Chicago Press.

Morgan, M. A., Hall, D. T., & Martier, A. (1979). Career development strategies in industry: Where are we and where should we be? *Personnel,* 13–30.

Noer, D. M. (1993). *Healing the wounds: Overcoming the trauma of layoffs and revitalizing downsized organizations.* San Francisco: Jossey-Bass.

Rogers, C. R. (1961). *On becoming a person.* Boston: Houghton Mifflin.

Sherman, S. (1994, August 22). Leaders learn to heed the voice within. *Fortune.*

Smith, L. (1994, July 25). Burned-out bosses. *Fortune.*

Spera, S. P., Buhrfeind, E. D., & Pennebaker, J. W. (1994). Expressive writing and coping with job loss. *Academy of Management Journal, 37,* 722–733.

Steele, C. M. (1988). The psychology of self-affirmation: Sustaining the integrity of the self. In L. Berkowitz (Ed.), *Advances in experimental social psychology* (vol. 21, pp. 261–302). San Diego, CA: Academic Press.

Tajfel, H., & Turner, J. (1979). An integrative theory of intergroup conflicts. In W. G. Austin and S. Worchel (Eds.), *The social psychology of intergroup relations* (pp. 33–47). Pacific Grove, CA: Brooks/Cole.

Weiner, B. (1980). A cognitive (attribution)-emotion-action model of motivated behavior: An analysis of judgment of help-giving. *Journal of Personality and Social Psychology, 39,* 186–200.

Wiesenfeld, B. M., Brockner, J., & Martin, C. (1995). *A self-affirmation model of individual reactions to organizational change.* In preparation.

CHAPTER 4

Integrated Human Resource Development
Building Professional Competencies and Communities

Edward M. Mone
Melissa A. Bilger

In today's large companies there is certainly an emphasis on decentralization and being close to the customer, while shrinking the centralized corporate function. As a result, many professionals, including those in engineering, systems, marketing, and human resources, are working apart from a majority of their colleagues in divisions or business units around the country, if not around the world. This raises at least two questions: how to ensure consistent and appropriate development for all members of a professional group and how to create in them a sense of membership in their professional community.

This chapter is a case study about one such group of professionals in a large, global company. It details how the authors and company leaders worked together to answer these questions as they tried to develop a community of world class professionals. This case study will be of particular interest to human resource managers and industrial and organizational psychologists responsible for any or all of the following: professional or management development; assisting organization leadership in building a community of professionals within centralized or decentralized organization structures; supporting organization change through the design and implementation of human performance systems.

Developing Community

Organizations, as open systems, interact with their environments (Katz & Kahn, 1978). Successful organizations are those that adapt effectively to meet environmental challenges. Competitors, regulators, and customers typically provide significant challenges. However, this chapter details a more unusual challenge. We examine how the financial function of a major global corporation approached the problem of developing a world class professional *community*.

Dewey (1954) offers the following on community: "Whenever there is conjoint activity whose consequences are appreciated as good by all singular persons who take part in it, and where the realization of the good is such as to effect an energetic desire and effort to sustain it in being just because it is a good shared by all, there is in so far a community" (p. 149).

Begging the question of what is the "good" for this community, the challenge that makes this case study of particular interest is that the more than fifteen thousand employees in this financial function, when viewed as members of a community, can be said to be working in a postmodern organization (Harvey, 1989; Kvale, 1992). Much like today's social milieu, the members of this community exist in a world of fragmentation and multiple realities. For example, members of this community occupy places in more than twenty business units and divisions worldwide, in scores of geographically dispersed locations. Their membership can take many forms and can be expressed in layers, such as their work groups (the revenue journalization team), the functional groups they support (marketing, sales, public relations, and so on), their business unit or division (customer-focused organizations), the overall corporate entity, and finally their own financial community.

Because of this, many employees express uncertainty about community membership. Although the chief financial officer and staff of direct reports understand the need and value of a strong, competent financial community for the success of the overall company, the rank and file membership do not share in this understanding. For the leadership this left two major challenges.

The first challenge was to define and communicate the rationale for and purpose of the community; that is, to define the "good" that would unite a characteristically postmodern organization. The financial leadership concluded that the rationale for community was to better serve the business as a whole; its purpose was to promote information sharing, develop integrated solutions for customers, and ensure the development of its members. The second and related challenge was to determine for what and how to develop community members. Synonymous with what other global leaders have said, particularly those familiar with benchmarking (see Fitz-enz, 1993), the financial boss chose "world-class professionals" as the parameter for the "what." The authors, organization development consultants in the boss's human resources organization, led the officer and the direct report team in defining the "how."

To ensure the development of a world-class professional community, we partnered with the financial leadership in the design, development, and implementation of a human performance system (HPS), with a specific focus on development and career planning. HPS is defined as an integrated and comprehensive approach to the design of standard human resource functions to support the achievement of business objectives. In essence, human resource systems would focus on the business initiative of developing a community of world-class professionals.

More specifically, this case study describes and analyzes the implementation of a human performance system, with a specific emphasis on development and career planning, as one way to achieve world-class competency, aid in the building of a community ethos, and offer an alternative for managing employee development in a downsizing environment.

The balance of this chapter includes:

- Delineation of the human performance system (HPS) concept and its role in developing a community of world-class professionals
- Discussion of the nature and structure of the change

- Description of the competency-based development and career planning process and tools custom designed for this community
- Lessons learned in applying change management principles in an attempt to implement HPS and build a community
- The impact of downsizing on the implementation of HPS and the community

Evolution of the Human Performance System Concept

The concept of an integrated human performance system as a vehicle for supporting organization and community transformation is an outgrowth of our experience in facilitating large-scale organization change. Whether facilitating the introduction of a new leadership paradigm or supporting an organization's leaders in the transformation to a process quality management environment, we recognized that our client organizations' human performance practices were not being altered to support and sustain the respective changes. These practices had deep cultural roots and were extremely resilient to change. Therefore, by not supporting changes in these practices the organization's leadership inhibited rather than fostered their intended change efforts.

For example, although one organization desired to move to a process quality management environment that demanded teamwork for its ultimate success, its strategy and practice for compensation remained strongly individual-based (see London & Mone, 1994, for a case discussion of this organization's transformation efforts). As a result, organization members were reluctant to change the ways in which they worked because their perceptions about what would be rewarded remained the same.

In many ways, the recognition of the importance of human performance practices to organization design, change, and development is not new. Using the language of Porras and Robertson from their overview chapter on organization development, "diagnostic OD implementation theories" have referenced the key role of human performance practices and their necessary linkage to organization strategy and goals. For example, Kotter (1978) discusses organizational arrangements, including job design, measurement and reward systems, hiring and development systems; and Nadler and Tushman (1980) refer to the organization's human resource management system, which includes "processes for selection, placement, appraisal, training, rewarding, etc." (p. 274). Porras and Robertson also define a category called "organizing arrangements," which includes goal setting, administrative systems (specifically personnel management systems), and reward systems (pay, benefits and performance appraisal). It was our experience, however, that human performance system practices were being underemphasized, if not neglected, in most organization change efforts.

One of our earlier attempts to emphasize the need for integrated human performance practices to support organization change (Mone, 1988) was to argue for the redesign of goal setting, development, performance management, appraisal and compensation processes in order to institutionalize a specific managerial role of "developer." Others have also highlighted the need for explicit changes in human performance practices in order to achieve organization change success in support of business objectives. Schuler (1992), in writing on strategic human resources management, presents the 5-P Model as a framework for how organizations can ensure integration and synergy between their overall HR efforts and strategic needs of the organization. This model, similar in nature to the HPS concept described in this case, requires a clear articulation of and linkage among human resources philosophy, policies, programs, practices, and processes in support of the strategic needs of the business.

At this point we want to make explicit a key assumption: the proper design and integration of human performance systems practices, along with their successful implementation within an organization, are necessary for the organization to achieve its change initiatives and strategic goals.

Components of the Human Performance System

We suggest that ten key components are essential to an effective human performance system (later in this chapter, we focus on two specific components). These ten components have been selected because they can meet the following criteria:

- Each is largely under the control of a manager or supervisor to use.
- Each has face and content validity; that is, it seems to make sense given the strategic business goals.
- The linkage between each and all of the components is explicit.

From this perspective, any organization's human performance system will be contingent upon its specific needs and the strategic objectives it must achieve.

We generally represent the human performance system as is shown in Figure 4.1 It is a simple way to indicate and communicate its system aspects and the interconnection of the components.

We define each of the HPS components in Table 4.1. These are conceptual definitions that help members of the community understand each of the components.

Figure 4.1. The Human Performance System.

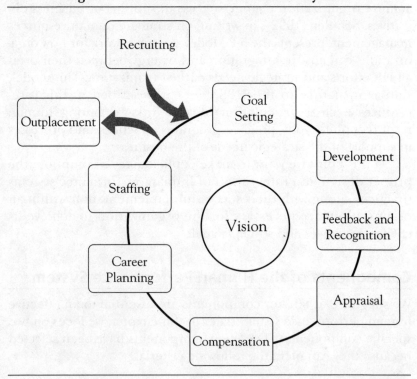

Table 4.1. Definitions of HPS Components.

Recruiting	Attracting and retaining a diverse mix of people to meet near- and long-term business needs; represents the input of human resources into HPS.
Goal Setting	Negotiating team and individual goals (behavioral as well as performance) linked to organization and corporate vision and strategic goals.
Development	Identifying requirements for and acquiring new skills and knowledge related both to current job goals and career plans.
Feedback and Recognition	Providing ongoing formal and informal feedback from multiple sources on performance relative to goals and recognition of key behaviors or progress toward goal attainment.
Appraisal	Documenting performance over an agreed-upon period (such as 1 year), representing the culmination of the ongoing feedback process and reflecting the degree of attainment of the negotiated goals.
Compensation	Providing base pay increases and/or bonuses to strengthen the relationship between rewards and team and individual goal attainment.
Career Planning	Identifying employees' skills, interests and desired career goals and matching them with future opportunities in the business.
Staffing	Matching employees with current job opportunities, both to capitalize on their existing skills to produce needed business results and to provide development opportunities in line with their career goals.
Outplacement	Helping employees exit the business as necessitated by changing business requirements, skills mismatches or limited career opportunities.
Diversity	Valuing the contributions people bring from different backgrounds and promoting equal employment opportunity in staffing and promotion decisions.

The HPS philosophy, policies, practices, and specific programs unique to this case of building a world-class professional financial community will be discussed later. In essence, this case serves as an example of how this human performance system concept can be implemented to support organization development and change.

The Nature of the Change

What is the role of HPS in this case? It was developed and implemented to support organization change. What is the change? Specifically, to create a community culture in a fragmented functional organization, and to focus on developing world-class financial professionals to support achievement of business goals. In the language of Porras and Robertson (1992), this change is both *second order* (it involves a shift in fundamental assumptions about the nature of relationships) and *planned* (it originates with a deliberate decision to improve functioning). Porras and Robertson classify this kind of change as *transformational*. Table 4.2 details the essence of this transformation.

Structure of the Change Process

The major sponsor for the change effort was the chief financial officer, who led a team of eight vice presidents, including the trea-

Table 4.2. Introduction of HPS: A Transformational Change.

Case Example: *Introduction of HPS*

Goal of Leadership	Provide world class financial counsel and services to business partners.
What was the change?	Create a sense of community and develop world class financial professionals.
What was specifically changing?	The financial leadership and HR partnered to create an integrated human performance system, focusing on development and career planning.
What was the expected outcome?	Provide support for professional development, create of a sense of urgency, foster the sense of community spirit.

surer, controller, and group financial officers; together, this group operated as a functional steering committee for the corporate financial organization (CFO). Directly reporting to these team members were more than fifty financial senior managers with functional responsibilities in the areas of accounting, auditing, treasury, controllership, financial services, and financial support. These fifty-eight financial leaders, along with the senior community quality and human resources officers, constituted a management council. A relatively new structure, this council was formed to help foster cross-boundary and cross-organizational support and communication, and to create a sense of community.

The approach for designing, developing, and implementing the human performance system was to establish teams, with members from the council partnering with selected human resource professionals. Membership on these teams was suggested by the officer group as a way to improve working relationships across the community; for some, the teams provided the initial opportunity to actually meet and work with their colleagues in the financial community. The authors and the human resource professionals on these teams were selected based on their areas of expertise and were asked to provide support both in terms of their specific functional area and in change management.

Five teams were created, eight to ten members per team, with some change in team membership and leadership during the eighteen-month period during which these teams met. Three of the teams focused on HPS components: (college) recruiting, development, and career planning. The fourth team focused on the financial leadership's goal of promoting diversity. The fifth team served as an integrating mechanism, coordinating the efforts of and ensuring consistency among the other teams. Leaders from each of the other functional teams, as well as the human resources leader, made up this team.

The reason for focusing on these four areas in depth was a strategic one: these areas would have the most impact in terms of fostering a sense of community. How each of the four areas contributed to community development is described in Table 4.3.

These four, arguably, would also most directly contribute to developing world-class professionalism. It was over these four areas as well that the leadership of the community felt they exercised the most control. For example, business units and divisions often had

**Table 4.3. The Role of HPS Components
in Community Development.**

Component	Role in Community Development
Diversity	Fosters recognition and valuing of differences that community members bring.
Career Planning	Provides common paradigm, as well as resources, for career management.
Development	Specifies the requirements for world class professionalism, and provides necessary resources.
Recruiting	Defines hires as members of a community, rather than as members of a specific business unit or division.

unique appraisal or compensation policies, plans, and processes that made sense for their strategic purposes. To impose a different, or worse yet, additional community process upon the financial people in these organizations would be viewed as an unnecessary administrative burden. As a result, principles rather than shared practices were articulated for the other HPS components in the belief that if these principles were followed, a stronger sense of community could be established.

Why, however, was there a more specific and in-depth emphasis on development and career planning in this community? The leadership had several reasons for choosing to focus on development and career planning. They had a clear sense that community members currently lacked the competencies to be world class, although they could not yet articulate what those needed competencies would be. They recognized that both current and future financial leaders needed much stronger people-management skills and a deeper understanding of their customers' underlying business, and that the leadership had historically undervalued and underdeveloped these competencies relative to functional, financial skills. Employee feedback, leadership assessments, and exit interview results all indicated weakness in developing employees for the future and providing meaningful career opportunities. And, finally, the leadership hoped that shared development and career planning processes would strengthen the sense of community among employees at all levels.

Defining "World Class": The CFO Competency Model

As previously discussed, the top leaders determined that they wanted to build a community of world-class professionals. However, they could not immediately articulate what specifically such professionals would know or be able to do. They looked to the HPS development team to fill in the gaps and define the competencies that would be present in a world-class organization community.

The financial directors on the development team agreed that the competency model needed to be future focused, and they recognized the importance of balancing their internally grown view of how the world worked with some external perspectives. As a result, their first step was to charter an analysis of the external and business environments and workforce trends. The directors spent a day together exploring the compiled trends and identifying the implications for the financial community and its managers. Building from those implications, they then created an initial competency model.

This model then went through multiple analyses and revisions. It was compared with other competency models from both inside and outside the corporation. Numerous teams of employees participated in reviews, helping to validate the competencies across management levels and develop behavioral descriptions of excellence for each competency. The model was also reviewed by the entire organization leadership team several times. As a result of this process, the final model not only had the support of the entire CFO leadership team and key managers across the community, but also included sufficient validated detail to enable the HR professionals to develop supporting tools.

The final version of the model included forty-one competencies grouped into three categories: leadership/managerial competencies (such as strategic thinking, building information networks, and energizing and empowering others), business environment competencies (corporate products and services, global economics and business trends, and business ethics) and functional/technical competencies (accounting, decision and risk analysis, and internal control). The final model clearly defined all of the competencies and provided specific descriptors of excellence for each, generally expressed as behaviors, skills, or knowledge.

The competency model has become instrumental in helping to bring about the desired community development. The actual process of developing the model caused the financial leaders to discuss and come to agreement on the "people" requirements for future success, a dialogue that had not previously occurred and which served to better align the leaders with each other and the desired future state. The model itself has provided the financial leaders across the business a common focus and language, which has continued to build their sense of connection to the community. Among the top leadership, the model has brought a new clarity to staffing and career planning discussions, as they learn to describe both key job requirements and members' qualifications in terms of this common language of competencies.

The impact of the model has extended well beyond the leadership team. To all community members, it represents the leadership's commitment to change in two ways. First, it explicitly articulates the requirement that leadership/managerial and business competencies be developed in balance with the more traditional functional/technical competencies (a major shift in priorities). Second, the competencies are consistent with the expressed vision and values of the community and, in fact, they make more explicit what it will look like when that vision and those values come to life.

On a more personal level for the community members, the model provides a clear sense of what the leadership is looking for, important input for development and career planning efforts. Because such information had not previously been available in any systematic way, and had not been consistent across the various financial organizations, the model also serves to create a greater sense of career opportunity for employees who previously had felt limited by their own organization's boundaries. Yet a real risk was that the competency model, although embraced by the leadership, would trickle down only inconsistently to the employees, especially given the community's generally poor communication track record. To the extent that this occurred, significant benefits would be lost.

For this reason, the development and career planning teams determined that they must provide tools to help community members take advantage of the opportunity provided by the model's existence, tools that would help employees focus their personal and career development efforts in the direction of the world-class competencies defined by the leadership. The two teams thus agreed to sponsor the creation of a joint set of tools for all members of the community.

In the following section we focus our attention on this joint product—the HPS Development and Career Planning Toolkit— how it was developed, the process and tools it provided, how it was implemented with employees, and how it supported the development of this community at multiple levels.

The Toolkit: A Resource for Building World-Class Competency

The purpose of the Development and Career Planning (D&CP) Toolkit was to help the organization community members continuously develop their skills and effectively plan their careers, thus preparing them and the community as a whole for continued success in the future. A secondary purpose was to introduce and put into use the new CFO competency model.

The D&CP Toolkit was designed and developed by a team of five human resource and organizational development professionals (including the two of us, who had the dual role of supporting the director-level HPS development and career planning teams). This team worked aggressively to involve employees at all levels across the community in various stages of the development of the Toolkit, to maximize both its effectiveness and ultimate acceptance. The final result of this extensive process was a D&CP Toolkit that financial managers commend as targeted precisely to their needs and both easy and rewarding to use.

The Toolkit begins with a booklet titled *Getting Started* that outlines the purpose, approach, organization, and contents. Because community members were using the terms *development* and *career planning* in many different ways, it was important to clarify the language to be used throughout the Toolkit. *Development* is defined as "a continuous, lifelong process in which you acquire or enhance the *competencies*—the skills, knowledge, behaviors or perspectives— important to your job, professional career and personal growth." *Career planning* is defined as "a deliberate process in which you engage to identify your personal career-related goal—based upon an examination of your interests, preferences, values, competencies and motivations—and to establish a plan to achieve that goal." The strong interrelationship of the two processes is emphasized in this booklet, as well as throughout the ensuing descriptions of the process stages and related tools.

The interrelationship and integration of the development and career planning processes (see Figure 4.2) serves as the basis for all that would follow in the Toolkit. The six process stages are expressed in reader-centered language (such as "Who Am I? What Do I Want?") to encourage employees to take personal ownership of each stage.

Each process stage is supported by tools, such as assessments, a planning portfolio, or resource, and by a booklet explaining how

Figure 4.2. The Development and Career Planning Process.

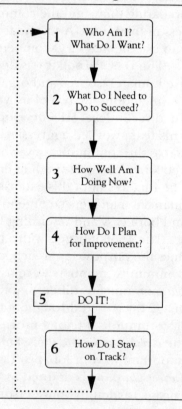

1. Choose your career goal by matching your preferences, interests, and values with career opportunities.

2. Identify which of the competencies you need to achieve job mastery, professional development, and your career goal.

3. Assess yourself on the competencies you identified in stage 2 and get feedback from others.

4. Create your development, plan, including activities to improve three or four competencies based on your assessment results.

5. Participate in planned development activities.

6. Reflect on what you are learning and consider revisions to your plan.

1 Who Am I? What Do I Want?

2 What Do I Need to Do to Succeed?

3 How Well Am I Doing Now?

4 How Do I Plan for Improvement?

5 DO IT!

6 How Do I Stay on Track?

to use the tools in the context of the activities and decisions involved in that stage. The Getting Started section of the Toolkit provides the *Getting Started* booklet mentioned earlier and several tools that could be used throughout the entire process: the CFO competency model with definitions and behaviors, the future trends analysis that was used in the development of the competencies, and an Integrated Planning Portfolio for documenting the results of development and career planning efforts.

The next six sections of the Toolkit relate to each of the six process stages, with each section containing the process guidelines booklet and tools for that stage. In Stage 1, "Who Am I? What Do I Want?" (the career planning stage), the tools include six career inventories with interpretation guidelines, a career goal analysis worksheet, and a resource describing key job families across the financial community. The inventories range from the standard (job characteristics, work environment, and career values) to the customized (behavior preferences and career interests based on the CFO competency model). Also included was a newly developed Career Motivation Inventory, based on London's (1983) career motivation typology.

In Stage 2, "What Do I Need to Do to Succeed?" a competency-targeting tool helps to determine which of the forty-one competencies are most critical for success in an employee's current job, desired career, or profession. This selection is the basis for Stage 3, "How Well Am I Doing Now?" which includes an assessment tool for each of the competencies. These assessment tools provide employees the opportunity to evaluate key behaviors associated with each competency along two dimensions: how effectively the competency is performed and how frequently the competency is demonstrated. This approach was based upon employee requests to help them differentiate between those behaviors they do not do well and those they do well but not often enough or in appropriate circumstances.

The actual work in this process stage involves preparing a customized assessment tool, selecting the assessments for the competencies identified as critical in Stage 2, and deciding how in-depth an assessment to do. The customized tool is then used to conduct both a competency self-assessment and to solicit feedback from others, including peers, subordinates and supervisor as appropriate.

An assessment summary tool is also provided to help aggregate the feedback from others and maintain key data for use in planning, such as specific problem behaviors within a competency and whether the problem is one of frequency or effectiveness.

In Stage 4, "How Do I Plan for Improvement?" three resource tools help the employee formulate a development plan based on the results of the Stage 3 assessments. All three of these tools work together to encourage employees to think differently about their development and, in particular, to consider a range of learning opportunities beyond traditional classroom training.

The first tool, Promoting Continuous Learning, helps employees to understand the elements that contribute to effective learning and to become more aware of their predominant learning styles. This tool also helps the employees determine the types of learning activities that might be most effective for them and how to maximize the outcome of a given learning activity. The next tool, the Resource Matrix, provides a listing of internally available learning resources for each of the competencies, including courses, computer-based training, video and audio tapes, and books. In addition, the tool provides a list of professional organizations and, for many of the functional/technical competencies, contact information for organizations that conduct development or certification programs. A companion tool, On-the-Job Experiences, provides suggestions for how to develop each competency on the job, either in lieu of or in support of more formal development activities.

Stages 5 and 6, "Do It!" and "How Do I Stay on Track?" include no new tools of their own, relying instead on the results of the previous stages as summarized in the Integrated Planning Portfolio. Stage 6 also reinforces the cyclical nature of this process, encouraging employees to periodically review their plans, their progress toward achieving their career and development goals, and whether, in fact, their goals are still meaningful, and directing them back into the process as needed.

The Toolkit also includes two other resources that are unique in their intended audience. The process stages in the Toolkit had been focused on and written toward the perspective of the individual employee. Yet we realized and acknowledged early in the Toolkit that the success of the overall development and career planning process and the employees using it also depended upon the support provided by supervisors and the leadership of the organization. Thus the final section of the Toolkit provides a Supervisor's Guide, which reaffirms the supervisor's support responsibilities and provides coaching tips for each stage in the process, and a Leader's Adaptation Guide, which helps each organization leader customize the process and tools for maximum success in the specific environment without losing the sense of community.

Introducing the D&CP Toolkit

The implementation of HPS across the financial community, and the introduction of the D&CP Toolkit as one element in that overall implementation, were as complicated as one would expect in a postmodern organization. With the financial organizations fragmented across the corporation and the "community" still more conceptual than real, the leaders found it virtually impossible to agree on a unified approach. They decided that all of the financial officers would plan their own implementation strategy, including the specific practices they would use in implementing the HPS component principles. They did agree to shared practices in the areas of recruiting and diversity and to use the new competency model, but other practices and tools were deemed optional—including the D&CP Toolkit.

Despite this decision, the HPS project leadership continued to believe that to bring about the overall desired change, other key common elements needed to be in place. Among these were the commitment of the leadership to this as a major long-term change rather than a "program of the month," the shared vision of the community we were striving to become, and the need to create ownership in the employees for their own development and career planning. The project leadership saw the various HPS products, including the D&CP Toolkit, as vital mechanisms to get those key common elements in place and to strengthen the sense of community across the fragmented financial organizations. The challenge was one typical of customer services: how to influence the customer (the financial officers) to use your products and services (to include our key elements and products in their implementation plans) when they have a range of other options.

The task of making this happen fell to the two of us. We had to identify what implementation products the customers wanted and then design them, market them, and make them quickly available and easy to obtain and use—all before the officers got so far in their own plans that they would no longer be interested. Drawing on our relationships within one officer's organization, we were able to collaborate with those directors and HR representatives who had the greatest desire to move forward with HPS and the clearest sense of their own requirements. These partnerships proved invaluable to the overall implementation effort, not only because they yielded us the information we needed to create effective implementation products, but also because many of the other financial directors were very willing to follow the lead these first directors set.

The resulting set of implementation products covered a range of potential customer needs and included the following:

• *HPS implementation workshop.* This workshop, designed in modular format so that directors could easily customize it to their specific needs, introduces two HPS Toolkits intended for all employees (including the D&CP Toolkit). In the first half day, the workshop participants explore the meaning of community and shared values as a foundation, review the HPS vision and principles, and explore all of the HPS components, emphasizing how they are linked and how practices in each area would be improved. In the second half day, the participants learn about the D&CP Toolkit and how and why to begin using it. They also discuss performance management, what they and their leaders jointly commit to do around the various HPS components (such as goal setting and feedback) in the upcoming year, and create a personal action plan.

• *D&CP workshop.* Assuming some previous introduction to HPS, this workshop focuses on the D&CP Toolkit and why and how to use it. This workshop provides more hands-on experience with the development and career planning tools than is possible in the more general HPS workshop; the degree of practice desired determines whether this is a half day or longer.

• *HPS introductory video.* This video introduces the key themes of community, shared values, and vision, and introduces the HPS components, principles, and Toolkits. With the associated discussion guide and the HPS Primer Toolkit (which provides basic information about HPS), this video could be used by work groups as a substitute for the first half of the HPS implementation workshop.

- *Consultative services.* This includes a diverse range of services, such as helping organization leaders and their HR representatives plan their implementation strategy and activities, facilitating the HPS and D&CP workshops, and training their line managers to deliver the workshops.

- *Pro forma implementation plan.* This tool coaches leaders through the implementation process, which includes identifying their organization's HPS needs, deciding their implementation strategy, and putting it into operation. The tool also, not incidentally, outlines our ready-to-use implementation products and who to call to obtain them. Copies of this tool were provided to all members of the corporate financial community's HR group, who generally were doing most of the HPS implementation planning for their officers.

Did we succeed in developing and marketing the products our customers needed before they could meet the need themselves? For the most part, yes. The same factors that made the community and its desired change complex acted in our favor, buying us time as individual organizations struggled at different paces to identify their needs and move ahead. One officer launched his HPS implementation efforts before our workshop and video were available, but subsequently became our first and recurring customer for the D&CP workshops. Another officer group focused the majority of its implementation efforts around our HPS workshop, and many of the officer's direct reports have requested follow-up D&CP workshops as well. Others have moved much more slowly, but none has rejected our support or failed to use some portion of our products.

In addition, the feedback from employees is encouraging. Despite their well-grounded cynicism based on past change efforts, employees in the organizations whose implementation we supported have begun to demonstrate a growing sense of personal empowerment around their development and career planning and some optimism about the success of the larger HPS initiative.

Barriers to Change

As Beckhard and Harris (1987) discuss, resistance is normal and to be expected in any change effort; it takes many forms and must be analyzed to reduce it and gain commitment to the change. All change efforts meet with some resistance, and to be successful, barriers must be overcome. Six of the key barriers encountered in this change effort are identified below. Coincidentally, the first three potentially meet the criteria of conditions for failure described by Beckhard (1969, pp. 93–96):

- When a discrepancy exists between top management statements of values and styles and how they actually behave.
- Believing in a short-term time frame.
- Searching for the easiest or quickest available solution—a cookbook answer.

1. *Questionable sponsorship.* Relating to the first of Beckhard's conditions above, the chief financial officer's sponsorship was questioned by members of the management council because of the espoused commitment to the change effort but what appeared to be the lack of extensive, visible actions. The financial chief's commitment was unfailing, but unfortunately at the same time he was charged to head negotiations for a significant acquisition, which became his major focus while this change effort was under way. This left the HPS teams questioning whether they should remain emotionally committed and just how much of their time should they actually allocate to the HPS initiative. What helped the teams through this was regular testing of support for the project with the finance head, who continued to allocate extensive resources to the effort and espouse the same level of commitment.

2. *Believing in a short-term time frame.* The financial management team could be characterized as highly task oriented, and initially worked hard at trying to "get the project over with." In addition, many members were uncomfortable working with the "softer issues," which added to hastening their efforts. Finally, some team members conceived of this effort as a project, (the introduction of some new forms, workshops, or processes, to improve func-

tioning) but not as a change effort to create a new climate and culture. Constant coaching by us and other human resource team members helped these financial executives come to the realization that this was a long-term change effort.

We also presented change management techniques that could help facilitate the process and provided readings in organization development and change to increase the financial executives' overall familiarity with the process. Finally, the human resource team argued that the overall effort was not about new forms and procedures, but about creating a community that would be successful and attractive to all.

3. *Searching for the easiest or quickest available solution—a cookbook answer.* In connection with a short time frame approach, the HPS teams wanted to, in effect, steal best practices from other organizations. Fundamentally, they believed that best practices existed out there in a vacuum; therefore, they should not have to spend their time analyzing the nature of their current practices and determining how to improve them. However, as Fitz-enz (1993, p. 192) states, "A best practice is not defined by the way a process is structured or carried out. It is a function of a set of background values, strategies, and interactions. These are the constants. These are the driving forces. These are what make organizations best." This point of view is also expressed by Cook and Yanow (1993) in their essay on culture and learning organizations. "Organizational know-how is not meaningfully transferable from one shop to the next; it is deeply embedded in the practices of each workshop" (p. 381).

We attempted to convey these points of view and asserted that it was more important to focus on the strategic needs of the community and to develop an integrated system of human resource practices than to collect best practices. To demonstrate the point, the human resource team actually benchmarked some major organizations. When the results were shared, the financial executives realized that many of our current practices were more advanced than could be found elsewhere. This aided in convincing them of the need to be internally focused, to work within their own context, and to be oriented to the human performance system.

4. *HR credibility.* Because of their legitimate power and positions in the hierarchy, many of the financial executives believed

that they had the "right answers" to solve human resource problems, and they tended to discount the expertise of the human resource professional team members who possessed expert power but held positions lower in the hierarchy. The truism that "everyone is an HR expert because HR is just common sense" held in this situation. As a result, the progress that could have been achieved through a collaborative effort of hands-on leadership expertise and human resources professionalism was slowed. Eventually, through careful coaching and helping the financial executives learn from their experience in trying to solve HR problems, all of the human resources professionals "earned" the credibility that they always possessed.

5.   *Focus on details and not the big picture.* The financial executives were selected for these teams because of their business and leadership expertise, and not for their human resources expertise. However, because of their overall discomfort with their project roles, their penchant for details, and their task focus, many of the executives wanted to understand and debate the finer points, such as the number of steps in the recruiting process or whether a career planning workshop should be two or three days in length. This orientation prevented them from focusing on the big picture of how to make this change effort an overall success. It put product before strategy, as they pressed to deliver what was referred to as "low hanging fruit," or the visible changes they could produce quickly to create an impression of action.

We were able to overcome this barrier by encouraging these managers to focus on creating some specific products that satisfied their personal need for action. We cautioned, however, against introducing those products in a piecemeal fashion. After they had a product or two under their belts, they were better able to focus on the overall change effort.

6.   *Resistance to learning.* The culture was dominated by the belief that you did not admit the need to learn something. If you admitted this need, you were considered to have a deficit and were therefore less of a leader than your peers. As a result, the financial leaders had to behave as if they had all of the right HR answers. They turned to their own experience—five, ten, up to thirty-five years earlier in their careers—to find a worthwhile answer or per-

spective on a given situation. There is nothing essentially wrong with relying on experience, but this was done in direct opposition to expert HR opinion, employee survey data, or best-practices findings.

The resistance manifested itself in several ways: discounting of HR's informed perspective, refusal of the teams to admit their struggles to one another, and not recognizing that "learning" was progress that a team should have felt positive about. We and the other HR professionals on the teams did help some of the leaders to recognize the value of individual, team, and organization learning, but by and large the need to learn and the actually learning were minimally discussed.

Enablers of Change

Although authors such as Beckhard and Harris (1987) identify strategies, processes, and techniques for managing change, we would like to highlight two key factors that we believe helped to make the overall implementation of HPS and the development and career planning component a success. The first of these has to do with the perspective transformation experienced by the senior financial managers; the second, unflappable HR support.

Perspective Transformation

As defined by Mezirow (1991, p. 167): "Perspective transformation is the process of becoming critically aware of how and why our assumptions have come to constrain the way we perceive, understand and feel about the world; changing these structures of habitual expectation to make possible a more inclusive, discriminating and integrating perspective; and, finally, making choices or otherwise acting upon these new understandings."

As described earlier, the senior managers held a certain perspective about the field of human resources, human resources expertise, and the implementation of a human performance system. As internal consultants on the project, we knew that these views would be a challenge to overcome. We needed to move these senior managers toward a more inclusive paradigm based on the following assumptions: (1) there is a body of knowledge that makes human resources a profession and (2) the implementation of a new human resource system requires a change-management approach. Once the senior managers experienced this transformation in their perspectives about the entire change event, it became easier to move the overall project forward. But how did this transformation occur?

We would like to believe that it was through our personal charisma, expertise, and consulting skills; however, although we did help to facilitate critical reflection, two factors were largely responsible for the change in perspectives. The first was the team members' collective realization that they were on the project for the long run, and that their normal approach to the management of special projects would not work. The second was the private testing of some of the concepts, ideas, and practices that we suggested during many of the team meetings. For example, a team member may have tried to conduct a staff meeting in a less autocratic fashion, or counsel subordinates about career options rather than telling them what jobs to take. In the safety of their own environments the team members tested and were successful—they learned—and as a result, their perspectives about the value of effective HR practices started to shift.

Perhaps the most notable example of perspective transformation occurred when, during a combined meeting of all the HPS teams, the overall team leader stated that after almost a year on the project he finally realized that the implementation of HPS was about culture and organization change. He acknowledged that one of us had been counseling him about the nature of the change effort since the beginning of the project but he hadn't truly understood what it meant until recently. From that point on, this team leader became a true supporter of the change effort. His perspective had been transformed.

Ironically, then, the change effort was affected in a negative way because of the lack of knowledge the financial leadership had, or thought they should have had, about the field of human resources, but was affected favorably by their gaining a different kind of knowledge or learning—a perspective transformation.

Unflappable HR Support

We were involved in the overall change event from its inception. In essence we played roles as change generators, change implementers, and change adopters (London, 1988). As change generators, we approached the leadership with the HPS concept as a way to support the achievement of the community vision. As change implementers, we worked with the leadership to establish the HPS teams, counseled the teams throughout their tenure, and developed or co-developed HR practices and resources. As change adopters, we personally demonstrated how to behave in accordance with the community vision, used the new HR practices not only in our own organizations but also in application with the teams, and encouraged our HR leader to be the first to implement the overall HPS approach.

The end-to-end support that we provided was important. What enabled us, as well as some of the financial managers, to weather the change process can be understood in terms of resilience. A component of career motivation (London, 1983) and a characteristic of management success, *resilience* refers to having a sense of self-confidence, a desire to achieve, and a willingness to take risks (London, 1988, p. 6). To not only endure organization change but to be successful in facilitating it, a high degree of resilience is essential.

Burke (1982, pp. 353–354) articulates ten primary abilities important to effective organization consulting, which are also consistent with having high resilience. Of these, the ability to tolerate ambiguity, to conceptualize (for instance, key relationships, such as cause and effect), and to teach or create learning opportunities was particularly relevant during this change effort.

Lessons (Re)Learned

Although in the practice of change-management consulting for some time, we continue to learn from our own experiences and to expand (transform) our own perspectives. As any practitioner knows, this can be a humbling experience. As a result, we want to share some of the lessons (re)learned during this change process.

The first, a personal one, is recognizing that our own greatest strength is as agents of change, being catalytic. This is what Barker (1992) refers to as paradigm shifters, and in specific, one category of shifter, the *maverick:* "an insider, a practitioner of the prevailing paradigm who sees the problems on the shelf, understands the present paradigm will not work to solve them, and leads the charge to change paradigms" (p. 63).

As a result, when the senior financial managers began to truly grasp the nature and direction of the change, we recognized that we began to grow restless, as if our purpose had been achieved. Obviously, we knew we had a long way to go to be successful, but the recognition helped us to reenergize for the work that remained. Knowing one's strengths and weaknesses and being able to capitalize upon them—having insight—is another dimension of London's career motivation typology (1983) and an important characteristic for change agents to possess.

A second and related factor is that the organization change takes its own course. Both the process of the change and the content or practices being implemented will be subject to the culture of the organization. For example, our vision was to address all ten components of the HPS at the same time, but as the change was under way, the leaders decided to focus on four of the components that they believed would directly promote community building. Was this a good idea gone bad? Maybe, but as Di Bella (1993) argues, practices must be adapted to fit the culture of the organization, otherwise the change will meet resistance and fail. So although we held a different view about which components to begin with, we recognized the value of adapting the HPS concept to fit the needs and culture of the financial community.

Third, this change effort, which seemed to be a change for the good—it was moral, ethical, and humanistic in nature—still met with great resistance because it suggested a shift in power, a political shift. For example, defining and making public the competencies deemed important for success in the community, apparently a positive step for promoting effective career and development planning, meant that it was more difficult to make staffing and promotion decisions based on the informal network and who had served well in the past. Being truly competency based in personnel decisions provides for greater clarity about what is expected and tends to remove some of the ambiguity about what it takes to get ahead in the organization. For us this meant being increasingly aware of how some of the simpler suggestions for HPS practices may still have met with resistance because of how they affected the power structure. We had to reflect upon our own set of assumptions, which were largely within a human resources frame (Bolman & Deal, 1991), and test whether our clients were working within the same the set of assumptions or frame, or within the structural, political or symbolic frames.

Fourth, we authors had to recognize the strength of the legitimate power held by the senior financial managers. Legitimate power, according to French and Raven (1959), is power granted by the position one holds, and the higher in the organization hierarchy, the greater the legitimate power. For example, the senior financial managers were more inclined to listen to their bosses than to act on expert HR input when change-related decisions had to be made. Other bases of power identified by French and Raven include reward power, coercive power, and those we most exercised: expert power (based on our professional expertise and experience) and referent power (based on likability).

Fifth, what we saw very vividly in this case was the need for senior management to visibly support the change and to role model the new behaviors with their own direct reports and within their organizations. This helped to overcome the basic skepticism about HPS as "change program of the year" and suggested to community members that everyone was in this together. For example, when community members understood that their leaders were being appraised and compensated based on their successful implementation of HPS and the role modeling of associated behaviors, they became more actively engaged in activities, such as workshop participation and trying new practices.

Epilogue to the Change: Coping with Downsizing and Its Impact on the Community

The development of a world-class community, the implementation of HPS, and the introduction of the D&CP Toolkit were ideas conceived when the revenue and profit pictures for the company were extremely strong. The company's stock price hit record highs, market-leading products were being introduced, and the company's key strategic alliances appeared promising. Optimism prevailed.

The economic and competitive pressures of 1993–1994, however, forced the need for significant downsizing, and a companywide declaration of a reduction in force was made about six to eight months into the change. We describe below what we experienced and learned, as well as the actions taken, about the time the force management plan was announced in the financial community.

As you might expect, we found that the members of the financial community were frightened and feeling insecure. For most, the immediate concern was to ensure continuous employment with the company, and many did not consider career and development planning important to this task. Their focus was short term. Finding a job was on their minds. In contrast, they saw the HPS D&CP Toolkit as a resource that could help them only in the long run, once they found another job. While facilitating either the HPS workshop or the D&CP workshop, we learned that most were reluctant attendees; they said they did not see the value of career and development planning at this time and that downsizing was inconsistent with the financial leadership's desire to build a community. We were able to respond in ways that not only helped individuals cope but also helped to reinforce the value of community.

First, we shifted our focus in how we communicated about the Toolkit. During the workshops, we demonstrated how the career planning assessments could be used to help make choices about next job opportunities. We helped employees to realize that deeper insight about their values, interests, and preferences could help them to better sell themselves in the job marketplace. We showed them how they could use this information in their resumes, cover letters, and job interviews. In some of the workshops, we literally renegotiated expectations with the participants and taught them a wide variety of job search strategies. Using the model presented by Kubler-Ross (1969), we also helped them to realize that they could expect to feel a wide range of emotions comparable to those experienced when grieving the death of a loved one. As a result, many of the workshop participants began to feel more in control of their futures and less anxious about the threat of job loss.

To most community members, development planning also appeared too future-focused. During the workshops, we had to show community members that by focusing on assessing their competency now, they could establish and act on short-term development plans that would result in helping them to be more competitive for jobs and ensure their employment continuity with the company. This was particularly important because, along with performance appraisal information, the competencies detailed in the Toolkit were also used for assessing whether or not employees were to be considered "retained" or "at risk."

Second, we helped members of the community to see that they were not alone, and that if they worked together, by sharing job leads, coaching each other on interview strategies, critiquing each other's resumes and development plans, they would have a much greater chance of success than if they were to work alone.

Overall, our efforts to meet the immediate needs of the community members by changing the focus of these HPS-related workshops literally increased the demand for them, and significantly enhanced the perceived value of the D&CP Toolkit as well as HPS. On a larger scale, we were also influential in helping the financial leadership to see the need to act immediately to ensure that all community members were treated fairly and with respect during the downsizing.

This involved not waiting for the supporting corporate resources to become available later in the process. Specifically, the leadership took steps to support job search workshops for members of the community before they were officially labeled at risk of losing their jobs and also made funding available for competency-related training. In addition, the HPS career team was asked to create a special placement process to help at-risk community members find new jobs somewhere in the company, if possible. Finally, each financial director was asked to participate in a new program called "Coach a Colleague," which offered guidance and mentoring to members of the community who were having difficulty in the job search process.

In essence, the trauma of downsizing helped to increase the overall strength of the community as its members united around the "good" of trying to ensure employment continuity.

Final Note: HPS, Development and Career Planning, and Building a Community

In this chapter we have attempted to document a case study about organization change, specifically developing a world-class professional community. We noted that the organization can be described as characteristically postmodern, and that building a community required coming together around a common good.

First, we outlined the evolution of the HPS concept, a strategic approach for supporting organization change, and described the nature and structure of the change. Second, we detailed a specific resource designed to support the financial function's overarching goals and the development of a professional community. This resource, the D&CP Toolkit, served to focus the career planning and development efforts of all community members around a core set of competencies important to the success of a multinational financial community. The Toolkit is also an enabling resource in that it provides specific direction and how-to's for achieving business goals.

Third, we described the factors that we considered barriers to the change, including questionable sponsorship and a short-term focus, as well as those enabling the change, including having a perspective experience and strong professional support. We further described what we have learned—and must admit, relearned—as the prime change agents in this case. Finally, we described the impact of organization downsizing on the implementation of HPS and its effect on members' perceptions of the D&CP Toolkit.

In conclusion, we would like to note the fragility of the community concept. Although this effort has gone a long way toward strengthening the community ethos, there is still much work to be done. To understand the notion of community requires continuous consensual validation as members grow, change, and enter or exit the community. It is not easy to operationalize behavior in a community of more than fifteen thousand members that is consistent with the notion of appropriate community action. This is a challenge not only for the leadership, but for all community members. Therefore, everyone has a choice. Success is everyone's responsibility.

References

Barker, J. (1992). *Paradigms: The business of discovering the future.* New York: HarperBusiness.

Beckhard, R. (1969). *Organization development: Strategies and models.* Reading, MA: Addison-Wesley.

Beckhard, R., & Harris, R. T. (1987). *Organizational transitions: Managing complex change* (2nd ed.). Reading, MA: Addison-Wesley.

Berquist, H. (1993). *The postmodern organization: Mastering the art of irreversible change.* San Francisco: Jossey-Bass.

Bolman, L. G., & Deal, T. E. (1991). *Reframing organizations: Artistry, choice, and leadership.* San Francisco: Jossey-Bass.

Burke, W. (1982). *Organization development: Principles and practices.* Boston: Little, Brown.

Cook, S. D. N., & Yanow, D. (1993). Culture and organizational learning. *Journal of Management Inquiry, 2,* 373–390.

Dewey, J. (1954). *The public and its problems*. Athens, OH: Swallow Press.

Di Bella, A. (1993). The role of assumptions in implementing management practices across cultural boundaries. *Journal of Applied Behavioral Science, 29*(3).

Fitz-enz, J. (1993). *Benchmarking staff performance: How staff departments can enhance their value to the customer*. San Francisco: Jossey-Bass.

French, J. R. P., & Raven, B. H. (1959). The bases of social power. In D. Cartwright (Ed.), *Studies in social power*. Ann Arbor, MI: Institute for Social Research.

Harvey, D. (1989). *The condition of postmodernity: An enquiry into the origins of social change*. Cambridge, MA: Blackwell.

Katz, D., & Kahn, R. (1978). *The social psychology of organizations* (2nd ed.). New York: Wiley.

Kotter, J. (1978). *Organizational dynamics: Diagnosis and intervention*. Reading, MA: Addison-Wesley.

Kubler-Ross, E. (1969). *On death and dying*. New York: Macmillan.

Kvale, S. (Ed.). (1992). *Psychology and postmodernism*. London: Sage.

London, M. (1983). Toward a theory of career motivation. *Academy of Management Review, 8*, 620–630.

London, M. (1988). *Change agents: New roles and innovation strategies for human resource professionals*. San Francisco: Jossey-Bass.

London, M., & Mone, E. M. (1994). Managing marginal performance in an organization striving for excellence. In A. H. Korman (Ed.), *Human dilemmas in work organizations: Strategies for resolution*. New York: Guilford Press.

Mezirow, J. (1991). *Transformative dimensions of adult learning*. San Francisco: Jossey-Bass.

Mone, E. M. (1988). Training managers to be developers. In M. London & E. M. Mone (Eds.), *Career growth and human resource strategies: The role of the human resource professional in employee development*. New York: Quorum.

Nadler, D., & Tushman, M. (1980). A congruence model for organizational assessment. In E. E. Lawler III, D. A. Nadler, & C. Cammann (Eds.), *Organizational assessment: Perspectives on the measurement of organizational behavior and the quality of work life*. New York: Wiley.

Porras, J., & Robertson, P. (1992). Organization development: Theory, practice, and research. In M. Dunnette & L. Hough (Eds.), *Handbook of industrial and organizational psychology* (2nd ed.) (pp. 719–822). Palo Alto, CA: Consulting Psychologists Press.

Schuler, R. (1992). Strategic human resources management: Linking the people with the strategic needs of the business. *Organizational Dynamics, 21*, 18–32.

PART 2

New Patterns of Employment

The second section of the book reviews new patterns of employment. These patterns are emerging because organizations can no longer be counted on as sources of long-term employment.

Harold Kaufman introduces this part by examining organizational approaches to recycling existing employees in his chapter on obsolescence, retraining, and redeployment of technical professionals. He considers technical professionals' willingness to be retrained, government support for retraining, and industry retraining programs. He describes retraining and redeployment efforts in two companies and then outlines guidelines for implementing such programs. He highlights the importance of top management involvement, the value of keeping retraining and redeployment voluntary, the need for careful selection of employees for the program, the value of counseling, and the importance of realistic job previews so redeployed professionals know what to expect.

In Chapter Six, Daniel Feldman notes that the growth of part-time and temporary employment, the increased demographic diversity of the labor force, and the proliferation of new types of contingent work arrangements have made the management of part-time and temporary workers a significantly more challenging task. He examines the reasons for the increased growth and diversity of contingent work, the subsequent changes in expectations that part-time and temporary employees now bring to the workplace, and the implications that these trends have for the effective recruitment, development, and management of part-time and temporary workers.

James Smither focuses in Chapter Seven on contingent workers who are full-time, permanent employees in a company and are given different job assignments as needed. These technical, professional, and managerial employees are managed centrally by a department called Resource Link, which operates as an internal temporary services unit to meet the variable workforce needs of the company's business units and divisions. While the program was originally aimed at employees whose jobs had been declared at risk due to downsizing, about half of the more than 450 current Resource Link employees, called "associates," volunteered to join as a way of gaining more experience and advancing their careers. Smither describes how this method of "inplacement" benefits the company and the employees. He outlines the recruitment and selection system, the information database used to track and match employees, and guidelines for employee appraisal and compensation. The chapter suggests how other firms can implement similar programs to enhance employee flexibility and career development opportunities in changing organizations.

The last chapter in this part, by John Eggers, recognizes that new start-up firms are being created by disillusioned or displaced Fortune 500 employees, women executives who have grown tired of the corporate glass ceiling, and recent college graduates and dropouts. The chapter examines research on characteristics of successful and unsuccessful entrepreneurs. By focusing on what successful entrepreneurs do, Eggers outlines ways to encourage, teach, and facilitate entrepreneurship. In particular, he considers the entrepreneur's motivating vision and recognition of opportunity, expertise, expectation for reward, and environmental support. He examines the concept of intrapreneurship—starting enterprises within an existing organization. Organizations may want to develop entrepreneurial skills as a way to foster the growth of the organization and prepare employees for second careers outside the organization.

CHAPTER 5

Salvaging Displaced Employees
Job Obsolescence, Retraining, and Redeployment

Harold G. Kaufman

In this age of intense global competition, we hear with increasing urgency that the future well-being of America depends on the retraining of its workforce. At one end of the spectrum, unskilled workers are being retrained and upgraded to meet critical skill shortages in industry. A national survey revealed that retraining is already the primary method that U.S. industry is using to cope with shortages of skilled labor in manufacturing ("Manufacturers respond," 1992).

At the other end of the spectrum, technical professional workers have entered an era in which radical career change has become a way of life that increasingly requires retraining and occupational mobility (Carnevale, Gainer, & Schulz, 1990; Kaufman, 1982). In addressing the issue of retraining, this chapter will focus primarily on the approximately 5 million technical professionals in the United States, among whom are about 3 million engineers, scientists, and computer specialists. This large and growing workforce

Note: This chapter was adapted from the first Lydia S. and Samuel S. Dubin Endowed Lecture presented by the author at the Pennsylvania State University on June 2, 1993, and published in the Spring 1994 issue of the *Journal of Continuing Higher Education.*

is a national asset whose utilization and development are critical to the future economic and social well-being of this country.

Technological Change and Obsolescence

The need to retrain technical professionals is driven by rapid changes in the external environment, especially advances in technology, that have resulted in the obsolescence of knowledge and skills. Obsolescence among professionals has been defined as the degree to which they lack the up-to-date knowledge and skills necessary to maintain effective performance in either their current or future work roles (Kaufman, 1974). It is possible to differentiate job obsolescence—pertaining to one's current work role requirements—from professional or potential obsolescence—the capability to be effective in future work roles. Professional obsolescence could be a serious problem that requires retraining when the individual experiences either extensive work role changes or job loss.

From the model of obsolescence depicted in Figure 5.1, it can be seen that environmental change is all pervasive, directly affecting not only obsolescence but also organizational climate in terms of policies and practices, the nature of the work carried out, and characteristics of the professional employees themselves. While all of these factors can affect obsolescence, the organizational climate and the work itself appear to play key roles in motivating technical professionals to keep up-to-date (Kaufman, 1974, 1979, 1989).

Rapid technological change has been a major force driving the need for retraining technical professionals. It is ironic that the technical professionals, who are primarily responsible for technological change, are also most vulnerable to its consequences: obsolescence and the need to continually update (Kaufman, 1974, 1975).

The half-life is the amount of time it takes for half the knowledge and skills acquired in a professional's formal education to become out of date. In the 1960s, the half-life of an engineering degree was about five years (Zelikoff, 1969). By the late 1980s, the half-life was estimated to be as low as two and a half years in some technical fields, such as software engineering (National Academy of Engineering, 1988). During that period, professionals at Hewlett-Packard reportedly were becoming obsolete in three years

Figure 5.1. A Theoretical Model of Obsolescence.

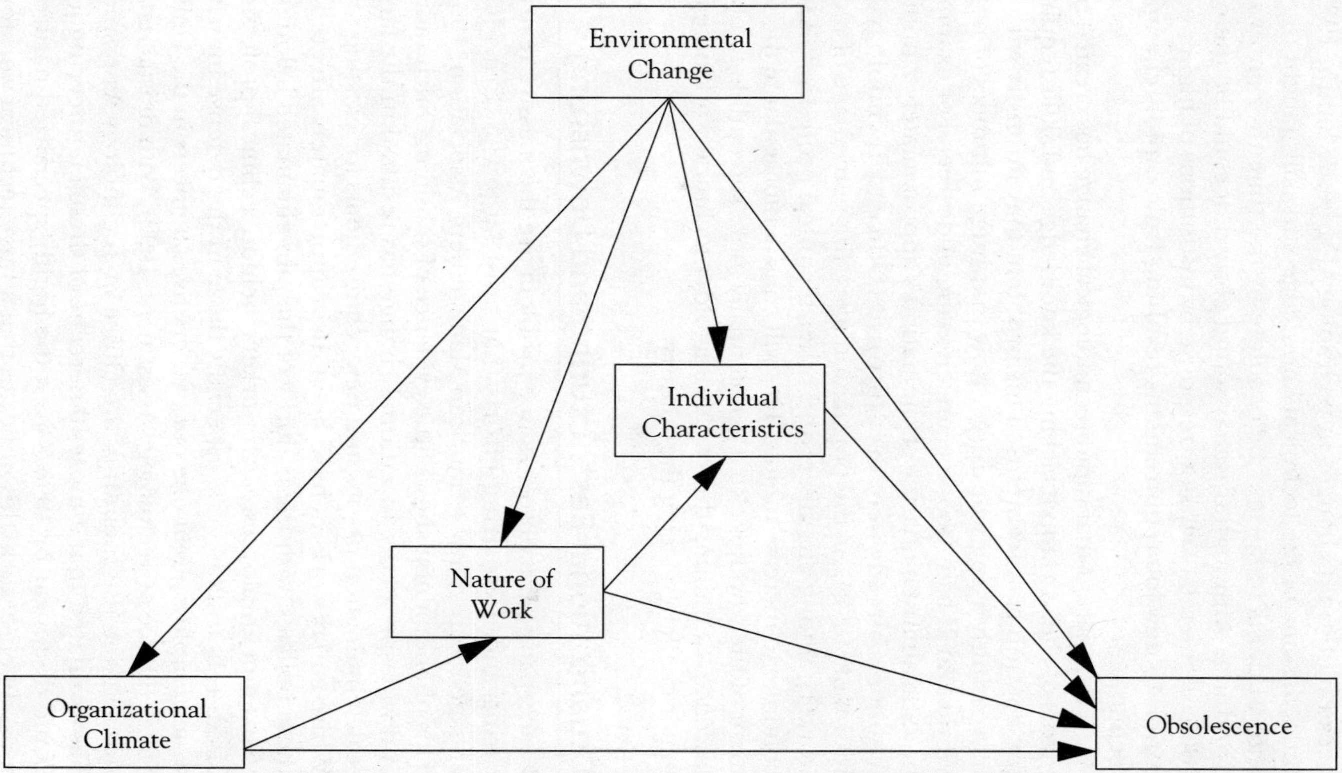

because of rapid changes in technology (Miljus & Smith, 1987). Indeed, some of the technical knowledge and skills taught to college students today may be obsolete by the time they enter the workforce. Although this may sound absurd, it could be the outcome of the relatively slow response by institutions of higher education to new job requirements resulting from rapidly changing technology.

It is apparent that rapid technological change has created segments of the workforce lacking the knowledge and skills required for new job requirements. This problem may intensify with an increasingly aging workforce, now that huge numbers of post–World War II baby boomers are entering midcareer. For example, by 1986 almost a quarter of the nation's approximately 2 million engineers already were over fifty-five (Office of Technology Assessment, 1992). As the population ages, the percentage of older workers among engineers and other technical professionals will continue to increase rapidly. This will considerably enlarge the segment of the workforce that is potentially more susceptible to obsolescence. Retraining this expanding older technical workforce is a major challenge facing the country.

Organizational Restructuring and Downsizing

Exacerbating the obsolescence problem are the massive restructuring and downsizing efforts that most large U.S. firms have engaged in recently (American Management Association, 1993). This phenomenon shows little evidence of subsiding. Such radical and widespread organizational change has resulted in the large-scale elimination of jobs and new requirements for existing jobs. White-collar workers have been disproportionately affected by these policies, with the majority of the jobs eliminated belonging to exempt employees. Such workers include technical professionals and their managers, especially those in the defense industry, which employs about one out of every five engineers in the United States (Office of Technology Assessment, 1992). With drastic reductions in defense spending, the Office of Technology Assessment has estimated that almost 40 percent of these engineering jobs could disappear by 1995. Given the highly specialized nature of most defense work, this indicates that a huge technical workforce will need to be retrained in the very near future.

A major consequence of organizational downsizing is the need to retrain the remaining workforce (Marks, 1993). However, the costs of retraining and other repercussions are part of what has been called the downside of downsizing, or even "dumbsizing" (Baumohl, 1993; Heenan, 1989). Although downsizing is implemented as a cost-reduction measure, it is "dumb" because there are often unanticipated consequences that can be costly to all concerned. In addition to the cost of retraining, the company must absorb the costs of lower morale, hiring of temporary workers and consultants, increased overtime, increased health care, outsourcing of entire functions, losing essential employees, severance payments that were greater than expected, and other unanticipated effects (Marks, 1993). Among downsizing firms surveyed by the American Management Association, employee morale declined in 77 percent, worker productivity did not increase or declined in 64 percent, and operating profits failed to improve in at least 47 percent (American Management Association, 1992). The more frequently a company downsized, the worse the aftereffects.

It appears that the widespread negative consequences of downsizing result, at least in part, from the fact that many employers who decide to reduce their workforce do so without retraining or redeployment policies in place to deal with the subsequent human resource problems (Cascio, 1993). Consequently, a heavy price is paid by all. This is especially true of the employees who are terminated (Kaufman, 1982).

Retraining of Unemployed Technical Professionals

For technical professionals who lose their jobs, a possible option has been to retrain for a new occupation. There is an established body of knowledge about the retraining of technical professionals who are out of work (Kaufman, 1982). In terms of motivation, it is clear that many would be willing to retrain. Table 5.1 shows the percentages of out-of-work technical professionals who believed that their knowledge and skills were "extremely or quite adaptable" to a variety of critical areas, including transportation, pollution control, urban development, and health care. Professionals who were reemployed in their field appeared to be just as adaptable as matched samples who remained out of work or who became underemployed.

Table 5.1. Potential for Retraining into Critical Areas.

Area of New Specialization	Employment Status		
	Unemployed (N=51)	Underemployed (N=52)	Reemployed in Field (N=54)
Pollution Control	37%	35%	46%
Public Administration	26	29	37
Transportation	51	37	45
Health Care	16	25	17
Law Enforcement	12	10	13
Urban Development	35	19	32

Source: Adapted from Kaufman, 1982.

The willingness of unemployed technical professionals to be retrained is widespread, especially if two conditions are met (Kaufman, 1982):

1. Financial assistance is provided for retraining to ease the transition to a new specialization. The unemployed are understandably reluctant to spend their own scarce resources on retraining that may or may not be successful.
2. A relevant job is assured at the completion of the retraining. Such an assurance could motivate even some of those more reluctant to accept retraining. The minimum objective here would be to avoid the worst-case situation of creating an unemployable retrained professional workforce.

Research shows that many individual factors affect unemployed professionals' willingness to retrain, including the following (Kaufman, 1982):

1. *Reluctance to relocate* is one of the most important factors in motivating retraining adaptability. Retraining is perceived as a likely path to reemployment without having to pull up one's roots. On the other hand, for those strongly committed to finding work in their occupation, relocation may be the only option. There are clearly trade-offs between retraining and relocation, so that resis-

tance toward one is compensated for by flexibility toward the other. Of course, a lack of retraining opportunities may also result in a greater flexibility toward relocation.

2.   *A perceived lack of jobs in one's field* is related to a greater willingness to retrain. Unemployed professionals who believe they are unable to return to their specialty may experience the "unfreezing" of their occupational identity. In this process they become more adaptable and willing to accept a career change. Such adaptability is common among those who already have had to make earlier career adjustments in response to termination.

3.   *Length of time out of work* is related to a willingness to retrain, but there appears to be a curvilinear relationship. The unfreezing of one's occupational identity appears most likely to occur after a long fruitless job search, typically about half a year. At this time many begin to feel that they are obsolescent and start to consider a major career change. Retraining becomes an acceptable option. However, for the very long-term unemployed professionals, many have resigned themselves to being in a jobless state and even become work-inhibited, similar to the hard-core unemployed. Even retraining may be unattractive to individuals who have become work-inhibited.

4.   *Staying professionally up to date,* especially through reading the current literature, is related to a greater retraining adaptability. Apparently those who keep themselves broadly abreast of new developments are more able to maintain a versatility and openness to change, making them better prepared to go through the retraining required to work in another specialty or applications area.

5.   *Age.* Jobless professionals in midcareer appear more willing to retrain to improve their employability than their younger colleagues. This is partly due to a greater reluctance to relocate among those who are more established and have deeper family roots in their community. However, for some, the opportunity to enter a new occupation at midcareer may be just what they were waiting for.

6.   *Certain personality characteristics* are associated with a willingness to retrain. Professionals who are more venturesome and

flexible (the high risk takers) or those who have a strong belief in their capabilities to effect change (those high in personal control) are more willing to make a career change through retraining. However, since the strength of these personality characteristics appears to decline with long-term unemployment, retraining should begin prior to a deterioration in flexibility and personal control.

Government Support for Retraining

To date, there has been very limited federal, state, or local government support for retraining terminated technical professionals (Kaufman, 1982; Office of Technology Assessment, 1992). Economic Dislocation and Worker Adjustment Assistance (EDWAA), the amended Title III of the Job Training Partnership Act, is the main government program currently providing training help to displaced workers. State assistance, funded under EDWAA, focuses on the needs of blue-collar workers and rarely provides resources for engineers and other professionals (Office of Technology Assessment, 1992).

One instance of EDWAA support for retraining of displaced technical professionals was the advanced CAD/CAM training provided to engineers who lost their jobs at McDonnell Douglas. However, this is the exception rather than the rule. Federally funded university-industry programs, such as those being supported by the Department of Defense's Advanced Research Projects Agency (1993), may be too little and too late. This has certainly been the case with other federally funded programs in the past (Kaufman, 1982).

Industry Retraining Programs

There are relatively few industry programs designed to retrain professionals who are being terminated or who have retired early. Some companies provide retraining or tuition grants as part of the severance package (Office of Technology Assessment, 1992). For example, GE Aerospace reimburses up to $5,000 in tuition costs for each of the two years following an engineer's termination. Other companies have similar, but typically less generous, tuition support programs for displaced professionals.

A creative approach to retraining early retired or displaced technical professionals is their conversion to certified math and science teachers for junior and senior high schools, where they are in great demand (Office of Technology Assessment, 1992). About twenty-six such retraining programs for teaching as a second career existed as far back as the late 1980s and included firms such as Digital Equipment, IBM, Kodak, Polaroid, and Rockwell International. These programs offer a highly attractive option for older technical professionals and appear to benefit society by addressing the critical shortage of math and science teachers.

Entrepreneurial training for displaced technical professionals who want to start their own business has been offered by some employers, typically with government assistance (Office of Technology Assessment, 1992). For example, McDonnell Douglas provided displaced engineers and other workers with federally funded short courses. The company also provided incubator space for the new start-up firms. It is too early to tell to what degree such entrepreneurial training programs are effective.

Industry Retraining and Redeployment: An Alternative to Termination

The retraining and redeployment or "inplacement" of employed technical professionals as an alternative to termination appears to be accepted by a small but growing number of firms. This is especially true for those firms that support a continuing education infrastructure, since they can extend or expand existing updating or upgrading programs. There is evidence that such an approach not only helps to maintain the loyalty and commitment of a workforce that is critical to the success of the firm but also can be highly cost effective. This was demonstrated by two carefully researched case studies of retraining and redeployment, one involuntary and the other voluntary.

Case Study 1: Involuntary Retraining and Redeployment

In the first case study (Zukowski, 1983), the GE Aerospace Electronics Systems Department was faced with two problems. The company was expanding into a new technology in which it had few knowledgeable engineers, while at the same time phasing out an old technology that would leave many engineers obsolescent. The traditional solution would have been to terminate the obsolescent engineers and hire others competent in the new technology. However, GE took an alternative approach by designing its Technical Renewal Program, which retrained the obsolescent engineers in the new technology and redeployed them in new positions.

The GE Technical Renewal Program was implemented and administered by the existing continuing engineering education infrastructure. The participants were selected by the immediate manager and approved by higher management. The program consisted of a series of intensive courses scheduled during working hours. Progress was monitored and evaluated by a final exam, with managers kept informed of results.

There was initial opposition by the engineers, all of whom were involuntarily assigned to the program. They were performing well and found it hard to believe that their job was no longer important. This initial opposition was largely overcome by communicating the need for the program and an understanding that the likely alternatives were a limitation of their growth potential or even termination.

The ultimate unfreezing of employee attitudes toward accepting a career change was attributed largely to the effort to make the retraining as productive as possible for the engineers. This was accomplished by integrating the following program components: support from top management throughout the program; careful selection of trainees with known development needs; highly qualified and credible instructors who provided two-way communication; tailor-made courses to meet the new job requirements, which eased the transfer of training from classroom to job; ongoing planning with management for continued career growth and development; and continuous evaluation of the program's acceptance, effectiveness, and cost by participants and management.

In spite of their initial opposition to the program, the majority of the participants were highly enthusiastic after completing the retraining. This enthusiasm was further reinforced by a rapid redeployment into jobs requiring the new technology. When the retraining approach was compared to the more traditional approach of termination and replacement with new hires, the results were very clear. Retraining was only 38 percent of the cost of replacement by new hires—a saving of 62 percent. In terms of productivity, over a five-year period sales grew 41.3 percent in uninflated dollars whereas the staff grew by only 23.7 percent. Retraining as an alternative to termination clearly provided a bottom-line benefit to the company. Moreover, in spite of the involuntary nature of the program, most of those retrained felt positive about their new jobs.

Case Study 2: Voluntary Retraining and Redeployment

The second case study focuses on voluntary retraining and redeployment in a high-tech multinational electronics manufacturing company with a long-standing commitment to employment security (Mitchell & Oltrogge, 1989). In this firm, advances in technology had produced skill imbalances and employee surpluses in many areas. A promote-from-within philosophy resulted in frequent job and career changes as the company norm.

The purpose of the study was to investigate a group of recently retrained technical employees in order to determine who volunteers for retraining, how they react to career change, and what factors contribute to a successful transition. The population studied involved over five hundred nonexempt customer engineers whose jobs were being eliminated and who voluntarily retrained into one of three exempt jobs—systems engineers (63 percent), programmers/systems analysts (25 percent), and sales/marketing support representatives (12 percent). Retraining was provided by the company and some of it was very extensive, with training sites often far from the initial employment site. The career change often involved a geographical relocation. All costs were assumed by the company.

The retrained employees represented about 10 percent of the workforce in their original job classification. They were mostly male (87 percent), four-fifths had at least some college education, and their median age was thirty-five, with about ten years of company tenure.

A comparison of those who volunteered for retraining with coworkers who did not reveals some interesting results. Retrained employees were more likely to be better educated, younger, and employed with the company for a shorter time period than their counterparts who chose not to retrain. There was also a tendency for more women to retrain, relative to the eligible population.

For at least 80 percent of those retrained, the change to a new occupation was primarily self-motivated. In addition, more than seven out of ten entered their first choice of new occupation and a similar proportion did so at their first choice location. Thus, the retraining and redeployment that occurred were what most of the employees desired. However, successful redeployment appeared to be a function of minimizing the "transitional distance" that the employee had to move in terms of new job, organizational unit, and geographical area.

Performance ratings of the redeployed employees were similar to those they had received in their former jobs. Moreover, their ratings in the new job were comparable to those of new hires as well as of all employees in the three relevant occupations. Therefore, performance was maintained at the expected level after redeployment.

Questions about the redeployment process indicated that the employees understood the need for retraining, had a good prior understanding of their new jobs, were assigned the jobs before retraining, and were very satisfied with the retraining process, especially the on-the-job training component. Reactions to the career change were generally quite positive and satisfaction measures were better than the population of nonretrained exempt employees. This discrepancy is especially noticeable in their overall job satisfaction as well as satisfaction with the company, which reached an incredible 99 percent for the retrained employees. It appears that company loyalty can be increased significantly through voluntary retraining and redeployment.

A Guide to Retraining and Redeployment

Guidelines for designing more cost-effective retraining and redeployment programs can be derived from the results of the case study research. In situations where retraining is an alternative to termination, the research suggests applying the following principles:

1. Top management support should be present from the inception of the program and maintained until the retraining and redeployment are completed. Such support can make a difference between success and failure of the program. Human resource professionals should be wary of any inplacement approach that lacks support of top management.

2. To the extent possible, retraining and redeployment should be voluntary. This applies to both job and location. In cases where the transition is involuntary, open communication of the need for retraining and the potential alternatives should enhance the acceptance of the program. Overcoming resistance to change is one of the critical problems and pitfalls facing human resource professionals involved with retraining and redeployment.

3. Candidates should be carefully screened and selected, using valid diagnostic techniques to determine individual development needs. Involving human resource specialists, especially industrial and organizational psychologists, in the selection process can help assure a better fit between the person and the job.

4. A good person-job fit would also be the objective of career counseling by human resource professionals. This counseling should begin early in the transition process, preferably as soon as the new jobs are identified.

5. Counselors should try to assure that the career change is not too great, that the "transitional distance" that the employee has to move in terms of new job, organizational unit, and geographical area is minimized.

6. Specific jobs should be assigned prior to retraining. Knowing the jobs in which people are going to be placed should enhance the relevance and effectiveness of their learning. Human resource professionals should be involved throughout this inplacement process.

7. Managers should provide realistic job previews with regard to the new job requirements, the new organizational setting, and relocation. In a voluntary transition, such previews could help improve the employee's decision about which career change, if any, is likely to be best. When the transition is involuntary,

the preview would create more realistic expectations and help in adjusting to the career change.

8. Instructors should be highly qualified in the subject matter they are teaching and should be perceived as credible by the participants. This will enhance the acceptability and effectiveness of the instructors. Opportunities for open two-way communication should be provided by the instructors to reinforce learning.

9. Courses should be tailor-made to provide subject matter designed to meet the new job requirements. This should ease the transfer of training from the classroom to the job. Human resource specialists in training methods could be effectively utilized in the design of courses and curricula.

10. Future career opportunities and growth potential in the new occupation or organizational unit should be emphasized. Having a knowledge of potential career paths from the new position can enhance commitment to the career change. Career planning with the help of counselors should be ongoing to enhance the possibilities of continued growth and development.

11. There should be a continuous evaluation of the program's acceptance, effectiveness, and cost. This evaluation should include inputs from both participants and management. Cost effectiveness of the program can be monitored through such an ongoing evaluation, in which industrial and organizational psychologists can make significant contributions.

Conclusion

It is likely that, as we approach the twenty-first century, radical changes in technology and organizational restructuring will continue unabated. The development of the "communication highway" will have a far-reaching impact on new technical knowledge and skills as well as on the functioning and design of organizations. Problems of obsolescence will be exacerbated and retraining will be required on a massive scale. This could necessitate large-scale cooperative ventures among government, industry, and educational institutions. All indications are that our future economic and societal well-being will be greatly affected by the degree to which these retraining efforts are successful.

References

Advanced Research Projects Agency. (1993). *Program information package for defense technology conversion, reinvestment, and transition assistance.* Washington, DC: U.S. Department of Defense.

American Management Association. (1992). *AMA survey on downsizing and assistance to displaced workers.* New York: American Management Association.

American Management Association. (1993). *1993 AMA survey on downsizing.* New York: American Management Association.

Baumohl, B. (1993, March 15). When downsizing becomes "dumbsizing." *Time*, p. 55.

Carnevale, A. P., Gainer, L. J., & Schulz, E. R. (1990). *Training the technical work force.* San Francisco: Jossey-Bass.

Cascio, W. F. (1993). Downsizing: What do we know? What have we learned? *The Executive, 7,* 95–104.

Heenan, D. A. (1989, November-December). The downside of downsizing. *Journal of Business Strategy,* pp. 18–23.

Kaufman, H. G. (1974). *Obsolescence and professional career development.* New York: AMACOM.

Kaufman, H. G. (Ed.). (1975). *Career management: A guide to combating obsolescence.* New York: IEEE Press.

Kaufman, H. G. (1979). Technical obsolescence: Work and organizations are the key. *Engineering Education, 68,* 826–830.

Kaufman, H. G. (1982). *Professionals in search of work: Coping with the stress of job loss and underemployment.* New York: Wiley-Interscience.

Kaufman, H. G. (1989). Obsolescence of technical professionals: A measure and a model. *Applied Psychology, 38,* 73–85.

Manufacturers respond to shortage of skilled workers. (1992, March). *HR Focus,* p. 10.

Marks, M. L. (1993, April). *Planning organizational transition—and recovering from it: The human resources perspective.* Paper presented at the Society for Industrial and Organizational Psychology Workshop, San Francisco.

Miljus, R. C., & Smith, R. L. (1987). Key human resource issues for management in high-tech firms. In A. Kleingartner & C. S. Anderson (Eds.), *Human resources issues for management in high tech firms.* Lexington, MA: Lexington Books.

Mitchell, M. E., & Oltrogge, C. G. (1989, August). Retraining of nonexempt workers: Successful solution for job obsolescence. Paper presented at the annual meeting of the American Psychological Association, New Orleans.

National Academy of Engineering. (1988). *Focus on the future: A national action plan for career-long education for engineers.* Washington, DC: National Academy of Engineering.

Office of Technology Assessment. (1992). *After the cold war: Living with lower defense spending.* Washington, DC: U.S. Government Printing Office.

Zelikoff, S. B. (1969). On the obsolescence and retraining of engineering personnel. *Training and Development Journal, 23*(5), 3–15.

Zukowski, R. W. (1983). Managing technological career transitions. In *Conference Record: IEEE Careers Conference* (pp. 38–41). New York: IEEE Press.

Managing Part-Time and Temporary Employment Relationships
Individual Needs and Organizational Demands

Daniel C. Feldman

Until fairly recently, the amount of concern given to part-time and temporary employees was best signified by the jargon used to describe them: "peripheral workers," "disposable workers," or "occasional laborers." While many organizations have employed part-time or temporary workers on a regular basis, these workers have often been viewed as relatively unimportant human resources whose comings, goings, and on-the-job performance warranted only minimal attention.

Over the past ten years, that situation has changed dramatically. The part-time workforce has expanded from 12 percent of the workforce in 1957 to almost 24 percent currently; there are over twenty million part-time employees working in the United States today. In fact, in many companies in the service industry (retailing, fast food service, and tourism) most employees are indeed part-timers. The growth of the temporary workforce has been even more remarkable. A decade ago, there were only one hundred temporary employment agencies in this country and only about 470,000 temporary employees. Today, the number of temporary employees is close to 1.6 million and the number of temporary help services is close to fifteen hundred (Fierman, 1994). Temporary employment is now a $20 billion a year business in the United States; Manpower, Inc., alone deploys over one hundred thousand workers a day. Indeed, between 1991 and 1993 over 20 percent of all the new positions created in this country were temporary jobs (Tilly, 1991; Ansberry, 1993; Morrow, 1993).

This growth in so-called contingent employment has been fueled by changes in both organizational demands and individual needs. From the organization's perspective, the demand for part-time and temporary employees has been largely driven by the desire to respond quickly to cyclical economic conditions. In light of the recession of 1989–1991 and the relatively slow economic recovery thereafter, organizations are more willing to add part-time and temporary workers to their payrolls than permanent full-time employees. In addition, given the tremendous increase in the cost of fringe benefits over the past decade, organizations view the hiring of part-time and temporary employees (who are typically given no medical insurance coverage whatsoever) as an effective mechanism for significantly lowering labor costs. Also, as the economy becomes increasingly service-dominated, many organizations are open for business seventy or more hours a week; part-time and temporary employees help these firms achieve efficient staffing levels at peak hours without chronic overstaffing (Ronen, 1984; Presser, 1986; Levine, 1987).

The demand for part-time and temporary work on the part of employees themselves has increased dramatically as well. Until twenty years ago, part-time and temporary jobs were largely held by married women with children and students currently enrolled in high school or college. For these workers, the attraction of contingent employment was flexibility of scheduling to accommodate other demands on their time: spouses, children, parents, leisure, and education (Greenberger & Steinberg, 1986; Gannon, 1984). However, the dramatic growth of the part-time and temporary workforce has been driven by new types of entrants into the contingent labor market, and they are far less sanguine about the typical contingent work contract.

As downsizing, corporate restructuring, and mergers and acquisitions became common during the late 1980s, there were increased numbers of laid-off workers who had no permanent employment possibilities and were forced into taking part-time and temporary jobs simply to make ends meet (Leana & Feldman, 1992). As increasing numbers of older workers took advantage of early retirement incentives (often as an alternative to layoffs), there were also significantly more older workers looking for some type of "bridge employment" between the end of their career-long occupations and permanent retirement (Doeringer, 1990). In addition, due to poor labor market conditions, growing numbers of high school and even college graduates are unable to obtain full-time employment; as a result, many more recent graduates are working in part-time and temporary jobs as a stopgap measure until they can find satisfactory permanent employment (Tiggeman & Winefield, 1984; Feldman & Turnley, 1994b). Finally, more and more women are using contingent work to reenter the labor market and retool to continue their careers; they hope to leverage their contingent jobs into full-time or permanent employment (Polivka & Nardone, 1989; Williams, 1989; Sheridan, 1990).

As a result of all these changes, then, the once-benign employment relationship between organizations and part-time and temporary workers has come under greater scrutiny. For many married women with children and part-time students, the traditional contingent employment relationship is still mutually satisfactory: flexible hours and short-term commitments in exchange for lower wages and fewer benefits. However, for many other part-time and temporary employees, the contingent employment contract seems far from fair.

Many employees have reported being terminated from their jobs and being offered "consultant" positions doing the exact same work at half the pay and with no benefits; others report working continuously as "temporary" employees for the same organization for two years or longer without receiving any of the benefits associated with full-time employment. Besides removal of the health insurance safety net, in many cases contingent work arrangements are also being used to decrease organizations' responsibilities for enforcing social legislation such as EEOC, OSHA, and the Family Leave Act (U.S. Senate Labor Committee Hearings, 1993). Thus, many social policy experts are concerned that part-time and temporary workers are stuck in a culture of underemployment, unable to get training or pay raises in dead-end jobs and unable to convert even those poor jobs into permanent positions (Levitan & Conway, 1988).

In a series of studies over the past few years, my colleagues and I have been examining the changing nature of part-time and temporary work arrangements. One set of studies utilized data collected from seven hundred part-time workers in medical care, retailing, and educational settings (Feldman, 1990; Feldman & Doerpinghaus, 1992a, 1992b; Doerpinghaus & Feldman, 1993). A second set of studies is based on data collected from two hundred temporary employees (from seven agencies) who performed clerical, light industrial, and service jobs (Feldman, Doerpinghaus, & Turnley, 1994, 1995). A third set of studies focuses on the experiences of 175 early retirees with bridge employment (Feldman, 1994; Feldman & Turnley, 1994a), while a fourth set examines the experiences of 250 recent college graduates who are underemployed (Feldman & Turnley, 1994b). These studies, when taken together with previous research on part-time and temporary employment, provide a robust picture of the new challenges involved in managing contingent workers and are the basis for much of the subsequent discussion.

The chapter is divided into four sections, each of which takes a different perspective on part-time and temporary employment. The first section examines the wide variation in types of contingent temporary work arrangements present in American corporations today and suggests that workers' expectations and motivations for taking these different types of contingent jobs largely influence their satisfaction and performance on them. The second section explores the role of demographic variables in understanding part-time and temporary employees' reactions to their jobs. Here we suggest that different demographic groups gravitate toward different types of contingent work arrangements, and that the observed demographic group differences in reactions to contingent employment are largely attributable to the different types of contingent work arrangements into which they self-select. The third section of the chapter outlines a variety of specific organizational strategies that corporations can use to more effectively select, develop, and manage part-time and temporary employees. In the fourth and final section of the chapter, we identify some new, emerging issues in contingent employment and the potential implications they may have for research and management practice.

Patterns of Part-Time and Temporary Employment

Earlier work on part-time workers focused on the differences between full-time and part-time workers (Jackofsky & Peters, 1987; Wakefield, Curry, Mueller, & Price, 1987). However, our thesis is that there are many more types of contingent work arrangements today than there were two decades ago, and that major differences among them account for the differences in motivation and satisfaction among contingent workers.

Contingent work arrangements can be arrayed along six different continua (Feldman, 1990):

1. *Part-time/temporary.* Permanent part-time workers are employed fewer than thirty-five hours per work on a continuing basis, whereas temporary workers are hired for limited periods of time to deal with fluctuating workloads or short-term personnel shortages.

2. *Organization-hired/agency-hired/self-employed.* Contingent workers may be recruited and hired by, and paid by, just one company or they may work for a personnel agency that places them in a variety of corporations and pays them directly. In addition, more and more contingent workers are becoming self-employed consultants and independent contractors to a variety of corporations.

3. *Year-round/seasonal.* Some part-time and temporary workers hold employment year-round, while others hold employment only during certain seasons of the year (such as the Christmas season or the summer vacation season).

4. *Main job/second job/multiple contingent jobs.* Some part-time and temporary workers are employed fewer than thirty-five hours per week in one job, which is their only source of salaried income; others ("moonlighters") work part-time jobs as second jobs to supplement their income; still others work two or more part-time jobs in lieu of working at one full-time job.

5. *Voluntary/involuntary.* Traditionally, the Bureau of Labor Statistics (Nardone, 1986) has distinguished between voluntary contingent workers (who hold this type of employment by choice) and involuntarily contingent workers (who hold this type of employment because of the unavailability of full-time, permanent employment.)

6. *Satisfactory employment/underemployment.* Labor economists also make a distinction between satisfactory employment and underemployment (Kaufman, 1982). Satisfactory employment refers to jobs where part-time and temporary workers are hired into positions consistent with their prior education and experience, while underemployment refers to jobs where individuals' skills and knowledge are underutilized.

Of these six dimensions, the ones that have received the most empirical investigation are part-time/temporary, voluntary/involuntary, and satisfactorily employed/underemployed (see Feldman & Doerpinghaus, 1992a, 1992b; Feldman, Doerpinghaus, & Turnley, 1994, 1995). The pattern of results is clear and consistent both among part-time and temporary workers. Workers who are permanently part-time have significantly higher levels of general satisfaction and internal work motivation and have greater intentions of remaining with their current employers than temporary workers. In addition, individuals who are voluntarily contingent workers report significantly greater levels of work motivation and job commitment and are significantly more satisfied with their jobs in general, their careers as contingent workers, their compensation, and with the work itself. The results are similar for the satisfactory employment-underemployment continuum; underemployed workers have significantly poorer job attitudes and attachments to their jobs.

Our results on types of contingent work arrangements highlight several aspects of the part-time and temporary employment picture. First, even within contingent work, there are still job hierarchies. Employees who hold the "better" contingent jobs—the permanent part-time jobs and the contingent jobs that require higher skill and experience levels—are considerably more satisfied and motivated on their jobs. (Consistent with this finding are our corollary findings that the longer people's organizational tenure and the more hours per week they work for an organization, the more likely they are to be given these permanent part-time jobs and jobs of higher responsibility.) Second, these "better" contingent jobs also provide significantly more wages and significantly less close supervision. Third, independent of the rewards of the contingent jobs offered, individuals who enter these jobs involuntarily or who enter these jobs as underemployed workers are likely to experience the greatest sense of deprivation.

Thus, to the extent that contingent workers are segregated into low-pay, low-challenge jobs, the traditional problems of managing contingent workers are exacerbated. However, if part-time and temporary workers are given opportunities to advance within the contingent job hierarchy, they are more likely to display the same attitudinal and motivational profile of full-time workers. Unfortunately, in any event, the prospects of developing a high-quality, high-involvement workforce among involuntarily and overqualified contingent employees are quite dim.

Role of Demographic Characteristics

Although the type of contingent work arrangement certainly has an impact on the attitudes and behaviors of part-time and temporary employees, it is also clear that individual differences, particularly demographic characteristics, play a major role as well. The variables that have been most closely explored in the context of contingent work are age (Bosworth & Holden, 1983; Soumerai & Avon, 1983), gender (Haring, Okun, & Stock, 1984; Rothberg & Cook, 1985), and marital status and number of children (Hart, 1987; Nakamura & Nakamura, 1983; Presser, 1986). In general, consistent with the organizational behavior literature on full-time employees, older contingent workers tend to be more satisfied than younger workers, females tend to be more satisfied than males, and married women with children and part-time students tend to have higher absence and turnover rates than other groups of contingent workers.

Feldman (1990), in a theoretical review of the literature, argues that different demographic groups might systematically gravitate toward different types of contingent work arrangements, which are, in turn, differentially reinforcing. For example, young high school students may end up being disproportionately represented in seasonal physical labor jobs, which have historically been low paying and of little intellectual challenge. In contrast, early retirees may be able to keep working on their previous jobs but on a part-time basis, allowing them to earn relatively high part-time wages on jobs of equal challenge (Feldman & Turnley, 1994a). Thus, the impact of demographic variables on the attitudes of part-time and temporary workers may be more indirect in nature; demographic variables may have a greater impact on the types of work arrangements contingent workers enter than on job attitudes themselves.

Our research has empirically examined this hypothesis in some detail. The results here are quite strong that different demographic groups do indeed gravitate to different types of contingent work arrangements, which themselves offer widely varying levels of reinforcement. For example, in our study of part-time employees (Feldman & Doerpinghaus, 1992a, 1992b), we found that married women with children are significantly more likely to gravitate into permanent part-time jobs that are consistent with their prior education and experience. Sixty-one percent of the married women with children in our sample, for instance, were satisfactorily employed in their part-time jobs, as opposed to only 32.5 percent of all other respondents. Along the same line, part-time students were significantly less likely to hold permanent part-time jobs and were significantly less likely to be satisfactorily employed. Only 29 percent of the part-time students in our study were permanently and satisfactorily employed, as opposed to 53 percent of all other respondents.

The results in the temporary work study (Feldman, Doerpinghaus, & Turnley, 1994, 1995) are similar. In the temporary worker study, women were significantly less likely than men to be involuntarily temporary workers and were significantly less likely to be looking for permanent jobs. Married workers were significantly more satisfied and committed to their jobs and were significantly more likely to gravitate into temporary work voluntarily than single workers (30 percent of married respondents reported working as temporaries out of choice, compared to 18 percent of the single respondents). Similarly, older employees were significantly more likely to gravitate into temporary jobs voluntarily and to be more satisfied and motivated by their work. In terms of education, 49 percent of those with a high school education, 56 percent of community college graduates, 72 percent of university graduates, and 79 percent of graduate school degree holders reported they were underemployed. Not surprisingly, more highly educated workers had significantly lower general job satisfaction, too.

In both studies, we also conducted hierarchical multiple regression analyses to determine the incremental amounts of variance accounted for in the dependent variables by the type of work arrangement and demographic variables. In both studies, type of work arrangement consistently accounted for more variance than did the demographic variables. Thus, while there may be some direct effects of demographic variables on the job attitudes of contingent workers (consistent with the general organizational behavior literature), their greatest impact may be indirect. Different demographic groups seem to gravitate toward different types of contingent work arrangements, which themselves provide significantly different amounts of rewards.

Strategies for Managing Part-Time and Temporary Employees

Along with collecting quantitative survey data from participants in our studies, we also obtained qualitative data about their work experiences. Those comments focused largely on how organizations can more effectively manage part-time and temporary workers. In particular, five themes emerged from participants' responses: (1) the need for better compensation practices; (2) the need for more comprehensive fringe benefit packages; (3) the desire for more supportive supervision; (4) the need for better training, orientation, and development; and (5) the desire for more accurate portrayals of employment contracts.

Compensation Practices

For many of the permanent part-time workers we studied, the trade-off between higher wages and flexibility of hours seemed fair. However, for many of the other part-time workers and most of the temporary workers, the wage differential between their jobs and their full-time colleagues' jobs seemed inequitable, both in terms of their relative contributions to the organization and in terms of their net income (after taxes, costs of commuting, and costs of child care had been subtracted.)

Two specific suggestions emerged from participants' comments. First, salary has to be high enough to compensate for the basic expenses enumerated above; otherwise, organizations will have trouble attracting and retaining high-quality contingent workers. Second, even if the base hourly rate for contingent workers is relatively low, organizations should consider pay raises based on a combination of merit and job tenure. Without any hope of additional financial incentives, contingent workers have little reason to improve performance—a particular problem for service organizations, whose survival depends on quality performance from workers.

Fringe Benefits

Perhaps no issue is of greater concern to contingent workers than fringe benefits. Among part-time workers in our study, the most frequently received benefits were free parking, vacation leave, and merchandise discounts. However, the most frequent complaint among part-timers was the lack of medical insurance; indeed, fewer than a quarter of the part-time nurses in our study received any medical insurance from their own hospitals! The fringe benefits problem for temporary workers is even more dramatic. Only 7.5 percent of our respondents received any employer contributions to medical insurance payments; only 13.4 percent even received the option of buying medical coverage through an agency-affiliated group. Fewer than 5 percent received life insurance, disability insurance, or paid sick leave; none received pension benefits.

Many organizations that hire large numbers of part-timers do make employer contributions to health insurance as a means of gaining long-term commitment. For example, Parisian (a chain of clothing stores headquartered in Birmingham, Alabama) provides prorated health insurance benefits to part-timers who work twenty or more hours per week. The health insurance picture for temporary workers is less sanguine. While temporary agencies like US Personnel have tried to experiment with providing health insurance benefits, most health care insurance companies have significant barriers to eligibility for temporary workers. For instance, most insurance companies require temporary workers to be employed more than thirty-five hours per week for three months before they are eligible for coverage. Given the nature of temporary work, that leaves the vast majority of temporary workers without much chance of getting health insurance benefits.

At this time, the freedom of employers to not pay contingent workers health care benefits is in serious jeopardy. In fact, one of the primary factors fueling the current health care debate about universal coverage is the high percentage of the so-called working poor who are essentially working forty-hour weeks yet receiving no medical insurance benefits. Whether government mandates to provide health care insurance to contingent workers will significantly decrease the demand for part-time and temporary employees in the future is certainly open to question.

Supervision

Consistent with the research on full-time employees, many of the part-time employees in our study were quite satisfied with their relationships with supervisors and co-workers. The opportunities for social interaction are a major attraction for many part-time employees, and in most cases those social interactions are positive in nature.

The suggestions of part-timers about improving relationships with supervisors focused largely on communication. First, part-timers felt that they were often left out of the communication loop about new procedures or current problems in their departments, and that supervisors should make greater efforts to bring them up to speed on important or relevant issues. Second, part-timers commented that supervisors were more likely to punish them in public than full-time employees. Like most workers, part-timers want supervisors to be more patient with them and to refrain from giving them negative feedback in front of others.

Unfortunately, the feedback from temporary employees about their experiences with supervisors and coworkers is less positive. These workers resent being referred to, and treated as, "just temps." Many temporary employees feel they are treated as things rather than as people, and with significantly less respect and courtesy than they deserve. Implementing organizational policies governing day-to-day treatment of temporary employees in the workplace (such as guidelines on sexual harassment and occupational safety) is not especially costly, and may, even in the short run, decrease liability for inappropriate conduct by full-timers.

Training, Orientation, and Development

While one of the benefits to organizations of using contingent workers is the lower costs for training, orientation, and development of human resources, there certainly appear to be cases where organizations have made insufficient investments in their contingent workers. With part-time employees, the most frequent complaint along these lines was the unwillingness of organizations to give them more training and autonomy. In particular, part-time employees expressed strong desires for more rotation of job assignments to alleviate boredom, more on-the-job training, and more control over their daily routines. While the nature of part-time work is such that there are fewer opportunities for employees to grow and develop professionally, at the minimum organizations need to design some mechanisms to combat obsolescence and lagging productivity, which may result from declining motivation.

For temporary employees, the problems here revolve more around miscommunication among employing organizations, temporary agencies, and temporary workers themselves. In some cases, employer organizations are not clear enough with temporary agencies about their exact job demands, and consequently temporary workers without the right skills get sent to inappropriate assignments. In other cases, temporary agencies do not really have the appropriate employees to send for a particular assignment but, not wanting to lose the business, send out temps anyway—much to the mutual frustration of employing organizations and the temporary workers themselves. In still other cases, the appropriate temporary workers show up for an assignment, but the employer organizations do not spend enough time orienting them to procedures to make efficient use of them. Better communication between employing organizations and temporary agencies, as well as better orientation of temps to their assignments, would result in greater satisfaction of organizational demands and greater motivation of individual workers.

Accurate Portrayal of Employment Contracts

With part-time workers, virtually all the employees felt that their job assignments had been fairly and accurately described. Even in the case of seasonal part-timers and occasional part-timers, the employees understood that their job assignments were only transient and were not going to convert into full-time jobs.

With the temporary workers, however, there were numerous discrepancies between what temps felt they had been promised and what had been delivered. Most temporary agencies make a distinction between "regular temps" (who rotate through a variety of short-run temporary assignments in multiple organizations) and "temp-to-perms" (whose temporary jobs are supposed to convert into full-time employment after some probationary period is over, usually six months.) In many cases, temporary workers had been recruited and signed up by agencies who had promised them temp-to-perm assignments, and only discovered later that no permanent jobs were going to be available. In other cases, organizations themselves had recruited and hired temporary workers with the understanding that temporary workers would get full-time positions in the near future or special preference for any new job openings. Again, in many cases, temporary workers felt they had been given false promises simply as a means of recruiting them and getting them to work harder.

Undoubtedly, in some cases temporary workers who were desperate for full-time employment may have "heard" promises that were never made, even implicitly. However, the frequency of these complaints from temporary workers suggests that both agencies and employing organizations need to be clearer and more explicit with temporary workers about the nature of their work contracts, and that more of these work contracts should be written rather than oral in nature.

Emerging Issues in Part-Time and Temporary Employment

In this final section of the chapter, we turn to consider future issues of interest in the area of contingent employment, both in terms of research on part-time and temporary workers and on management practice. In particular, we explore alternative forms of contingent employment that are emerging, the performance and productivity of part-time and temporary workers, the impact of contingent workers on the attitudes and performance of full-time employees, part-time and temporary employment for older workers, and the impact of contingent work on subsequent career development.

Emerging Forms of Contingent Employment

As the preceding discussion suggests, most of the work on part-time and temporary employment has examined part-time workers who are mainly employed by one organization and temporary workers who are mainly employed by one agency. However, there are increasingly large numbers of contingent workers whose jobs do not fall into these categories and about whose experiences we have very little systematic knowledge.

For example, there are growing numbers of individuals who work as consultants and independent contractors, some of whom are self-employed and others who are regularly attached to one or two organizations; the lines between contingent work and entre-preneurial work are becoming increasingly blurry. In the same vein, the lines between alternative work schedule arrangements and contingent work arrangements are becoming fuzzier as well. For instance, the original implementation of flextime allowed essentially full-time employees to allocate their hours at their work-places at their convenience. However, it is less clear whether job sharing is a scheduling innovation or an alternative form of part-time work. Even the relationship between contingent work and place of work is becoming more cloudy. As more and more indi-viduals become employed as "home workers" (performing their jobs at their residences instead of at the organization itself), the definition of contingent employment in terms of hours per week alone becomes more open to question.

In the years ahead, then, more and more research will be needed on these new forms of contingent work and hybrid forms of conventional work arrangements. Such research would sharpen our focus on how, and why, individuals and organizations label some types of employment "contingent" and others not, and the implications that these labeling processes have for both the self-management and the organizational management of these employees.

Part-Time Work, Temporary Work, and Productivity

While we are beginning to get a much clearer picture of how con-tingent work affects employees' attitudes, we are still a long way away from understanding the impact on performance. There is some evidence to suggest that motivation levels of part-time and temporary workers are lower than those of full-time employees, but even here, the motivation levels vary greatly across types of con-tingent workers.

Moreover, it is difficult to untangle the various potential causes of productivity differences between full-time and contingent workers. One possible explanation is that many of the individuals in the contingent labor force may have lower skill levels and thus may disproportionately self-sort into contingent jobs. Another possibility is that contingent workers receive less training or skill updating. Yet a third possibility is that contingent workers do not work long enough periods in a stretch to reach or sustain peak periods of productivity. In terms of service jobs, it is possible that contingent workers do not have the financial incentives to provide consistently high service or the time to develop meaningful client relationships.

Consequently, yet another important issue for the next decade will be examining the productivity levels of part-time and temporary workers and determining the factors that enhance or depress their performance. Particularly in the service sector, the ability to develop high-quality, high-involvement workforces may be seriously constrained by increasing reliance on lower-quality, less involved contingent employees. For example, the ability to attract and retain older, less transient sales help is substantially higher in upper-end stores (like Parisian and Burdine's), which offer generous fringe benefits to most employees, than in lower-end chains (like McDonald's and Burger King), which do not.

Impact of Contingent Workers on Full-Time Employees

A third emerging issue in the use of part-time and temporary workers is their impact on full-time and permanent employees. In her research on contract laborers, Pearce (1993) found that managers are more likely to assign temporary workers tasks that require little or no organization-specific knowledge while shifting more difficult assignments that require teamwork and task interdependence to full-time employees. In other situations, full-time employees are asked to take on tasks of greater complexity and responsibility for no additional pay so that their lower-skilled tasks can be given to contingent workers.

Equally interesting, Pearce found that the use of temporary workers and leased workers can negatively affect the job attitudes of regular full-time employees. As she notes, even though full-timers prefer their own positions and compensation packages to those of contract workers, they may perceive the organization as exploiting contingent employees. This perception may lead full-timers, Pearce writes, "to question the organization's fairness to the contractors today—and possibly to themselves tomorrow."

The effective utilization of contingent workers, then, has managerial implications above and beyond the employment relationship between organizations and contingent workers themselves. The increased use of part-time and temporary employees also raises questions about compensation equity, the quality of employer-employee relationships, and the meaning of organizational loyalty for full-time employees. Particularly as organizations engage in such practices as laying off workers, outsourcing them, and hiring them back as temporaries, they need to realize the potential negative impact these employment practices may have on their core workforce (Feldman, Doerpinghaus, & Turnley, 1994).

Contingent Employment and the Older Worker

In the United States, the number of people retiring before age sixty-five is increasing dramatically; today, only 54 percent of the men and only 33 percent of the women aged sixty to sixty-four are still on full-time jobs (*Employee Benefits Review*, 1990). However, although 33 percent of the workforce leave their long-term jobs by age fifty-five and 50 percent leave by age sixty, less than one in nine workers in this country has fully retired by age sixty. Instead, most of these workers take "bridge jobs" between the time they end their full-time jobs and the time they begin full-time retirement. Fifty percent of these bridge jobs involve changes in occupation and industry and most are heavily clustered in small- and medium-sized firms offering fringe benefits inferior to those in their last jobs (Doeringer, 1990).

As a result of these changes, older individuals are becoming an increasingly large part of the potential contingent workforce. However, with a few notable exceptions like McDonald's "McMasters Program," organizations seem to be having trouble recruiting and retaining these employees (Feldman, 1994; Feldman & Turnley, 1994a). In the case of large, declining manufacturing firms, there may be little incentive in trying to keep older workers in part-time or temporary jobs; in the case of small firms, there may not be inexpensive or obvious mechanisms for identifying and attracting them. In either case, there are tax disincentives that make contingent work for more than a day or two a week unattractive to older workers.

It is far from clear whether the shortages of labor highlighted by Workforce 2000 will actually take place. If these shortages do occur, however, older contingent workers are a prime source of additional labor. From a research perspective, we need much more data on why older workers choose to remain in the workforce and the economic and noneconomic incentives that most encourage their continued labor force participation (Feldman, 1994). From a practitioner perspective, we need much better strategies for identifying, attracting, recruiting, and retaining older workers in the contingent labor pool. It is possible, for example, that organizations should consider outward career paths, in which older workers could regularly transition from full-time employment to part-time employment to temporary employment to permanent retirement (Feldman, 1994). Companies like Days Inn and Travelers Insurance have been very active in efforts to keep older workers in their jobs in bridge employment (McNaught & Barth, 1992; Jacobs, 1986).

Contingent Work, Underemployment, and Career Development

Another issue that is likely to come to the forefront in the next decade, not only from an organizational perspective but from a public policy perspective as well, is the relationship between contingent employment and underemployment. More and more young high school and college graduates are turning to part-time and temporary work as a last resort after their searches for full-time employment fail; in many cases, these young graduates are ending up in jobs for which they are significantly overqualified in terms of education if not experience (Feldman & Turnley, 1994b). Their ability to exit from low-growth contingent jobs and to jump start their careers is in serious question; our evidence suggests that many are very discouraged and are beginning to wonder whether work can be, or should be, the focus of their lives.

The evidence on the career paths of laid-off workers is equally disturbing. As Leana and Feldman (1992) found, many laid-off workers end up in part-time and temporary jobs earning half their previous incomes and with virtually no hope of regaining their career trajectories. While these new contingent employees do not blame their current employers for their career misfortunes, contingent workers who have experienced layoffs do have considerably decreased enthusiasm for their jobs and considerably more pessimism about their careers in general. Moreover, as noted earlier, the likelihood of organizations developing long-term, productive relationships with contingent workers who are involuntarily part-time employees and who are seriously underemployed is very low, independent of the fairness of the compensation or the challenge of the jobs assigned.

From a research perspective, then, increased investigation of the impact of contingent work on subsequent career development is clearly warranted. To what extent does underemployment in early career result in longer-term underemployment and slower career progression? To what extent does contingent work taken voluntarily in midcareer (for child care or elder care, for example) result in slower subsequent career advancement? From an organizational perspective, too, much more exploration of mechanisms to integrate part-time and temporary work assignments into longer-range career paths is needed. Organizations need to begin exploring, as well, better ways of integrating contingent job assignments, flextime and job sharing programs, and home-based and off-site job responsibilities.

Conclusion

The topic of part-time and temporary work is becoming a hotly debated public policy issue. In the years ahead, we need to begin considering the implications of a large and growing contingent workforce for our present social legislation, originally written and intended to protect the rights of full-time, permanent employees. Unfortunately, the financial safety nets and protections of employee rights mandated by federal legislation are beginning to apply to an increasingly smaller percentage of American workers.

In recent Senate hearings on contingent employment, Senator Howard Metzenbaum noted: "When companies replace full-time employees with disposable workers to cut labor costs, these costs do not simply 'disappear'—they are borne by workers and by taxpayers. The more 'contingent' our workforce becomes, the more dependent workers will be on government programs for income assistance, health care, and retirement income. Ultimately, I am very concerned that if this trend continues, we may wake up one morning to find that the American dream has slipped away. . . . For many workers, that morning has already come" (U.S. Senate, 1993).

As researchers and practitioners in the field of industrial and organizational psychology, we have important roles to play in understanding the nature and consequences of part-time and temporary work, suggesting methods for more effectively using contingent workers, and helping frame reasonable public policy alternatives. If we do not, we may see the same cycle of events all too common in human resource management and labor policy repeat itself—prescriptive work preceding empirical investigation and public policy based on accumulated anecdote rather than on analysis.

References

Ansberry, C. (1993, March 11). Workers are forced to take more jobs with few benefits. *Wall Street Journal,* pp. A1, A9.

Bosworth, T. W., & Holden, K. C. (1983). The role of part-time job options play in the retirement timing of older Wisconsin state employees. *Aging and Work, 6*(1), 31–36.

Doeringer, P. B. (Ed.). (1990). *Bridges to retirement.* Ithaca, NY: Cornell University Press.

Doerpinghaus, H. I., & Feldman, D. C. (1993). Employee benefit packages for part-time workers. *Benefits Quarterly, 9,* 72–82.

Employee Benefits Review. (1990, August). *45,* 12–15.

Feldman, D. C. (1990). Reconceptualizing the nature and consequences of part-time work. *Academy of Management Review, 15,* 103–112.

Feldman, D. C. (1994). The decision to retire early: A review and conceptualization. *Academy of Management Review, 19,* 285–311.

Feldman, D. C., & Doerpinghaus, H. I. (1992a). Missing persons no longer: Managing part-time workers in the '90s. *Organizational Dynamics, 21,* 59–72.

Feldman, D. C., & Doerpinghaus, H. I. (1992b). Patterns of part-time employment. *Journal of Vocational Behavior, 41,* 282–294.

Feldman, D. C., Doerpinghaus, H. I., & Turnley, W. H. (1994). Managing temporary workers: A permanent HRM challenge. *Organizational Dynamics.*

Feldman, D. C., Doerpinghaus, H. I., & Turnley, W. H. (1995). Employee reactions to temporary work. *Journal of Managerial Issues,* forthcoming.

Feldman, D. C., & Turnley, W. H. (1994a). *Factors influencing intentions to retire: An empirical test of theoretical propositions.* Working paper, University of South Carolina, College of Business Administration.

Feldman, D. C., & Turnley, W. H. (1994b). *Underemployment among college graduates: An empirical investigation.* Working paper, University of South Carolina, College of Business Administration.

Fierman, J. (1994, January 24). The contingency workforce. *Fortune,* pp. 30–36.

Gannon, M. J. (1984). Preferences of temporary workers: Time, variety, and flexibility. *Monthly Labor Review, 107,* 26–28.

Greenberger, E., & Steinberg, L. (1986). *When teenagers work.* New York: Basic Books.

Haring, M. J., Okun, M. A., & Stock, W. A. (1984). A quantitative synthesis of literature on work status and subjective well-being. *Journal of Vocational Behavior, 25,* 316–324.

Hart, R. A. (1987). *Working time and employment.* Boston: Allen & Unwin.

Jackofsky, E. F., & Peters, L. H. (1987). Part-time versus full-time employment status differences: A replication and extension. *Journal of Occupational Behavior, 8,* 1–9.

Jacobs, B. A. (1986, May 26). Surviving retirement. *Industry Week,* pp. 113–114.

Kaufman, H. (1982). *Professionals in search of work.* New York: Wiley.

Leana, C. R., & Feldman, D. C. (1992). *Coping with job loss: How individuals, organizations, and communities respond to layoffs.* New York: Macmillan/Lexington Books.

Levine, H. Z. (1987). Alternative work schedules: Do they meet workforce needs? *Personnel, 64*(1), 57–62.

Levitan, S. A., & Conway, E. A. (1988). Part-timers: Living on half-rations. *Challenge, 31,* 9–16.

McNaught, W., & Barth, M. C. (1992, Spring). Are older workers "good buys"? A case study of Days Inns of America. *Sloan Management Review,* pp. 53–60.

Morrow, L. (1993, March 29). The temping of America. *Time,* pp. 40–47.

Nakamura, A., & Nakamura, M. (1983). Part-time and full-time work behavior of married women: A model with a doubly truncated dependent variable. *Canadian Journal of Economics, 16,* 229–257.

Nardone, T. T. (1986). Part-time workers: Who are they? *Monthly Labor Review, 109,* 13–19.

Pearce, J. L. (1993). Toward an organizational behavior of contract laborers: Their psychological involvement and effects on employee coworkers. *Academy of Management Journal, 36,* 1082–1096.

Polivka, A. E., & Nardone, T. T. (1989). On the definition of contingent work. *Monthly Labor Review, 112,* 9–16.

Presser, H. B. (1986). Shift work among American women and child care. *Journal of Marriage and the Family, 48,* 551–563.

Ronen, S. (1984). *Alternative work schedules.* Homewood, IL: Dow Jones–Irwin.

Rothberg, D. S., & Cook, B. E. (1985). *Part-time professionals.* Washington, DC: Acropolis Books.

Sheridan, J. M. (1990). Just passing through. *Industry Week, 239,* 20–26.

Soumerai, S. B., & Avon, J. (1983). Perceived health, life satisfaction, and activity in urban elderly: A controlled study of the impact of part-time work. *Journal of Gerontology, 83,* 356–362.

Tiggeman, M., & Winefield, A. (1984). The effects of unemployment on the mood, self-esteem, locus of control, and expressive affect of school leavers. *Journal of Occupational Psychology, 57,* 33–42.

Tilly, C. (1991). Reasons for the continuing growth of part-time employment. *Monthly Labor Review, 114,* 10–18.

U.S. Senate, Committee on Labor and Human Resources, Subcommittee on Labor (Senator Howard Metzenbaum presiding). (1993, June 15). Washington, DC.

Wakefield, D. S., Curry, J. P., Mueller, C. W., & Price, J. L. (1987). Differences in the importance of work outcomes between full-time and part-time hospital employees. *Journal of Occupational Behavior, 8,* 25–35.

Williams, H. R. (1989). What temporary workers earn: Findings from the new BLS survey. *Monthly Labor Review, 112,* 3–6.

CHAPTER 7

Creating an Internal Contingent Workforce
Managing the Resource Link

James W. Smither

In a conference concerning contingent workers, Labor Secretary Robert Reich said, "The new phenomenon of disposable workers is not good for Americans. I do not believe in the long term, it's good for American companies either. How do we build up the kind of competitive companies . . . that we need that are flexible and innovative, if employees don't feel loyal, and don't feel the company is going to be there for them?" (Rubis, 1994, p. A1). Similarly, the *Wall Street Journal* noted that "contingent workers . . . are the medium for a corporate America preaching a message of flexibility and cost cutting" (Ansberry, 1993, p. 1). The number of people working for temporary employment agencies has increased from 470,000 to 1.6 million over the past ten years (Fierman, 1994). Moreover, a 1994 poll of CEOs indicated that 44 percent had increased their use of contingent workers over the preceding five years and only 13 percent had decreased use (Fierman, 1994). Contingent workers are not confined to simple clerical positions. They can be found in technical areas, such as engineering, programming, and nursing. In fact, one Connecticut firm, IMCOR, provides companies with temporary senior executives.

However, the increasing reliance of companies on contingent workers has raised a number of concerns. From the workers' perspective, they may live riskier and less certain lives than permanent employees. Contingent workers often receive no benefits, such as medical coverage and pensions. Also, laws that were passed by Congress and many states to protect employees (such as those prohibiting job discrimination) may not protect independent contractors (Ansberry, 1993).

From the organization's perspective, the increasing reliance on contingent workers also raises doubts. One CEO has argued that excessive reliance on contingent (that is, temporary) outsiders can decrease productivity because they lack the loyalty and ownership that results from being a regular part of a team (Fierman, 1994). Richard Belous of the National Planning Association described a case study where contingent workers at a large manufacturer that was engaged in union negotiations had access to the employer's collective bargaining goals, fallback positions, and other strategies. The contingent workers leaked the company's entire game plan to the union. The fiasco made the company aware of how little power it had over a contingent workforce that had no reason to show loyalty to the company (Ansberry, 1993).

Robert Kuttner (1993), writing in *Business Week*, has stated, "If most of the people connected to the corporation no longer have job security, all the talk about teamwork, empowerment, investment in people and long-term orientation is a sham. Without a reciprocal commitment by management to a long-term relationship, the employee who buys into the partnership model is being romanced for a one-night stand . . . it is difficult to imagine a culture of mutual commitment when everyone is a temp."

Cost can also be a factor. Depending on the level of their skills, independent contractors can sometimes command higher hourly wages than permanent employees. And temporary agencies may charge corporate clients fees that are much higher (by 20 to 50 percent) than the hourly wage of regular workers. Thus, contingent workers are not necessarily less expensive than their permanent counterparts.

In sum, although the use of contingent workers is increasing, the workers are concerned about their relative lack of job security and benefits, and corporations have expressed concerns about the cost of such workers and their commitment to the goals of the company.

The Dilemma at AT&T

As the deregulation of the telecommunications industry accelerated in the 1970s and 1980s, the structure of AT&T has been radically altered. It has changed from a domestic company to one with significant international involvement and presence. Today, more than twenty business units (in areas as diverse as long distance services, credit cards, and microelectronics) have their own separate profit-and-loss responsibilities. These business units are supported by divisions (such as human resources, finance, public relations, government affairs, and information systems).

While some of these business units have grown, others have downsized. While shrinking business units paid severance, growing business units paid for recruitment and training. The process of reducing the number of employees in some business units (via layoffs and attrition) while recruiting and training employees in other units was very expensive.

A 1988 task force recommended that the company establish a resource management center (RMC) to help retain some of the people who might otherwise leave the business due to layoffs. To accomplish this, the RMC created a critical hiring process that required business units to first consider employees whose jobs were at risk due to downsizing in other parts of the business before hiring from the external market. However, the RMC did not have an adequate infrastructure to match "at-risk" employees to hiring needs of other business units. Thus, although business units dutifully submitted their job openings to the RMC, the RMC was able to match relatively few employees to available openings. As a result, some business units viewed the RMC as merely an unfriendly policy police force.

The situation became more severe in 1991 when AT&T acquired NCR, the multinational computer business, and therefore decided to dissolve its own computer systems unit. At this time, another task force was established to consider how the company could (1) address the reality that some business units were downsizing while others were growing, (2) retain talented employees who might otherwise be lost due to downsizing, and (3) address the company's growing reliance on contract and temporary employees. The task force benchmarked external companies, conducted internal focus groups, surveyed business units and divisions to determine their contracting activity, and researched workforce trends and issues.

Also, an external consulting firm was hired to conduct a survey to determine the experience of other companies with contingent workforce programs. Nineteen of thirty-seven corporations that were interviewed had contingent workforce programs in place; however, more than two thirds of them were composed almost entirely of clerical and administrative personnel. These in-house temporary pools typically consisted of a mix of former employees and outside staff hired directly as temporary workers. Several programs that originally focused exclusively on clerical and administrative positions were beginning to fill temporary openings requiring professional or managerial skills. Also, several programs focused on creating a temporary pool of retirees who wanted to continue working on a part-time, temporary basis.

Three programs had focused largely on professional, managerial, and technical workers (a group that was a major concern of the AT&T task force). Two of these programs had been discontinued. One program had used retirees to conduct training classes for newly hired permanent employees or to work as mentors with inexperienced engineers. Another program had consisted of twenty-six managers and engineers who had lost their jobs (due to restructuring) but were kept on the company's payroll. This group participated in an eight-week retooling program and reentered the company as self-managed, in-house consultants. They worked on project teams to address issues that, in the normal course of business, the company's management had no time to address, such as facilitating supplier-production coordination. This program was discontinued because it was viewed as too costly and unwieldy. In addition, it was difficult to implement the solutions that the "off-line" project teams had developed.

Another program identified in the survey uses an external subsidiary temporary unit that was established and is partly owned by the company. The company offered new, part-time careers to early retirees who were also given incentives to join the program (guaranteed ninety days of work per year for two years). The employees in this program, virtually all of whom are professional, managerial, or technical, may be given assignments in the company or with other firms. In addition to stringent selection requirements, the company continues to train employees who join the program.

It is noteworthy that virtually all of the contingent workforce programs identified in this survey were developed by relatively large corporations. Moreover, small organizations may not be able to capitalize on economies of scale sufficiently to support such a program.

Based on all of the data analyzed by the task force, AT&T decided to establish Resource Link, a temporary services unit that places on-payroll management-level employees in temporary assignments across the company. Resource Link was designed to (a) take advantage of the company's own employees, in preference to temporary employees from outside agencies, (b) increase the company's flexibility in meeting its staffing needs, and (c) provide employees with a greater sense of employment stability, as contrasted with stability in a specific job.

The task force recommended an entrepreneurial approach that included an orientation to actively marketing Resource Link's services and products—talented temporary employees—throughout the company. It also pointed to the need to provide value-added, rigorous screening of employees, rather than merely serving as a conduit for referring employees from one business unit to another. Finally, it was necessary to create a financial structure that could help accommodate the short-term staffing needs faced by many business units and divisions.

AT&T's Internal Contingent Workforce

The staff who managed start-up operations at Resource Link represented a blend of disciplines and expertise, including sales, recruiting, management information systems, finance, and operations. Perhaps the most important initial success factor was Resource Link's commitment to selecting only employees with strong performance records. It was critical that Resource Link not be perceived as a dumping ground for marginal employees. Thus, Resource Link is not a holding unit for employees affected by workforce reductions.

Resource Link was launched in the fourth quarter of 1991. It operates as an internal temporary services unit, using on-payroll employees, called associates, to help meet the variable workforce needs of the company's business units and divisions. Associates have permanent jobs with Resource Link (and AT&T); it is only their assignments that are temporary, typically from three to twelve months. There is no limit on the length of an assignment. Associates retain the same salary and benefits as other AT&T employees. They may perform short-term project work, temporarily fill a vacant position, satisfy a one-time customer need (such as a planning or development opportunity), or provide other interim managerial, technical, or consulting services.

As of mid–1994, there were over 450 associates on assignment in twenty-seven business units and divisions. Clients are billed at an hourly or monthly rate commensurate with the associate's skills. Most associates work on only one assignment at a time (although one organization development associate divided time each work week among three clients). Most assignments are at the first two levels of the management or technical/professional career ladder. About 40 percent of associates work in technical positions such as software development or systems analysis; the remaining associates fill a wide variety of management assignments.

The program was originally aimed at employees whose jobs had been declared at risk due to downsizing. However, about half of its current associates volunteered to join Resource Link for other reasons. That is, many employees have seen Resource Link as a way to advance their careers.

Associates who move from job to job in a variety of locations must be made to feel that they are being "supervised" in the traditional sense and being properly supported. Thus, each associate reports to a Resource Link staff manager. These staff managers are responsible for supporting and reviewing the performance of many associates whom they rarely see. (Details concerning the performance management and appraisal process are provided below.)

The following sample of job titles filled by Resource Link associates illustrates the wide variety of skills and positions encompassed by the program: systems architect, product manager, budget supervisor, programmer, project manager, business analyst, safety engineer, database administrator, administrative assistant, marketing manager, software developer, systems engineer, executive secretary, financial analyst, asset management supervisor, training manager, system administrator, contracts manager, sales program manager, document specialist, litigation project manager, quality measurements manager, consultant, LAN administrator, hardware design engineer, development lab administrator, system tester, leadership adviser, telemarketing coordinator, marketing consultant, customer service supervisor, EEO complaint manager, econometric specialist, quality process manager, broadcast/cable TV industry expert, instructional developer, senior account executive, business development manager.

Benefits to the Organization

Resource Link benefits the company in many ways. AT&T retains and develops talented employees, and spends less on severance payments and fees to temporary employment agencies. It has also helped business planners think more clearly about the value of distinguishing between a core and variable workforce.

It enables business units to quickly adapt to changing conditions. For example, when a new data center in New York needed to hire people skilled in networks and the UNIX operating system, it recognized that some people may be uncertain about working in New York, or about working in a twenty-four-hour-a-day, seven-day-a-week operation. The manager wanted to give people a chance to try the environment to see if they wanted to be a part of it. Usually, it would be very difficult to find highly skilled people to fill what amounted to trial positions. But Resource Link was able to fill the positions, and AT&T employees filled jobs that, in the past, may have gone to outside contractors. As the manager said, "If the operation is unsuccessful, I'm not committed to having people staffed to the business unit, and I don't have to make people surplus."

Resource Link also facilitates collaboration across business units. For example, to address a technical problem that concerns several business units, experts can be pulled together within Resource Link for a temporary period. At the end of such a project, the experts may simply return to their home business units.

Resource Link enables hiring managers to "try before they buy," evaluating associates' performance during a temporary assignment before offering some associates traditional, permanent positions. In fact, about 25 percent of Resource Link's associates have accepted traditional job offers in the company.

Also, the risks to managers of hiring temporary talent are reduced because Resource Link's associates are carefully selected (as described below) and are familiar with the culture of the company. Another manager who employs six associates (mostly software engineers) noted the advantage of not spending a lot of money to train consultants. He added, "If we're going to the trouble of training people, their skills ought to be transferable within AT&T. When the job is completed, I can let these people go off to another assignment. It's much easier to sign a contract with Resource Link for six months or a year than it is to transfer permanent employees in and then try to move them out a year later."

Resource Link also demonstrates to employees that the company does care about them and that it seeks innovative ways to lessen the pain of downsizing.

Most notable are the expense and revenue issues. To date, revenue (from clients) and cost savings (from reduced severance payments) have exceeded expenses (salary and benefits for associates and Resource Link's staff).

Resource Link benefits not only the company but also its associates. It provides them opportunities to enhance their skills, experience, and marketability and to acquire firsthand knowledge of the markets, products, and services associated with the different business units. Over 150 associates have obtained traditional jobs (over 10 percent of these positions were promotions) in nineteen business units or divisions. And many other associates have declined traditional jobs to take advantage of the variety of assignments offered to them by Resource Link.

Recruiting and Selection

Recruiting and selecting employees to work as Resource Link associates is characterized by two major issues not faced in more traditional contexts. First, unlike most temporary employment firms, Resource Link makes a long-term commitment to the employees it hires to work as associates. Resource Link cannot select an employee solely based on his or her ability to meet the requirements of a single assignment. Instead, employees are selected to join Resource Link when there is match for the short term (do skills match the requirements of a currently open assignment?) *and* the long term (are employees likely to be marketable for future assignments?). Assessing whether there is a long-term match requires determining whether the employee has work experience and technical skills that are compatible with a number of potential assignments, and also has the communication skills, adaptability, and customer orientation that are required to be successful in multiple temporary assignments.

Two selection tools (described below)—a behavior description interview and a detailed, comprehensive skills inventory—were developed by psychologists from the corporate human resources staff to assist in evaluating candidates for Resource Link.

The recruiting and selection process is managed by an account management and recruiting team that is part of the Resource Link staff. The recruiting process begins with the receipt of a written service request that includes a brief description of the temporary assignment, including location and expected length, and the specific skills the client is looking for. An account manager then contacts the client to verify the information and, if necessary, obtain additional detail and clarification. This information is passed to a recruiter who initiates a search for an employee who has necessary skills. Recruiters first determine whether any idle or soon-to-be-idle Resource Link associates have the skills required to fill the assignment.

Recruiters also use a computer database (Resource Link Operating Support System, R-OSS) to try to identify suitable candidates. R-OSS contains information on the skill sets of all Resource Link associates and applicants, obtained from a skills inventory that all applicants complete. Applicants circle, from detailed lists, information about their level of education, major field of study, professional licenses and certifications, foreign language skills, nontechnical experience (forty-one areas including finance, labor relations, purchasing, competitive analysis, database management, government affairs, product management), technical experience (thirty-seven areas including electrical engineering, economic analysis, systems analysis, statistical analysis, programming/software development, networking, LANs), computer skills (fifty-eight skills in areas such as applications packages, database administration, data communications, operating systems, and programming languages), and knowledge of fifty-one company products and services.

Unlike many skills inventories, applicants are not asked merely to indicate whether they either have or do not have each skill. Instead, they use rating scales to indicate the *level* of their skills. For example, foreign language skills in speaking and reading/writing are separately classified as either *elementary proficiency* (able to satisfy minimum courtesy requirements and understand simple questions and statements, with frequent errors in pronunciation and grammar), *limited working proficiency* (able to satisfy limited work requirements and routine social demands), *minimum professional proficiency* (able to participate in most formal and informal conversations with reasonable ease, read with relative ease, write well enough to be understood by a country national), or *full professional proficiency* (reading and writing proficiency equivalent to a college-educated country national).

Similarly, for each technical, nontechnical, and computer skill, applicants classify their skill level as *basic* (able to make limited use of this skill but need more training to apply it without assistance or frequent supervision), *intermediate* (functional proficiency sufficient to use this skill effectively without assistance and with only infrequent supervision), *advanced* (in-depth proficiency sufficient to assist, consult, or lead others in the use of this skill), or *expert* (proficiency sufficient to be recognized as an authority or subject matter expert in the use of this skill).

Recruiters indicate the level of specific skills they seek for a given assignment, and R-OSS can help identify a list of candidates who have rated themselves as meeting the skill requirements of the assignment. System limitations cause recruiters to also use more traditional methods to identify possible candidates. If no suitable candidate is identified at this stage of the recruiting process, recruiters will list the temporary assignment in a companywide electronic staffing system. Resumes of interested applicants are screened by recruiters, and applicants whose experience and skills seem to match the assignment requirements are contacted by the recruiter. At this point, the recruiter needs to adopt a marketing perspective and sell the applicant on the benefits of working for Resource Link. Interested applicants are asked to submit their two most recent annual performance appraisals.

Applicants with a history of good prior performance are then asked to complete the skills inventory and to participate in a structured, behavior description interview (Janz, 1982) developed for Resource Link by psychologists in AT&T's corporate human resources division. Recruiters use seven-point, behaviorally anchored rating scales to evaluate applicants in four areas: flexibility/adaptability, communication, customer/service/quality orientation, and work motivation and perseverance. For example, applicants may be asked to describe the most difficult transition they ever faced going to a new job, or to describe a time when they encountered an insurmountable problem on the job.

The interview is especially important in view of the fact that Resource Link does not hire employees merely for a single assignment. Instead, recruiters must be certain that all Resource Link associates have the kinds of skills and experience that will enable them to be successful in multiple assignments. Given Resource Link's extended commitment to its associates, it cannot afford to place an employee in an assignment if it appears that the employee will not be easily marketable for other Resource Link assignments.

Associates without a current assignment (idle time) receive full pay and benefits, and idle time of associates whose skills do not match assignment requirements can potentially be enormously expensive. In this regard, recruiters note that effective communication skills and flexibility/adaptability are critical requirements for the long-term success of Resource Link's associates. Stated differently, account managers and recruiters will need to continuously market each associate and associates will need to market themselves to obtain assignments in the future.

This long-term perspective has occasionally caused Resource Link to decline to fill a temporary position where the client had already identified an employee the client wanted to hire through Resource Link, but whom Resource Link evaluated as lacking the skills required for success in other assignments. In such a circumstance, turning down the revenue associated with placing the person in a short-term assignment seemed prudent given the likelihood that the employee would be likely to later accrue considerable idle time at substantial cost to Resource Link. This is another example of how Resource Link's recruiting and selection practices differ from those typically found among temporary employment firms who have no long-term commitment to their employees.

Applicants with low interview scores are generally eliminated from further consideration. During the interview, recruiters also review the skills inventory completed by the applicant. Specifically, recruiters note whether there are inconsistencies between the applicant's responses to the skills inventory and the applicant's resume (for instance, an applicant whose self-ratings on the skills inventory indicate an advanced level of project management skills but whose resume makes no mention of such a background). Recruiters can then question the candidate about such inconsistencies. Also, the recruiter reviews the skills inventory to determine whether the applicant's skills are not only suitable for the current assignment but also match the kind of skill requirements frequently found in Resource Link assignments.

It is also noteworthy that recruiters do not attempt to conduct an in-depth evaluation of applicants' technical skills. Clearly, given the breadth of positions and skills filled by Resource Link, it would be impossible to identify recruiters who have sufficient technical competence to evaluate candidates in terms of each of the skills clients seek. Instead, recruiters rely on the skills inventory as a method of identifying applicants whose skills apparently match requirements of the assignment. Recruiters then provide the client with information concerning those candidates who successfully completed the screens described above (prior performance appraisals, behavior description interview, skills inventory match). The client decides who to interview and evaluates the level of the candidate's technical skills. If all parties agree the candidate is a potential match for the client's assignment, the Resource Link recruiter extends a job offer to the candidate. Candidates who are not already Resource Link associates are then transferred from their business unit to Resource Link.

In sum, the selection process involves several elements: resume review, review of prior performance appraisals, a detailed skills inventory, a behavior description interview by a Resource Link recruiter, and an evaluation of technical skills conducted by the client. Except for the client interview, each element of the selection process is focused on evaluating both the applicant's fit for the current assignment and the long-term fit, given the type of skills most frequently sought by Resource Link and the need for each associate to be marketable over time.

How effective are these recruiting and selection procedures? To date, several factors have enabled Resource Link to recruit an ample number of applicants for its openings. In addition to employees whose regular positions have been declared at risk due to downsizing, some employees have been attracted by the project-oriented nature of the work, and others were no doubt attracted by the opportunity to obtain experience in a variety of business units—an opportunity not otherwise readily available to most employees. Also, until recently, Resource Link's incentive compensation plan (described below) enabled its associates to earn up to 110 percent of their regular salary. This feature also helped recruiters sell applicants on the benefits of working for Resource Link. The effect that removing the incentive compensation plan will have on recruiting is not presently known.

Resource Link identifies potential assignments in several ways. A companywide policy requires that business units contact Resource Link before searching for nonpayroll (contract) employees through outside employment firms. A good deal of information about the program has also appeared in company publications. Finally, account managers and a customer request center with an 800 telephone number help develop placements.

Although no formal validation study about the selection process has been conducted, several pieces of evidence suggest that it has been generally successful. For example, of the hundreds of associates placed in temporary assignments, less than a handful have been returned by the client to Resource Link due to unsuccessful performance. In fact, information from performance appraisals (described below) indicates that over 70 percent of associates exceed client expectations.

Also, as of March 1994, idle time among associates was less than 5 percent (only 17 of 378 associates were not currently employed in a temporary assignment). Idle time may be as brief as one or two days and usually does not exceed three or four weeks (although a layoff policy, described below, has been implemented to deal with the few associates who are unable to obtain assignments for a long period of time). The low level of idle time also suggests that associates possess the skills that have enabled them to be successfully placed in temporary assignments. Finally, annual customer satisfaction surveys (from 1992 and 1993) found that 90 percent of clients were satisfied or very satisfied with how well candidate qualifications matched job requirements. Taken together, these data suggest the selection process has generally been successful.

Although no validation study has been conducted concerning Resource Link's behavior description interview, research has shown good levels of validity for these kinds of interviews in particular (Janz, 1982; Motowidlo et al., 1992; Orpen, 1985) and structured interviews in general (Campion, Pursell, & Brown, 1988; Huffcut & Winfred, 1994).

When developing and validating selection procedures for a program such as Resource Link, companies should collect job analysis information concerning the variety of assignments that associates are likely to fill. In addition, it is important to consider skills and characteristics, such as adaptability, that may be especially important for people working in temporary assignments. When developing the behavior description interview for Resource Link, AT&T's psychologists had access to a large job analysis of entry-level management and technical positions. Also, input on skill and behavioral requirements of associates had been gathered via focus groups with potential clients. The dimensions assessed in Resource Link's behavior description interview were selected based on this job analysis information.

Less is known about the accuracy with which candidates are likely to evaluate their own skill levels on a detailed skills inventory. One Resource Link recruiter noted that some candidates appear very conservative when making such self-ratings, whereas others provide obviously inflated self-ratings. The latter tendency seems consistent with the literature on self-appraisals, which reports that employees often rate themselves more leniently than others would (Farh, Dobbins, & Cheng, 1991; Yu & Murphy, 1993), and finds less agreement between employees' self-ratings and ratings by others than between ratings of the employee provided by different sources such as peers, subordinates, and supervisors (Harris & Schaubroeck, 1988). However, most of this literature has focused on appraisals of work performance in general rather than on employees' ability and willingness to accurately evaluate their technical skills.

Kehoe (1994) compared applicants' self-ratings of skills to ratings of the same skills made by trained interviewers. After first completing self-evaluations of their proficiency (using anchors similar to those described above for Resource Link's skills inventory) on five to fifteen skills identified as important for a given job category, applicants were evaluated in each skill area by trained interviewers. Kehoe compared 1,061 applicant self-ratings with the corresponding 1,061 interviewer ratings for 200 applicants in four job categories. Of the skills rated low by applicants, 63 percent of the interviewer ratings were also low (and only 18 percent of the interviewer ratings were high). Of the skills rated high by applicants, 66 percent of the interviewer ratings were also high (and only 14 percent of the interviewer ratings were low). Stated differently, there was a reasonable level of agreement between self-ratings and interviewer ratings, and high disagreement between applicants and interviewers occurred in less than 20 percent of the ratings. Clearly, additional research in this area could help recruiters calibrate employees' self-evaluations and better evaluate the extent to which employees' skills match job requirements.

Training and Career Planning

At present, the typical Resource Link associate is allocated from three to five days per year for training. Given the nature of their work, it seems noteworthy that many associates have obtained further training in project management skills. However, to date, most training has been invested in acquiring or enhancing technical skills rather than general management skills such as time management and supervision.

Resource Link is implementing more formal career planning procedures. Although opportunities for promotion may be unavailable to many associates, Resource Link seems an ideal setting in which to acquire a variety of developmental assignments that broaden the employee's value to the company. Approaching this career planning and development process in a more systematic way will require consideration of several issues. It is not clear, for instance, whether career planning and training needs will be similar for associates who joined Resource Link after their jobs had been declared at risk versus associates who volunteered to join

Resource Link for other reasons. Perhaps associates whose prior jobs had been declared at risk are more likely to come from parts of the business that use technologies that are in low demand or are outdated. If so, they would have a greater need for training that develops new knowledge and skills rather than merely enhances existing knowledge and skills. Also, it may be difficult to balance the need for training that will meet the short-term needs of clients with the need for training that will meet the long-term needs of Resource Link and its associates.

Performance Appraisal and Compensation

Performance appraisal and compensation practices of Resource Link follow many of the same procedures used with other company employees, but several modifications are required to fully address unique issues faced by Resource Link. For example, in addition to the associate's performance on each assignment, appraisals need to take into account the associate's productivity (billed hours divided by available hours) and other administrative issues described below.

The performance appraisal process begins at the start of each assignment when the client establishes performance objectives for the associate. Moreover, establishing performance objectives is a natural part of Resource Link operations. In fact, the ability to clarify the client's performance expectations is a critical consultative skill for associates, especially when the client seems reluctant or unable to explicitly define the associate's role and objectives.

With respect to appraisal and compensation matters, it is noteworthy that Resource Link views itself (not the client) as the supervisor of each associate. Associates receive midyear feedback from a Resource Link manager, based on written feedback from clients concerning completed and current assignments. Clients are asked to rate the associate's performance using the same five-point rating scale used throughout the company: unsatisfactory, partially met objectives, fully met objectives, exceeded objectives, or far exceeded objectives.

Because clients are not responsible for determining the associate's pay increases or performance bonuses, clients sometimes appear to be lenient in rating the job performance of associates.

When this occurs, a Resource Link manager discusses the associate's rating with the client. For example, the manager may ask the client to focus more attention on the extent to which each performance objective was met, or the client may be asked to consider how he or she would have rated the associate in comparison to other employees.

At the end of each fiscal year, each associate receives a written performance appraisal based on three factors: (1) clients' ratings of the associate's performance on assignments throughout the previous twelve months (weighted 70 percent), (2) the associate's productivity (weighted 15 percent), and (3) an administrative rating (weighted 15 percent) completed by Resource Link managers concerning other important aspects of the associate's performance, such as timely reporting of hours worked (via a conversant phone technology that enables associates to call a central number and use the phone keys to enter hours worked), bringing in new work for Resource Link, commitment to personal development, and adhering to various administrative procedures. Low ratings in the administrative category can lessen the compensation increase and performance bonus of an otherwise high-performing associate.

All of the data needed to complete the appraisal process are gathered and compiled by managers on Resource Link's associate support staff. However, to provide face-to-face appraisal feedback to hundreds of associates in less than one month, Resource Link uses its recruiters and account managers (whose primary job is to identify temporary assignments and market Resource Link to the business units) to supplement its associate support staff (whose job is to provide support and general supervision to associates on assignment). Moreover, completing end-of-year appraisals for a growing number of associates will become a logistical nightmare, and this has caused Resource Link to consider variable timing for the annual appraisals (on the anniversary of each associate's date of hire) and a simplified rating scale.

Resource Link provides an increase in base salary and a performance bonus to all associates with satisfactory performance or better. Salary increases are based on a combination of the associate's annual appraisal and the associate's current base pay relative to a reference pay rate established for each salary grade. Associates' annual performance bonuses are based on their performance appraisal and salary grade.

One area of concern with the current appraisal process involves the number of rating categories used. Because the managers from Resource Link's associate support staff do not provide day-to-day supervision of associates, they must rely on ratings provided by clients. As noted above, such ratings occasionally appear to be lenient. Presently, about 50 percent of associates are rated "exceeded objectives" and another 20 percent are rated as "far exceeded objectives." Moreover, there are questions about whether Resource Link can reliably determine the difference between an associate who has exceeded objectives and one who has far exceeded objectives. For employees in other parts of the company, higher-level managers are often in a position to review ratings provided by different supervisors and ensure that one supervisor is not substantially more lenient or severe than others. Unfortunately, it is very difficult for Resource Link to know when a client's ratings are unreasonably lenient or severe.

Taken together, these factors create concerns about the accuracy of appraisals, and these concerns are causing the appraisal process to be reexamined. One possibility is to have a simpler rating process in which clients do not provide an overall rating for each associate, but instead merely indicate whether the associate did or did not meet each assigned objective. Similarly, annual appraisals for associates would simply indicate whether the associate's performance was satisfactory or unsatisfactory. This may be fairer than pretending to be able to make more fine-grained distinctions among associates.

It is interesting to note that associates were originally compensated based on an incentive plan that rewarded those with high productivity. Under this plan, associates received 80 percent of their previous salary as base pay and 20 percent of their previous salary was placed at risk. If productivity dropped below 85 percent, the associate would begin to lose some of the salary that was at risk. However, when productivity was above 90 percent, the associate would earn up to an additional 10 percent above previous salary. Thus, an associate with 100 percent productivity could earn up to 110 percent of previous salary, whereas one with poor productivity could earn only 80 percent of previous salary.

Several problems developed. For example, each associate's productivity was computed based on a rolling twelve-month average. As a result, it took a long time before associates saw their idle time reflected by a noticeable reduction in their pay. Also, productivity during the time this plan was implemented was much higher than had been anticipated—close to 98 percent. Many associates were being paid well above their previous salary, and the plan was costing Resource Link far too much. Also, one reason the incentive plan was originally established was to help attract employees to join Resource Link. However, as Resource Link has grown and gained credibility, this factor has become less of an issue. As a result of all of these factors, the incentive compensation plan was recently discontinued.

Recruiters have reported that the incentive compensation plan helped them attract qualified employees to join Resource Link. The effect of discontinuing the plan on recruiting and retaining associates is yet to be determined.

Layoff Policy

Even a successful program needs to develop a mechanism to deal with employees who cannot obtain an assignment for an extended period of time. The current layoff policy specifies that any associate who is forty-five days beyond the completion of his or her last assignment without obtaining a new assignment will receive a letter indicating he or she will go off payroll in ninety days. Thus, the present layoff policy creates the possibility that associates could go 135 days without an assignment before being laid off from the company. To date, eight associates have entered the ninety-day window but only two have been laid off.

Employee Attitudes

Results from a 1993 companywide employee opinion survey found that job attitudes of Resource Link associates compared favorably with attitudes of employees throughout the company who held more traditional job assignments. Resource Link associates provided more favorable responses (at least 5 percent higher compared to other employees) in categories dealing with management leadership, respect, teamwork, dedication to customer, quality process, performance management, operating efficiency, competitive position, and satisfaction with the company. In all, associates' responses were more favorable than responses from other employees in fourteen of the sixteen categories on the survey. One area where associates' responses were less favorable was items dealing with employment security—not surprising, given the temporary nature of associates' assignments and the fact that about half of associates came from jobs that had been declared at risk.

Unfortunately, survey results did not provide a way to distinguish responses made by associates who joined Resource Link after their jobs had been declared at risk versus responses from associates who volunteered to join Resource Link for other reasons. Researchers have hypothesized that job attitudes of part-time workers will be more favorable when their employment arrangement is voluntary (Feldman, 1990). Similarly, job attitudes may differ between associates who felt pressure to join Resource Link as a last resort and associates who volunteered to join for other reasons. Investigating differences between these two groups in terms of attitudes, performance, and turnover constitutes an important direction for future research.

Expanding the Resource Link Concept

The Resource Link concept has recently been extended in several interesting ways, including efforts to address needs of the nonexempt) workforce and to place associates in temporary assignments in other companies.

Resource Link has recently entered into a strategic alliance with an external firm, Management Recruiters International (MRI). As part of this alliance, AT&T may bring in temporary employees from MRI (after it has been determined that no AT&T employees are available), and Resource Link associates may receive temporary assignments at other firms through MRI.

AT&T has also initiated programs to make better use of nonexempt employees who face separation from the company. Those who have received notice that they will be laid off may be given several options. One (traditional) option is to leave the job and the company on the date they are designated to go off payroll, and take their severance pay in a lump sum payment at that time.

Alternatively, they may elect to take an extended compensation option (ECO) that enables them to receive their severance pay in weekly increments. Although ECO employees no longer have a regular job, they remain on payroll and continue to receive benefits until they have received all their severance pay, at which time they have to leave the company. Also, this additional time on payroll is credited toward their pensions. During this time, ECO employees may continue to use internal staffing mechanisms to obtain a permanent position, and they must be available to be placed in temporary work assignments in the company. ECO employees who are placed in temporary assignments, receive their weekly pay plus assignment pay, which is equal to the fee that AT&T would have paid an external temporary agency to fill the temporary assignment.

There have been 710 ECO participants since the program began in 1992. During its first seventeen months of operation, seventy of these employees obtained traditional, permanent jobs through the company's internal staffing mechanisms. Also, about 17 percent of ECO employees have been on temporary assignment (and therefore receiving assignment pay) at any given time.

In a trial program initiated in 1994, a small nonmanagement employee pool has been populated with new hires and employees who have received notices that their jobs are at risk. This pool of employees fills temporary assignments that could not be filled with available ECO employees. In the past, these temporary assignments would have been filled by outside employment agencies.

In the future, Resource Link could ultimately serve as a valuable mechanism by which external recruits may be rigorously screened and given temporary, rotational assignments in several parts of the company before receiving a regular job in a specific business unit.

Limitations

The Resource Link concept is not without limitations and problems. For example, due to the variable duration and nature of assignments, opportunities for promotion are limited. Also, pricing services to clients can be a problem because Resource Link must recover each associate's overhead, including substantial health and retirement benefits.

Despite the advantages of the approach, it may not be appropriate or feasible for many firms. For example, small organizations may not be able to capitalize on economies of scale sufficiently to support such a program. Also, because many individuals may be reluctant to move, they may be unwilling to accept distant assignments. Therefore, a successful program requires proximity between the jobs and the pool of interested and skilled employees.

Other companies have addressed similar problems with other innovative approaches. In 1988 Hewlett-Packard began a "flex-force" that includes about 7 percent of its ninety-five thousand employees. Flex-force includes internal temporary employees kept on Hewlett-Packard's payroll, but it also includes external temporary workers from third-party suppliers and independent contractors (Rubis, 1994).

Company have taken several other approaches in designing internal contingent workforce programs. Unlike Resource Link, most of these programs focus on filling temporary clerical openings from an in-house pool of temporary employees. These programs are established primarily to reduce or eliminate fees paid to outside agencies. The in-house pool is generally composed of former employees (retirees, laid-off employees) and staff hired directly from the outside for temporary assignments. Other companies have used a dedicated management approach in which temporary assignments are handled by a dedicated manager supplied by an outside agency. This dedicated coordinator usually operates on the client's site with office space and support provided by the client's employment department.

Finally, companies need to be aware that a program such as Resource Link can be very costly to the firm when many associates are on payroll but not placed in temporary assignments (when idle time increases). In this regard, success is very dependent on effective marketing coupled with rigorous screening to ensure that associates have the skills to meet client needs.

References

Ansberry, C. (1993, March 11). Workers are forced to take more jobs with fewer benefits. *Wall Street Journal,* pp. A1, A9.

Campion, M. A., Pursell, E. D., & Brown, B. K. (1988). Structured interviewing: Raising the psychometric properties of the employment interview. *Personnel Psychology, 41,* 25–42.

Farh, J. L., Dobbins, G. H., & Cheng, B. S. (1991). Cultural relativity in action: A comparison of self-ratings made by Chinese and U.S. workers. *Personnel Psychology, 44,* 129–147.

Feldman, D. C. (1990). Reconceptualizing the nature and consequences of part-time work. *Academy of Management Review, 15,* 103–112.

Fierman, J. (1994, January 24). The contingency workforce. *Fortune,* pp. 30–36.

Harris, M. M., & Schaubroeck, J. (1988). A meta-analysis of self-manager, self-peer, and peer-manager ratings. *Personnel Psychology, 41,* 43–62.

Huffcut, A. I., & Winfred, A. (1994). Hunter and Hunter revisited: Interview validity for entry-level jobs. *Journal of Applied Psychology, 79,* 184–190.

Janz, T. (1982). Initial comparisons of patterned behavior description interviews versus unstructured interviews. *Journal of Applied Psychology, 67,* 577–580.

Kehoe, J. F. (1994, April). *Automated employment processing at AT&T.* Paper presented at the annual conference of the Society for Industrial and Organizational Psychology, Nashville.

Kuttner, R. (1993, November 18). *Business Week,* p. 16.

Motowidlo, S. J., Carter, G. W., Dunnette, M. D., Tippens, N., Werner, S., Burnett, J. R., & Vaughan, M. J. (1992). Studies of the structured behavioral interview. *Journal of Applied Psychology, 77,* 571–587.

Orpen, C. (1985). Patterned behavior description interviews versus unstructured interviews: A comparative validity study. *Journal of Applied Psychology, 70,* 774–776.

Rubis, L. (1994). Contingent worker protections urged. *HR News, 13*(3), 1.

Yu, J., & Murphy, K. R. (1993). Modesty bias in self-ratings of performance: A test of the cultural relativity hypothesis. *Personnel Psychology, 46,* 357–363.

CHAPTER 8

Developing Entrepreneurs
Skills for the "Wanna Be," "Gonna Be," and "Gotta Be Better" Employees
John H. Eggers

We are experiencing a fundamental paradigm shift in the contract between workers and their organizations and the way jobs and careers are understood. While corporate America has been "down-sizing and right-sizing," smaller entrepreneurial companies have been amazingly adaptable, often growing at the expense of their larger competitors and creating jobs while other larger organizations have been eliminating them. In fact, almost all new jobs created in the past few years have come from companies with fewer than twenty employees. At a seemingly ever-increasing rate, new start-up companies are being created by disillusioned or displaced Fortune 500 employees, women executives who have grown tired and frustrated of the corporate glass ceiling, and recent college graduates and dropouts. They and others have discovered that self-reliance through entrepreneurship is a viable option and a part of the new rules of this changing world at work. This trend has created a renewed interest in the topic of entrepreneurship with a primary focus in how to develop it in oneself and others.

There seem to be three primary clusters of people driving this:

1. "Wanna be" entrepreneurs—people interested in entrepreneurship but not yet committed.

2. "Gonna be" entrepreneurs—individuals who have chosen entrepreneurship as a career option but are still in the early stages of development and skill.
3. "Gotta be better" entrepreneurs—those who already own or run organizations but want to increase their skills and abilities in order to keep growing and not stagnate.

Each of these groups has special interests and needs and we will explore aspects of each.

What Makes an Entrepreneur?

A Definition and Some History

As a foundation, one must first acknowledge the multitude of definitions of entrepreneur and entrepreneurship. The word *entrepreneur* is derived from the twelfth-century French verb *entreprendre*, roughly translated to mean "to do something." In this early usage the word was used to describe people who provided services. Economists in the late 1700s further defined the word to mean an individual who was a risk bearer in business but minimized the risks taken through innovation and invention. John Stuart Mill (1806–1873) is credited with popularizing the term in English and regarded entrepreneurs as capitalists who through rational thinking tried to maximize profits.

Three recurring ideas seem to capture the essence of most definitions of entrepreneurship: risk, managerial competence, and creative opportunism (Duchesneau & Gartner, 1988). More specifically, I define an entrepreneur as a person who creates value by finding innovative and creative ways to meet current needs or discovers new needs to be met through innovation or adaption.

Personality Traits

In attempts to understand and replicate the entrepreneurial process, one of the most studied areas for the last twenty years has been the characteristics and personality traits of successful entrepreneurs. Unfortunately, like many areas in the field, this one too has been plagued with a multitude of research limitations, including varying definitions of who is an entrepreneur, resulting in a variety of different study populations, questionable measurement methods, instruments and research designs, small nongeneralizable sample sizes, and lack of theoretical frameworks (Cooper, 1993).

Many different attributes have been explored as possible predictors; the most common are a high need for achievement, internal locus of control, and risk taking (Eggers & Smilor, 1995). Additional characteristics that are frequently associated with entrepreneurs are a need for autonomy, preference for change, tolerance for ambiguity, above-average level of dominance, high levels of energy and social adroitness, a preference for learning by doing, a preference for intuitive perception combined with deductive rational thinking, and an innovative creativity style. However, out of all the personality variables studied, only need for achievement stands out as a clear predictor of entrepreneurial motivation and behavior (Shaver & Scott, 1991). The study and identification of these personality variables have provided some insights into the entrepreneurial process; in separating entrepreneurs from other members of the business community, overall results have been disappointing. However, one construct that has shown promise is "creativity style," as defined and measured by the Kirton Adaption/ Innovation Inventory.

Entrepreneurs are more innovative than corporate managers, preferring to focus on problem definitions and finding new ways to do things rather than to fine tune. Among entrepreneurs, some interesting differences have also been noted. Adaptive entrepreneurs are more likely to continue operating their businesses over the long term, whereas innovative entrepreneurs are more likely to start more businesses. While running the business, adaptive entrepreneurs allocate 45 percent of their time to administration compared to 18 percent for innovative entrepreneurs.

Thus, entrepreneurs do tend to differ from the mean on psychological variables; however, as yet no generally accepted model of entrepreneurial personality or profile of the typical entrepreneur has emerged. This is primarily because of the mixed results in regard to the value of using psychological characteristics as predictors of success and group membership (Low & Macmillan, 1988). One key reason for this is that the same traits associated with successful entrepreneurs are also found in successful managers;

they are not exclusive to the entrepreneurial population (Sexton & Bowman, 1988). The current consensus is that psychological traits act in predisposing the individual to entrepreneurial behaviors but are not predictors. Thus, overall this research stream has had little meaningful impact in actually enhancing entrepreneurship or assisting entrepreneurs in useful and practical ways (Bygrave & Hofer, 1991).

However, it is important to note that the current lack of useful data might be due only to the flawed methodology used in most previous research (Low & Macmillan, 1988). There is a small but growing body of research that has addressed these issues and has had some success in demonstrating personality preferences as significant predictors of behavior, contradicting the current wisdom.

What these studies reveal is that the way we have measured personality constructs in the past may have been the primary problem with prediction, not necessarily the personality variables themselves. All previous studies have used general or questionable global personality measures to predict specific future behaviors. This intermixing of domain-general instruments and domain-specific behaviors has been shown previously to dilute or miss important relationships. Thus, the current disappointing state of affairs may be due solely to measurement errors (Shaver & Scott, 1991).

The Entrepreneurial Process

However, even if that proves to be the case, as Bygrave and Hofer (1991) point out, we might learn more about entrepreneurship by shifting our focus from characteristics of entrepreneurs to a focus on the nature and characteristics of the entrepreneurial *process*. Taking a little creative license, and again slightly modifying an established definition, I will define the entrepreneurial process as all functions, activities, and actions involved in the perceiving of opportunities and the creation and management of organizations either created or focused on pursuing them (adapted from Bygrave & Hofer, 1991). Identifying key aspects of this process will be the focus of the balance of this chapter.

By taking this approach we focus on what successful entrepreneurs do rather than what they are. This focuses our efforts on what can be learned and thus taught. It does little to actually end the debate over whether or not entrepreneurs are made or born, but it does provide insights. Most important, it does provide hope and a tangible avenue of action to those who wish to engage in the process and also for those who wish to teach the process.

In developing ways to teach entrepreneurship, at least three key themes are useful. First, entrepreneurship and small business growth are processes on a continuum of ever-increasing complexity encompassing every aspect of the business. Along this continuum are critical problems and challenges the entrepreneur must solve if the organization is to survive. Successful entrepreneurs are able to identify, acknowledge, manage, and transcend these critical transition points and key events in the growth of their organization. Failure is often directly associated with an inability to either acknowledge or manage these transition points effectively. A continuum also implies that the process is dynamic and often chaotic at times, with both linear and nonlinear patterns of growth (Eggers, Leahy, & Churchill, 1994; Eggers & Smilor, 1995).

Second, to effectively manage the ever-increasing complexity of their organizations and the challenges they face, successful entrepreneurs are continually learning. The very process itself requires a lifelong approach to learning and change.

Third, entrepreneurs learn differently when compared to other people in the workforce. They prefer to learn by doing and interacting in real time rather than reflecting. In this vein entrepreneurs at any level of development prefer to learn through interaction with other entrepreneurs.

Any attempt to help foster entrepreneurship and the development of entrepreneurs must take these three principles into account in order to maximize its usefulness.

One way to understand the process and identify the key tasks critical to success is to break the continuum into a series of management phases. A recently revalidated model designed to accomplish this is the Six Management Phases of Entrepreneurial Growth (Eggers, Leahy, & Churchill, 1994; Eggers & Smilor, 1995), built upon the classic model of the Five Stages of Small Business Growth. Within the model, early phases of development that capture the challenges of creation, establishment, and survival of the venture are on the left side of the continuum, whereas later challenges such as growth and maturity are on the right side. The model acknowledges the chaotic and often discontinuous nature of growing entrepreneurial companies; as Figure 8.1 shows, hypergrowth is often balanced by backsliding.

Conception and Establishment Phases

In the first phase of the entrepreneurial process, conception, the focus is on creation of the venture. Since personality traits alone have not been able to account for venture creation by themselves other variables have been explored. Bull and Willard (1993, p. 188) hypothesize four conditions necessary for venture creation:

Figure 8.1. Six Phases of Management.

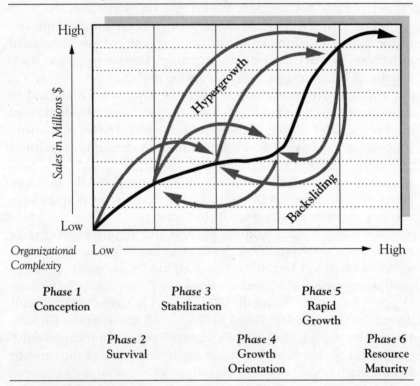

Source: Eggers, Leahy, and Churchill, 1994; Eggers and Smilor, 1995. Used by permission.

1. Task-related motivation—some vision or sense of social value embedded in the basic task itself that motivates the individual to act.
2. Expertise—present know-how plus self-confidence, so the person can obtain know-how needed in the future.
3. Expectation of gain for self— either economic or psychic benefit, or both.
4. A supportive environment—conditions that either provide comfort and support to the new endeavor, or that reduce discomfort from a previous endeavor.

Task-Related Motivation

The individual must urgently want to create the business and be willing to dedicate massive amounts of time and energy to do so. The most commonly cited reason in the business literature is an intense inner desire to work for oneself and be independent. The second most common reason is increased income potential. This desire may be heightened by situational events that have led to current job dissatisfaction, a feeling of alienation, or the perception of limited future opportunities. Inherent in this is the individual's ability to accept responsibility for problem solving and goal setting, and a tolerance for ambiguity and moderate calculated risk (Bull & Willard, 1993).

A vision of the future organization and its success has been shown to be a correlate of future current sales ($r = .20$, $p < .001$). In a series of focus groups, established entrepreneurs reported that having a clear vision of what the future organization could be was critical to their decisions to initiate their ventures (Eggers & Leahy, 1994). This future vision often takes the form of visual imagery, which produces the enthusiasm and excitement needed to overcome the inevitable obstacles in starting the venture (Bull & Willard, 1993).

The process of developing the vision and identifying the opportunity on which the vision is built is commonly referred to as "opportunity recognition." Situational factors and personality traits act as the catalysts to motivate a person to look for an opportunity, but they do not address how that individual would decide that any particular opportunity is the right one. Shaver and Scott (1991) suggest that this process is best explained as a cognitive heuristic, and they look to the social cognition literature for suggestions. They make a case that because people are not good intuitive statisticians, opportunity judgments are most likely influenced by at least three cognitive heuristics: availability, representativeness, and anchoring.

"A person who just read about another restaurant's closing in the morning paper will give a higher estimate of failures than will a person who has not seen such a story in a long time"—the availability heuristic. "A person for whom Restaurant X is typical of successful establishments will make a lower guess about failure than will a person for whom Restaurant X resembles failures"—the representativeness heuristic. "Finally, a perceiver who knows that three local restaurants have failed will make a smaller estimate than a perceiver who has been told that 10,000 restaurants have failed nationally"—the anchoring heuristic (Shaver & Scott, 1991, p. 33).

Shaver and Scott also point out that this process may be used to explain many decisions that are currently explained either in situational or social-learning terms. Unfortunately, little research has been done exploring the area of venture creation and opportunity recognition outside of situational variables and personality traits that would test their arguments.

Regardless of how the vision is created, formal planning beyond visualization has been found to enhance the initial success of start-up organizations (Duchesneau & Gartner, 1988; Van de Ven, Hudson, & Schroeder, 1984). This usually takes the form of a business plan, where obstacles to success can be identified and dealt with before they happen. Getting feedback on the plan from outside sources has also been shown to be related to organizational performance once the plan has been initiated (Van de Ven, Hudson, & Schroeder, 1984). The business plan acts as a reality check before actual implementation and provides a way to overcome possible cognitive processing errors, which could lead to major business problems and possible failure.

Expertise of the Individual

It appears that expertise comes through a combination of real-world experience and education. Thus, the network of relationships and the experience people need to start a business successfully often come from previous employment and both have been shown to be frequently related to survivability and growth.

This expertise does not have to come from previous experience exclusively, however. Other options are to gain expertise through a formal business incubator program, where the entrepreneur can gain expertise through advisers and consultants to minimize costly mistakes. In addition, in these programs the entrepreneur gains credibility, minimizes overhead costs, and gains a local and assessable peer support network.

Expectation of Gain

The initiation of a venture is often the interaction of cultural, personal, and social factors. This interaction may take the form of negative displacement such as losing a job, being bored, going through a divorce, being frustrated, or feeling partial social alienation. It may also take the form of a positive displacement, such as identifying a great opportunity unrecognized or unknown to others or encouragement by friends of potential customers. It can also take the form of being in between jobs or careers, having just finished school, or getting out of the armed services (Bull & Willard, 1993).

In addition to the situational factors influencing the individual, Shaver and Scott point out that the internal process may take the form suggested by exchange theory. This approach assumes that individuals try to maximize their own outcomes in any situation. Two internal standards are used to compare possible outcomes. The first is termed the comparison level, the perceived average outcomes from similar past experiences. The second standard, termed comparison level for alternatives, is the perceived best available alternative to the present circumstances.

Applying this approach to the question of expectations for gain, if someone has just lost her job and starting a business offers options that are perceived to be better than other possible replacement jobs based on her experience, then she will be motivated to start the business. If, however, other job options are more attractive based on her experience and the outcome of starting the business is either unknown or is not as attractive, then she will not be motivated to start a new venture because her expectation for gain will be lower than other perceived options.

An alternative explanation of new venture creation, combining both personality preferences and situational input, is a new two-factor theory of risky choice (see Shaver and Scott, 1991, for a discussion). In this theory, the first factor influencing the individual is his preference for security versus potential. Security seekers weigh the worst outcomes more heavily, whereas potential seekers weigh the best outcomes more heavily.

The second factor is aspiration level, defined by the current environment. The environment provides usable information about what might be a probable expectation, options being considered are compared in the context of other options available, and future goals can influence how actions are carried out. This final decision is based on an interaction of the two.

A Supportive Environment

The last condition to consider in new venture creation is a supportive environment. This may take the form of access to suppliers, a skilled and affordable workforce, role models of past success who show how to overcome obstacles, or family members who provide encouragement. Obviously, the availability of financial support is critical. During the conception phase this may come from personal savings, family loans, personal credit cards, and venture capital "angels" who will make a loan for equity in the unestablished company (Eggers & Leahy, 1994).

Survival Phase

Once the new venture is started, the next phase of development is focused on establishing the new entity and developing a large enough customer base and cash flow stream to survive (Eggers, Leahy, & Churchill, 1994; Eggers & Smilor, 1995). As entrepreneurs face the challenges that arise at this developmental phase, the process they use to explain success and failures is of interest. Shaver and Scott (1991) suggest that attribution theory provides a useful framework for understanding the process. The key elements of task performance within this framework are ability, intention, effort, task difficulty, and luck. If an action is intentional, successful performance depends on two external variables—task difficulty and luck—and two internal variables—ability and effort. A successful outcome is created when acceptable levels are reached in each of these areas or one area is so high that it can carry lower-performing variables.

In studies of successful entrepreneurs at this developmental phase, aspects of attribution theory have been shown to be related to growth. In a study of 340 entrepreneurial firms Eggers and Leahy (1994) found that firms led by entrepreneurs with high levels of skill, ability, and effort grew at substantially greater rates than those led by entrepreneurs of lower abilities, skills, and effort. This relationship was constant regardless of the level of resources the organization had to begin with. However, initial survival is also influenced by the organization's starting level of resources (financing, personnel, customers) and by the market viability of its products or services (Eggers, Leahy, & Churchill, 1994).

Critical skills and abilities of the entrepreneur at this phase are (listed in order of importance): financial management, communication, marketing, the development and implementation of organizational vision, and the motivation of others both within and outside the organization. The more skilled the entrepreneur is in each of these areas, the greater the growth of the young company (Eggers, Leahy, & Churchill, 1994).

When the company is small, the entrepreneur uses these skills in a very hands-on way. However, it appears that the more the entrepreneur is able to create a culture that allows for the empowerment of others, letting them do the daily tasks of the organization, the greater the future potential for growth (Eggers, Leahy, & Churchill, 1994).

Stabilization Phase and Growth Orientation Phase

As the new organization grows and is able to reach a point of stabilization, the entrepreneur reaches a point on the developmental continuum where she faces a series of management paradoxes. If these paradoxes are managed and resolved then the entrepreneur is poised for growth, referred to as growth orientation. At this point of development, skills and abilities that were once critical to the success and growth of the organization now actually get in the way. Hands-on types of activities that were once handled by the entrepreneur herself must now be delegated to others, ideas once viable must now be let go. This requires adaptability and the capacity to give up control and directly opposes the needed tenacity and high control desires that enhanced the early success of the organization (Eggers & Smilor, 1995).

This transitional process is further complicated by a sense of invulnerability many entrepreneurs develop as their organizations reach this point of growth. In the earlier phases, entrepreneurs face a seemingly countless series of "nos" and "can't be dones" from others surrounding them: customers, bankers, friends, and family members. Entrepreneurs work through these by sticking unquestionably to their vision and taking action frequently powered by only sheer will, since there is usually little positive reinforcement from the environment in these early phases. As the new organization becomes established and the vision becomes something tangible that these others can now see, the entrepreneur's confidence grows. Once-negative feedback from the environment now turns to positive, enhancing this self-confidence and healing the entrepreneur's often battered and bruised sense of self.

This rebound process frequently is overgeneralized by the entrepreneur, producing a false sense of invulnerability that can lead to serious trouble in managing the fledgling organization. The most common manifestations of this are a lack of appreciation, inability to let go of control, and the delegation of critical tasks to others, which can cripple the growth of the organization and in the extreme cases push it back into survival and even premature death.

Even in cases where this sense of invulnerability does not lead to organizational problems, entrepreneurs still struggle with this transition. Since the entrepreneur is the company in its earlier phases of development, this transition represents a major change in the role for the entrepreneur. At this point entrepreneurs often comment they don't know what their job is any longer. The critical challenge now is to allow others to be the company, with the entrepreneur's role shifting from daily doer to creator, coach, and shepherd of the organization's culture. The focus now shifts from them to others; see Table 8.1.

Highly successful entrepreneurs develop and fuel the growth of their organizations at this point by defining company values and a climate that enhances and promotes tangible actions by others toward accomplishing the entrepreneur's vision (which has now become the employees' vision). In a study of highly successful entrepreneurial companies Eggers and Leahy (1994) found

Table 8.1. CEO Critical Skills.

	Phase 2: Survival	Phase 3: Stabilization	Phase 4: Growth Orientation	Phase 5: Rapid Growth	Phase 6: Resource Maturity	Summary Across Phases
Organization Cultural Norms	Vision: Establish a direction. Communicate the vision and keep employees focused on it. Values: Keep employees informed. Develop and maintain employee morale. Be open to the ideas of others. Address problems before they become a crisis.	Vision: Share the dream with employees. Stay focused on the big picture. Keep on track. Develop a long-range strategic plan. Values: Keep lines of communication open with employees. Gain group support for goals. Keep group morale up. Treat everyone fairly and impartially. Promote development through learning.	Vision: Clarify the vision for the future. Share the vision. Keep focused. Values: Remove barriers to communication and performance; encourage debate. Foster buy-in and consensus. Have and communicate a company philosophy. Be open to employee ideas. Trust your employees.	Vision: Develop a vision for growth. Communicate the vision—develop commitment and discipline to continue regardless of circumstances. Values: Keep employees informed. Reward performance. Promote strong work ethic. Show compassion, respect, fairness. Support employees, require accountability.	Vision: Share the success with employees. Maintain a clear sense of purpose. Instill purpose in employees. Act in alignment with the vision. Values: Customer service and satisfaction. Integrity, honesty, and fairness. A clear set of values and principles. Enjoyable, positive and open work environment.	Vision: Primary guidance and measurement tool. Values: Customer satisfaction. Performance. Honesty, fairness, respect. Openness, clarity, compassion. Teamwork and individuality.

Table 8.1. CEO Critical Skills, (continued).

	Phase 2: Survival	Phase 3: Stabilization	Phase 4: Growth Orientation	Phase 5: Rapid Growth	Phase 6: Resource Maturity	Summary Across Phases
Organizational Structure	Provide performance incentives. Budget finances and maintain cash flow. Control expenses.	Maintain cash flow and reserves. Manage receivables. Make sure incentive plans are effective.	Communicate routinely with all levels. Monitor effectiveness of incentives, benefits, and promotion and developmental opportunities. Institute financial/cost controls. Develop effective hiring practices.	Provide performance incentives. Monitor cost controls, cash flow, receivables. Monitor performance of plans.	Maintain profitability and financial strength. Make sure employee incentives are meaningful.	Financial and cost control systems. Employee development. Human resource selection and placement. Reward systems. Group problem solving.
Group Behavior and Process	Build a strong team. Get "buy in." Identify and set objectives. Assess problems logically to decide the best course of action. Provide for employee development.	Maintain and build harmonious teams. Provide performance feedback. Set goals for company and individual performance. Analyze before making decisions, but then make them quickly. Provide training and education.	Maintain a strong team focus. Set goals with employees. Monitor goals and results and adjust actions accordingly. Let employees solve the problems who are closest to the job. Provide effective education and training.	Maintain a strong team. Support management decisions. Identify and set objectives. Hire and retain the right people. Identify talent and ability in employees and promote and place them effectively.	Draw out the ideas of others. Get employee involvement. Allow discussion of problems and "challenge-ups." Encourage participation, independent action planning, and performance.	Team focus, yet respect for the individual. Participative decision making using logical and empirical methods. Open environment. Clear goals and accountability. Supportive work environment.

Personal Behaviors and Self-Presentation	Be clear and direct. Encourage, praise. Persuade. Listen first.	Listen first. Acknowledge and praise effective performance. Demonstrate empathy, understanding, respect, and caring for people.	Stay self-focused on the vision. Be an effective company spokesperson. Listen to employees and develop trust, and credibility. Model empathy, compassion, caring. Know when to let employees go and promote.	Lead by example; model core values. Praise and reward employees. Demonstrate positive attitude and image, confidence, and enthusiasm. Listen and stay accessible to all.	Stay optimistic, enthusiastic, and upbeat. Set the example. Be decisive, think clearly, assess risks. Be tenacious and persistent. Be an active listener.	Model the core values. You are the role model; what you do is what others will do.
Knowledge/ Skills Personal Expertise	Accounting skill. Industry/product/technical skill. Current knowledge of industry's laws. Operations experience.	Invest wisely. Develop impressive public speaking skills. Stay current on technology and trends. Coach to develop people.	Maintain good banking relationships. Learn skilled financial analysis and forecasting. Demonstrate managerial skill.	Networking. Strategic planning. Developing organizational culture.	Networking. Developing organizational culture. Decision making and risk assessment. Strategic planning.	Majority are learned interpersonal skills and industry expertise.
Environmental Input and Output	Know the competition. Understand the market. Identify customer needs. Establish solid relationships with customers and vendors.	Maintain banking relationships. Understand, know, and adapt to the market. Target customer needs. Network work with others in the industry.	Networking; keep up with contacts, professional associations, and industry alliances. Assess future technology and business climate changes. Stay close to customers; determine needs.	Maintain credit lines and banking relationships. Stay sensitive to environmental changes. Identify "core" problems. Network with peers.	Strengthen customer service orientation. Listen to needs/ wants/feedback on products and services. Maintain good relations with banks, suppliers, community.	Must create an organizational culture that is open and supportive of adapting to environmental change.

that this was accomplished by developing in the organization a team approach to accomplishing the daily tasks of the business, an approach founded on values of mutual trust, honesty, and respect for others. This allows employees to learn by doing as they take tangible actions toward accomplishing the organization's vision. It also allows employees to make reasonable mistakes as they enhance their skills and abilities, maintaining a continuous learning mode. And when employees make measurable progress toward accomplishing the organization's vision they are rewarded in tangible ways, with the entrepreneur sharing the economic rewards.

Rapid Growth Phase and Resource Maturity Phase

With this culture in the organization the company typically enters the rapid growth phase of development and then resource maturity. If the entrepreneur is able to maintain this approach, the resulting culture is open and responsive to environmental inputs that allow the identification of new opportunities and the capacity to take advantage of them maintaining the viability of the organization. If, however, the entrepreneur grows complacent or lacks the skills to maintain this, then the organization is vulnerable to backsliding (Eggers, Leahy, & Churchill, 1994). Each of these phases has a distinct matrix of critical skills and developmental challenges for the entrepreneur, summarized in Table 8.1.

Developing Entrepreneurs

Various educational techniques are available to help entrepreneurs develop the needed skills. Choosing the appropriate one requires being aware of the organization's current phase and also the desired phase of development the entrepreneur wishes to reach. Approaches must be sensitive to the limited time the entrepreneur has to devote to this process, always keeping in mind that any approach must be engaging, relevant, and focused on real time.

Table 8.2 summarizes the delivery techniques and focuses of various curriculum programs for the three groups of entrepreneurs: "wanna bes" (interested but not committed), "gonna bes" (decided but still in early stages), and "gotta be betters" (established but interested in continuing to grow).

Table 8.2. Entrepreneur Populations and Curriculum Design.

Type of Customers	Curriculum Delivery	Curriculum Focus
"Wanna be" entrepreneurs	Audiotapes, TV, computer, video program $\frac{1}{2}$ to 2 hours long	What is entrepreneurship
"Gonna be" entrepreneurs	Startup incubators	How to do entrepreneurship
"Gotta be better" entrepreneurs	Convened training	Why and where of entrepreneurship
	2–3-day seminars to two-week mini-MBA programs	Mastery Application

Source: Kauffman Foundation/Center for Entrepreneurial Leadership, Inc., 1993. Used by permission.

For "wanna be" entrepreneurs, the basic skills of vision, financial management, and opportunity recognition are the most critical. For this group, one of the new college classes in entrepreneurship is an excellent approach; for example, the University of Saint Paul; the University of Missouri, Kansas City; Babson College; and Harvard University (there are of course many others). The curriculum of these classes not only teaches many of these basic skills but allows the potential entrepreneur to develop a comprehensive business plan in a supportive environment providing critical feedback.

The process of developing the business plan allows the individual to experience the challenges and rewards of entrepreneurship with little risk and provides a realistic preview of the process. Many discover that the reality of starting and running a business is not as attractive as they thought. Critical to this process is that it allows the individual to make mistakes with limited liability and resource drain. Many potential disasters and fatal business mistakes can be identified before they are implemented. Thus, this approach has been shown to enhance the success of the individual, resulting in many viable new organizations for those that successfully complete these classes.

For "wanna be" entrepreneurs this approach is too time intensive, and the skill-building process must take a different approach. Information on critical skills is best disseminated through one-day seminars, audiotapes, or videos. This provides the future entrepreneur with access to the information. Many times this takes the form of listening to an audiotape while driving.

The "gotta be better" group desires and demands not only time sensitivity to the delivery of information, but also who delivers it. Established entrepreneurs want to learn from other entrepreneurs who have shown by their success that what they say really works. They have little regard for academics or anyone who has not started and run a business. This complicates the skill-building and information-dissemination process.

Eggers and Leahy (1994) found in a series of six focus groups of established entrepreneurs held across America that one attractive approach to skill development was peer problem-solving meetings. Entrepreneurs found it very useful to get together with small groups of other entrepreneurs where they could discuss problems they were currently struggling with and receive peer feedback on solutions others had tried. This process met their needs for learning from other entrepreneurs, keeping activities in real time, and giving them tangible "take-aways" that were directly relevant to managing their organizations. This process was even more attractive if one or two members of the group were highly successful entrepreneurs who could act as mentors or coaches and role models. This approach also provides what appears to be another need of established entrepreneurs; they often feel isolated and even lonely because they have few if any people to share the problems they face within their organization. These groups provide not only practical solutions to problems but also social support.

This activity appears to be enhanced when entrepreneurs also receive feedback on their skill levels by employees in the organizations they lead. This can range from individual leadership feedback using survey instruments designed to measure critical skills to more global feedback on the organization's climate and culture. Unfortunately, this process is currently hampered by a lack of valid survey instruments designed for entrepreneurs and their organizations.

This group also uses audiotapes frequently to gather information and new skills. Established entrepreneurs also use audiotapes to keep their personal morale high as they work through problems.

Audiotapes focusing not only on skill building but personal motivation are frequently used in an effort to stay pumped up (Eggers & Leahy, 1994).

Intrapreneurship

New venture creation in established organizations is often referred to as intrapreneuring or corporate venturing. As large organizations struggle to revitalize themselves in the changing environment they are increasingly turning to intrapreneurship as a possible solution. Large organizations face not only all of the challenges facing entrepreneurs outside large organizations, but also a series of additional challenges. Although overcoming all the serious challenges incumbent to this process is beyond the scope of this chapter, a few are worthy of mention.

One of the major challenges facing the intrapreneurial process is that established norms, traditions, and ways of doing things in the large organization are often directly opposed to the intrapreneurial effort. The current operating paradigm of the established organization often blocks the recognition of new ideas and opportunities. New ideas are often viewed with suspicion, seen as challenges to established stakeholders and the status quo.

There is tremendous pressure within the established structure to conform. Thus, if an idea is to survive and gain support and the necessary resources to be implemented, there must be political support for it within the organization. This support frequently comes from either the intrapreneur himself or other champions with political or position clout within the organization who can provide the necessary access to critical resources.

Due to these pressures many large organizations have had difficulty in becoming intrapreneurial. A growing trend within large organizations is to establish independent intrapreneurship funds and boards that act as internal business incubators. This approach allows the individual who is championing the idea to present a business plan to the administrators of the fund and if approved receive the necessary financial resources to implement the plan. The new start-up then operates as an independent organization, thus escaping the internal pressures to conform. Several Fortune 500 companies I have observed have had great success using this approach.

Conclusion

Can entrepreneurs be developed? This chapter has illustrated that indeed they can, since the critical activities that enhance entrepreneurial success are skills and behaviors that can be learned. This process can be enhanced by paying attention to teaching the skills that really make a difference in establishing and running an entrepreneurial organization, keeping in mind the context of its current developmental phase, and delivering the information in a way that is engaging and attractive to entrepreneurs.

References

Bull, I., & Willard, G. E. (1993). Toward a theory of entrepreneurship. *Journal of Business Venturing, 8,* 183–195.

Bygrave, W. D., & Hofer, C. W. (1991). Researching entrepreneurship. *Entrepreneurship Theory and Practice, 16*(2), 13–22.

Cooper, A. C. (1993). Challenges in predicting new firm performance. *Journal of Business Venturing, 8,* 241–253.

Duchesneau, D. A., & Gartner, W. B. (1988). A profile of new venture success and failure in an emerging industry. In B. Kirchoff, W. Long, W. E. McMullan, K. Vesper, & W. Wetzel Jr. (Eds.), *Frontiers of entrepreneurship research* (pp. 372–386). Wellesley, MA: Babson College.

Eggers, J. F., & Leahy, K. T. (1994). Entrepreneurial leadership in the U.S. *Issues and Observations, 14*(1).

Eggers, J. H., Leahy, K. T., & Churchill, N. C. (1994). *Frontiers of entrepreneur research.* Wellesley, MA: Babson College.

Eggers, J. H., & Smilor, W. R. (1995). Leadership skills of entrepreneurs: Resolving the paradoxes and enhancing the practices of entrepreneurial growth. In W. R. Smilor (Ed.), *Entrepreneurship and leadership.* Westport, CT: Quorum/Greenwood.

Low, M. B., & Macmillan, I. C. (1988). Entrepreneurship: Past research and future challenges. *Journal of Management, 14*(2).

Sexton, D. C., and Bowman, U. D. (1988). *Entrepreneurship: Creating and growth.* New York: Macmillan.

Shaver, K. G., & Scott, L. R. (1991, Winter). Researching entrepreneurship. *Entrepreneurship Theory and Practice,* pp. 23–46.

Van de Ven, A. H., Hudson, R., & Schroeder, D. M. (1984). Designing new business startups: Entrepreneurial, organizational, and ecological considerations. *Journal of Management, 10*(1), 87–107.

PART 3

Economic Development and Revitalized Careers

This final section of the book concentrates on career opportunities for displaced workers. The authors emphasize the individual's role in the job-creation process, with the right support from human resource professionals and others. The chapters describe training to support a positive attitude and effective job-search behaviors, learning experiences that demonstrate how individuals can show their capacity to add value to an organization and develop job opportunities, and groups of unemployed workers joining forces to foster business initiatives and thereby create employment opportunities in the community.

Although social and economic policies need to address the problems that result from unemployment, various community efforts can be undertaken to reduce the impact of unemployment at the local level. These efforts could transform the crisis of job loss to an opportunity for individual development and growth. The JOBS Project at the University of Michigan was designed as a research and evaluation initiative to test a preventive intervention for unemployed persons. In Chapter Nine, Richard Price and Amiram Vinokur describe how this intervention was designed to provide participants with social support and a promotive learning environment to acquire job-search skills and at the same time to inoculate the participants from common setbacks that are part of the job-seeking process. The intervention goals were to prevent the deterioration in mental health that often results from unemployment and to promote high-quality reemployment, thus contributing to individual growth. These goals were achieved in the first generation of the JOBS field experiment (Curran, 1992; Vinokur, van Ryn, Gramlich, and Price, 1991).

The second generation of the JOBS field experiment focused on the effects of the intervention on job losers who were identified in a screening procedure as having high risk for depression. Analyses of the data from the second-generation field experiment, the JOBS II study, is presented to determine the differential effects of the intervention with respect to mental health and reemployment on high- versus low-risk job losers.

In Chapter Ten, Larry Last, Robert Peterson, Jack Rappaport, and Carin Webb describe the creation of the Center for Commercial Competitiveness. Funded by state and federal sources, the project helps displaced workers and local industries create new ventures that in turn generate job opportunities. Displaced workers are trained in developing markets and products for industry. They are also trained in how to work in self-directed, quality-oriented teams. The center makes teams of displaced workers available to industry, often in support of defense industry conversion into commercial markets. This demonstration project validates the concept that a designed integration of dislocated workers, entrepreneurial competitiveness training, and regional industries can create jobs and enhance regional economic development.

Next, in Chapter Eleven, Gerrit Wolf, Joseph Pufahl, Jeff Casey, and Manuel London report the results of a government-funded retraining program for displaced engineers from the defense industry. A premise of the program was that the usual outplacement strategies (writing a strong resume, learning how to be interviewed, and networking) are insufficient when job openings are few and far between. These authors believe that displaced workers need to be involved in demonstrating their worth and creating new opportunities. In their project, two groups of displaced engineers participated in two separate programs. Each program focused on basic management skills (such as communications and business strategy) and the management of emerging technologies (such as computer integrated manufacturing systems and electron micro-spectroscopy) and offered fifteen graduate-level credits over a six-month period.

The first group (fifty-six participants) was exposed to a series of company representatives presenting costly problems faced by their firms. The purpose was to engage the participants in impor-tant, real-world issues that would allow them to demonstrate how they could add value to an enterprise. The second group (eighteen participants) engaged in unpaid internships in the firms working on problems the organizations needed to solve. Here again the focus was on helping the managers understand how they could contribute to the organization—the hope being that the added value would lead to job creation. Successful participants adopted an entrepreneurial mindset that they could apply in making a con-tribution to new and existing enterprises, thereby creating employ-ment opportunities for themselves.

In addition to describing the retraining program, the chapter reports the results of assessment and outcome variables. At the start of the programs, the participants were assessed on a number of personality, attitudinal, and behavioral measures associated with reactions to job loss and job search strategies—measures used initially by Leana and Feldman (1992). The same measures were completed by a comparison group of twenty displaced engineers not in the program. (Also, data from comparison groups of full-time employees and students were collected for the personality measures.) Multiple outcome measures captured participants' reac-tions and attitudes toward the program, ability to create a value-added role for themselves, and success in securing employment.

The study found that the displaced engineers varied consider-ably in their attitudes about the job-search process and their roles in job creation. Some expected to be handed a list of job oppor-tunities and be placed in the assignment where they were needed. This was the model they had followed for years in the bureaucratic environments of large defense contractors. Other participants were willing from the outset to learn new skills and prove their value. Some were malleable in willingness to learn new skills and exper-iment with new behaviors. Still others remained depressed and unable to risk new learning and new ventures. The results have implications for selection of displaced individuals for graduate-level retraining programs and for the design of programs that create opportunities by demonstrating worth.

The Philadelphia Naval Shipyard and Base is slated for closure in 1996, with most operations ceasing by September 1995. In Chapter Twelve, Robert Vance and David Day describe a project to develop a computerized outplacement counseling program to assist in transitioning 7,500 employees to training programs and private-sector employment. The project is unprecedented in that the U.S. Navy has never closed a shipyard. The political and economic contexts affected project activities and outcomes. Successful large-scale transitioning of federal defense workers to private-sector employment requires a multidisciplinary approach, with close cooperation among diverse players and constituents, including employees, unions, managers, politicians, government officials, private industry, and community leaders.

Finally, in Chapter Thirteen, Carrie Leana and Daniel Feldman discuss the considerable attention that the topic of job loss has received from researchers over the past decade. They examine factors that predict individuals' propensities to engage in this collective form of coping, and the effects of such efforts on adjustment to job loss. They also discuss different types of collective job-creation efforts that are originated and pursued by laid-off employees, either through new organizations they create for that purpose or through various institutions such as unions, local government bodies, and educational institutions.

Unions have a stake in the continued employment of their members and opportunities to expand membership. Recognizing technological and competitive trends that pressure organizations to reduce employment, some unions have been working with management to limit downward trends and maintain jobs. Employee development is an important part of these initiatives. Model programs have been operated during the last ten years by the United Auto Workers with Ford and GM and by the Communications Workers of America with AT&T. These programs, usually jointly funded by management and the union, help employees prepare for reemployment in the face of a layoff or they help employees acquire new skills so they will have increased employment opportunities within and outside the firm. The decision about what training to provide is often made at the local level by the employees themselves, who decide what they need. Local colleges or companies' in-house facilities provide the training. This chapter describes these efforts and evaluates their success from the standpoints of the unions, management, and the employees. The chapter considers difficulties these programs have confronted in translating training into job opportunities.

References

Curran, J. (1992). *JOBS: A manual for teaching people successful job search strategies.* Ann Arbor: Michigan Prevention Research Center, Institute for Social Research, University of Michigan.

Leana, C. R., & Feldman, D. C. (1992). *Coping with job loss: How individuals, organizations, and communities respond to layoffs.* New York: Lexington.

Vinokur, A. D., van Ryn, M., Gramlich, E. M., & Price, R. H. (1991). Long-term follow-up and benefit-cost analysis of the JOBS program: A preventive intervention for the unemployed. *Journal of Applied Psychology, 76,* 213–219.

CHAPTER 9

Supporting Career Transitions in a Time of Organizational Downsizing

The Michigan JOBS Program

Richard H. Price
Amiram D. Vinokur

Consider the plight of the corporate manager or industrial worker who receives a notice that she or he no longer has a job. As painful as this reality is, it is increasingly prevalent on the American work scene. That person faces two major challenging uncertainties. First, there is the uncertainty that, perhaps sooner rather than later, he or she will experience major changes in financial circumstances and, perhaps, serious financial hardship. This newly jobless worker also faces a second major uncertainty: how to search for a new job. After all, this was one skill that was never taught in school, and very likely not even talked about in any formal educational setting.

Uncertainty about searching for a new job has a number of elements, each of which adds to the complexity and threat of the task. The jobless person may be unaware of which skills are most marketable. In many cases the person will not know where to look. Are those ads in the paper really of any use? Does a brother-in-law have some inside information? And even if one had a clear sense of which skills are marketable and where to look, there remains the question of how to present yourself in the job search. Is the resume the key to success? How eager should one be in a job interview? Finally, it is likely that the job seeker will have to face numerous setbacks before a new job is won. The setbacks may be as subtle as a long silence in response to job inquiries or as explicit as being told "you're overqualified" or "don't call us, we'll call you." If setbacks create a sense of discouragement and hopelessness, the person is defeated virtually before he or she starts to make any progress toward regaining employment.

All of these challenges in the job search amount to this: Searching for a new job is a long-term, uncertain, coping activity that requires the use of complex strategies, substantial self-control, and self-regulation skill, all of it punctuated by discouragements and setbacks that present major motivational challenges of their own. These setbacks can be triggers to more serious problems among vulnerable individuals, including the onset of depression, drinking problems, and family conflict (Kessler, Turner, & House, 1988; Price, 1992).

Unfortunately, this scenario is becoming all too common. As a nation we appear to be in a major period of organizational downsizing with a consequent epidemic of job loss. Careers are changing as well (Reich, 1991). In the future, workers will not expect a single career with a single company, but instead will experience multiple career changes in which job transitions will occur frequently (Price, forthcoming). Job-search skills will become part of a repertoire of career transition skills that all workers will need. This repertoire of skills will be used to move in the labor market, both within one's own organization and outside it as well. Career transitions will not only be from company to company, but also may be from one industry to another; from a marketing job in the automotive industry, for example, to a job requiring marketing skills in the insurance industry. The new workers, whether skilled in management or at a craft, will need to be agile. They will need to be vigilant about opportunities, continuously building bridges in anticipation of future organizational changes. They will also need a ready set of skills for the search process itself.

For organizations the need is equally compelling. Organizations need the capacity to adapt in a variety of ways, including the ability to redeploy workers from one sector to another without incurring the substantial costs of rehiring and retraining. A work-force that can adapt to new work roles can be a key strategic advantage for companies and for national competitiveness (Reich, 1991). Companies that are able to redeploy their internal labor markets for competitive advantage will need programs that help workers make internal transitions effectively and transitions to other firms with minimal organizational and personal costs (Price, 1990; Price & D'Aunno, 1983).

In this chapter we outline nearly a decade of research on the Michigan JOBS Program, which helps people who are experiencing job loss with the transition to reemployment.

No matter how carefully designed, and regardless of their effectiveness under optimal conditions, human resource innovations such as the JOBS program must be implemented in organizations ready and able to adopt them and must be replicated with high fidelity to their original model if they are to be effective (Price & Lorion, 1989). The remainder of the chapter describes a theoretical model of organizational readiness and procedures.

The Michigan JOBS Program: Research on Program Effectiveness

A major project within the Michigan Prevention Research Center (MPRC) has been the development of the JOBS project for successful job transitions. The goals of the project have been to develop and test a program designed to help people experiencing job loss cope with the job loss itself and develop successful strategies for finding high-quality employment.

Some of the major findings early in this project evolve from studies of job loss conducted at the Institute for Social Research (Kessler, Turner, & House, 1987, 1988, 1989; Price, 1987; Vinokur & Caplan, 1987; Vinokur, Schul, & Caplan, 1987). These initial studies showed that the mental health of people who lose their jobs often deteriorates. The studies also indicated that when unemployed persons find work again they regain their previous levels of mental health and well-being (Vinokur, Caplan, & Williams, 1987). Research conducted by MPRC also indicates that a primary long-term goal of preventive programs for the unemployed should be to provide participants with personal resources and skills that promote reemployment (Caplan, Vinokur, Price, & van Ryn, 1989; Price, 1990; Vinokur, Price, & Schul, 1994). These skills and resources not only aid in the initial task of finding a new job but are available to help people cope with subsequent job transitions.

Based on the experience gained from these earlier studies, two large-scale, randomized field experiments testing the JOBS preventive intervention were conducted in 1986 and 1991. What impact has the JOBS intervention had? The field experiments to test the impact of the program indicated the JOBS intervention yields more rapid reemployment, higher-quality jobs, and better mental health for program participants and job losers (Caplan, Vinokur, Price, & van Ryn,1989). They also indicate that the economic benefits derived from the program exceed its costs (Vinokur, van Ryn, Gramlich, & Price, 1991).

Two and a half years after the completion of the randomized trial, people in the experimental group showed significantly lower numbers of episodes of depressive symptoms (Price, van Ryn, & Vinokur, 1992). The JOBS intervention was most successful precisely with those people who were at highest psychological risk for episodes of depression (Price, van Ryn, & Vinokur, 1992; Vinokur, Price, & Schul, 1994). These were people who were at risk for experiencing higher levels of economic hardship, already displayed some depressive symptoms, and who showed lower levels of social assertiveness.

These research results make it clear that a carefully designed preventive program can produce beneficial effects both in terms of mental health and economic outcomes. The nature of the JOBS program itself not only emphasizes the acquisition of sense of mastery through the development of new job skills, but also provides social support for participants as well as inoculation against adverse setbacks associated with the stressful job-search process.

Key Ingredients of the JOBS Program

A successful job-search program must meet several formidable challenges. The program must recruit individuals who are shaken by their recent job loss, uncertain about their financial and career futures, and frequently haunted by self-doubts about their marketability. Having recruited these often fragile candidates, the program must gain their trust, help them discover their own marketable skills and appraise the barriers facing them in their job search, develop their job-seeking skills and increase their confidence in the job-search process, support them in actively engaging a sometimes unfamiliar job market, inoculate them against the inevitable setbacks they will face, and finally, help them make career decisions that will launch them into the next phase of their working lives.

Figure 9.1 summarizes the Michigan Prevention Research Center JOBS program and the theoretical elements and instrumental skills and knowledge that are its foundations. This set of skills and knowledge depends in part on knowledge of the local labor market conditions, and is aimed at helping people recognize the optimal fit between their own background and skills and the job market.

The motivational and coping processes outlined on the left-hand side of the figure are theory-derived psychosocial coping skills for coping with challenges in the face of uncertainty and maintaining skilled performance and high levels of motivation in the face of multiple challenges and setbacks over time. These two sets of cognitive and behavioral skills are combined into a single learning and performance repertoire in the JOBS program. By themselves, neither the motivational and coping repertoire on the left side of Figure 9.1, nor the skills and procedural job-search knowledge repertoire on the right side of the figure, is adequate to the task of successful job search. The two skill repertoires must be forged into a single programmatic set of strategic learning activities (Zimmerman & Bonner, forthcoming) to be effective and result in a successful job search.

Motivational and Coping Processes

Figure 9.1 identifies motivational and coping processes that must be activated and sustained through the long-term challenge of job search, which is itself frequently punctuated by multiple setbacks. Caplan and colleagues (1989) have described these processes in detail.

The person facing the coping task of job search is often filled with uncertainty and is considering the possibility of engaging and

Figure 9.1. The Michigan JOBS Program.

| Motivational and Coping Processes | JOBS Program for Employment Transitions | Instrumental Skills and Procedural Knowledge |

Motivations/ Expectancies
- Trust in trainers
- Belief in trainer expertise
- Expectations of success

Discovering marketable skills

Self- and Market Appraisal
- Identifying marketable skills
- Assessing market opportunities
- Identifying career options

Problem Appraisal
- Barrier appraisal
- Expectations to overcome barriers

Presenting job skills and thinking like an employer

Enlarging the Job Environment
- Network mapping
- Obtaining contacts
- Information interview
- Self-presentation skills
- Communicating one's job skills and assets

Skill and Efficacy Enhancement
- Job-search skill and efficacy enhancement
- Expectations of successful outcomes

Finding job openings

Resume, contacts, and getting an interview

Job-Search Outcome Management
- Setback management
- Choosing among job options

Support Mobilization
- Emotional support
- Instrumental support

The complete search process, planning for setbacks, and decisions about offers accepting help from an expert. Initial expectations of trust, a belief in the expertise of the helper, and a belief that the effort will lead to success all must be activated. French and Raven (1959) and Caplan and colleagues (1989) have described these as motivational expectancies based on *referent power and expectations of expertise.* It is these initial expectations that must engage a potential recruit to the program and set the stage for a later cognitive and motivational activation.

A second set of cognitive and motivational processes are activated by *problem appraisal.* Initial appraisal of the barriers to be faced in the job search and the motivation to overcome these barriers are critical in this stage of coping and motivational activation (Caplan, Vinokur, Price, & van Ryn, 1989). A critical aspect of problem appraisal at this stage is the recognition that the coping process in the job search is fundamentally transactional in nature (Heller, Price, & Hogg, 1990) and that understanding the expectations of those with whom one is to engage, such as potential employers, is critical for success. In the actual program this is translated into the reminder to participants that they must learn to "think like an employer."

Following problem appraisal is a group of cognitive behavioral (skill building) and motivational changes aimed at *efficacy enhancement.* This includes expectations regarding one's developing skills and expectations regarding positive outcomes if these skills are successfully mobilized (Bandura, 1977; Zimmerman & Bonner, forthcoming). Self-efficacy has been identified as a critical ingredient for successful coping in a wide range of social and personal tasks requiring the skilled deployment of effort in the face of uncertainty and setbacks.

Another key component in the coping repertoire is the *inoculation against setbacks* (Meichenbaum, 1985). The recognition that even the most skillfully enacted coping strategies will meet with periodic failure and rejection requires that the individual anticipate setbacks in the job search and rehearse alternative coping strategies. Anticipatory problem solving inoculates the individual against setbacks and mobilizes coping strategies more rapidly and effectively when setbacks are actually encountered.

Finally, a cluster of skills that we describe as *support mobilization* is a critical ingredient for coping. This includes not only mobilizing the support of one's personal social network including families and friends (Heller, Price, & Hogg, 1990; Vinokur & Caplan, 1987), but also mobilizing more instrumental forms of support, including help with practical tasks and financial demands that become even more acute following job loss.

Instrumental Skills and Procedural Knowledge

As valuable as this set of generic coping skills and motivational processes is, by themselves it is no guarantee of a successful job search. To it must be added a repertoire of procedural knowledge and pragmatic skills. Three major clusters of such skills are required for job-search success and have been incorporated into the JOBS training program.

The first has to do with *self-appraisal and market appraisal* (Curran, 1992). People must be able to identify their own marketable skills. This is not as simple as it sounds, particularly for someone considering a transfer from one labor market or industrial sector to another. Basic job skills often go unrecognized, and procedures are needed to highlight their existence and usefulness. At the same time, market appraisal skills are needed to evaluate viable job opportunities when they emerge. Each of these two sets of skills needs to be combined into a tentative plan identifying a career track or sector in which jobs are likely to be available.

A second cluster of skills involves *engaging the environment*. Active networking skills (Lin & Dumin, 1986; Granovetter, 1974)— skilled abilities to contact prospective employers, the capacity to conduct information interviews, to make further contacts—and self-presentation skills are required once an initial self- and market appraisal has been conducted (Curran, 1992). These skills are acquired and mastered through *active learning* and *role playing* (Zimmerman & Bonner, forthcoming). Furthermore, an effective program requires that they be exercised *in situ* during the course of the program, with results being brought back for review to provide effective feedback for additional attempts to refine these skills.

Finally, even after an effective self- and market appraisal and skillful engagement in the job market environment, outcomes of these efforts must also be skillfully managed. Two sets of outcomes are critical here, the first of which we have already described. Setbacks must be effectively managed and procedures for *inoculation against setbacks* must be established, both to maintain motivation and to make maximum use of opportunities that exist even in the face of setbacks (Meichenbaum, 1985). At the same time, a persistent skilled job search will generate more than a single job, and the *management of job choice* (Power & Aldag, 1985) is also critical since the first job that one is offered is not necessarily the best job for long-term career management and well-being. In short, evaluating the potential jobs for their future promotion potential, short-term and long-term provision of economic resources, their "stepping stone" qualities to yet another job—this is all part of the complex decision making that must occur during a successful search process (Power & Aldag, 1985; Soelberg, 1967).

Five Sessions, Five Interlocking Goals

A combination of distilled research knowledge from social and organizational psychology and pragmatic skills and procedural understanding described above is embodied in the JOBS training program itself (Curran, 1992). The program can be delivered in public- or private-sector settings and is designed for people experiencing job loss who are recruited and trained to cope with the transition back into work.

The pragmatics of the JOBS program begin with recruiting participants in some central organizational settings such as an employment office or an outplacement program in a corporate human resources division. The JOBS program itself consists of five four-hour sessions distributed over one to two weeks. The five sessions are designed to provide an intensive learning experience using key *active learning techniques* focusing on modeling, role playing, and the application of general behavioral principles to the unique circumstances of each participant (Caplan, Vinokur, Price, & van Ryn, 1989; Zimmerman & Bonner, forthcoming).

The JOBS program is delivered to groups of fifteen to twenty participants using an interactive group-process format. Typically, a pair of trainers, one male and one female, guide the group sessions. Each session involves broad orienting introductions, dramatizations and modeling sessions in which trainers enact both successful and unsuccessful strategies at each stage of the job-search process, and specific exercises in which participants may test their newfound knowledge and their newly recognized skills in structured but supportive role-playing exercises. Each session begins with a structured training problem. Participants develop a cognitive framework regarding a specific job-search problem and then act both as observers and active learners, providing supportive suggestions and constructive feedback to one another (Curran, 1992).

The program begins with trainers establishing a sense that they can be trusted with this critical task and that they have the expertise needed to help participants succeed at it. Trainers discuss their own job-search experiences to illustrate both that they have been there and that they have the knowledge that it takes to mount a successful job-search campaign (French & Raven, 1959). Also, at this early stage an expectation of success in coping with the job-search process requires that participants develop a framework by learning to "think like an employer." This message establishes the idea that successful job-search activities require the development of a transactional perspective in which the job seeker learns to anticipate the needs and concerns of a perspective employer. At the same time, participants begin to identify their own marketable skills and to identify ways to translate those skills into new job or career lines.

Participants then learn to present their own job-search skills while at the same time continuing to think like an employer. They identify personal barriers that must be overcome in presenting their skills to an employer. For example, older workers learn to present their long careers as reservoirs of experience that can be used in new job settings rather than signs of aging and decline.

As these preliminary skills to present oneself effectively in the job market are honed, attention moves to engaging the job-search environment. The key topics for this stage are identifying network contacts, finding job openings, and conducting initial information interviews with perspective employers, focusing in particularly on what the candidate can do for the employer rather than the reverse (Curran, 1992).

By the fourth session new skills in self-presentation are emerging—developing a resume, building a bank of contacts, and securing interviews. At this time, initial training inoculating participants against the inevitable setbacks they will encounter begins in earnest (Meichenbaum, 1985). Participants are asked to share their anticipation of setbacks with the group. These are used to think through, generate, and refine alternative solutions to reach the goals in the face of setbacks. Evaluations of these alternative courses of action and banking them for coping with future setbacks are also a key to inoculation.

For example, one often-mentioned cause for setbacks is employers' reluctance to hire older workers or younger ones. The group discussion may focus on what employer concerns might lead them to reject older or younger workers. As the session progresses, participants generate a list of these concerns, such as older workers' health issues and adaptability to new technologies and younger workers' lack of experience and demonstrated responsibility. Once these concerns are outlined, participants proceed to devise ways of counteracting these concerns by using more skillful presentation methods in the resume and job interview to address the employer's concerns. For example, older workers may emphasize their good health record in their resume and interview—"not missing a day due to illness in the last three years"; younger workers may emphasize their past experience as volunteers and any activities that demonstrate that they have been trusted and responsible, such as "coaching a little league baseball team."

Finally, in the later stages of the program a complete enactment of the search strategy, including rehearsal and critique of the job interview itself, is conducted, with the participants providing supportive feedback and suggestions for improvements for each candidate. Typically, in the final session a number of job leads will have already been obtained and a number of job interviews will either have been scheduled or information interviews already obtained.

By the end of the program, typically participants report considerable confidence that they know what to do even when initial efforts fail and reversals are experienced. At this point, most participants have not simply internalized a fragmented set of job-search skills, but have gone through an experience of strategic learning (Zimmerman & Bonner, forthcoming) that increases the likelihood of obtaining job offers and also helps sustain them along the rocky and sometimes prolonged road to reemployment.

Keys to Effective Implementation of Innovative Programs

A program is only as good as its actual implementation. Even the most carefully constructed program, based on our best understanding of social psychological and organizational principles and aimed at enhancing practical skills and procedural knowledge for job search, is of little value unless it can be delivered with high fidelity to organizations that are receptive to it and willing to support it (Van de Ven, 1986). Like all organizational innovations involving technology that is largely psychological and organizational, meeting the dual challenges of fidelity and organizational receptiveness is critical in successful implementation of the JOBS program for reemployment.

Organizational Readiness

Price and Lorion (1989) have argued that organizational interventions are more likely to succeed in host organizations that have certain critical attributes. These attributes can and should be assessed before program implementation is carried out.

Figure 9.2 presents a model that begins with the hypothesis that organizational readiness depends in part on the environment of the organization to adopt an innovative program. For example, corporate decision makers may be more ready to adopt the JOBS program for outplacement purposes if key agencies in the environment of the organization produce incentives for corporate outplacement.

Furthermore, awareness, acceptance, and ownership of the problem by top managers in the organization are also hypothesized to be critical components of readiness. For example, a vice president for human resources may recognize that there are major corporate costs associated with downsizing efforts that do not include an effective outplacement program. The vice president may realize that the lack of an outplacement program may result in demoralization of those workers who remain (see Chapter Three), and she may therefore be more likely to champion a program such as JOBS. In addition, the attitudes, beliefs, and practices of corporate managers and staff or public agency officials in the local organization can also be a critical dimension of readiness. If local human

Figure 9.2. A Model of Organizational Readiness to Launch Prevention Programs.

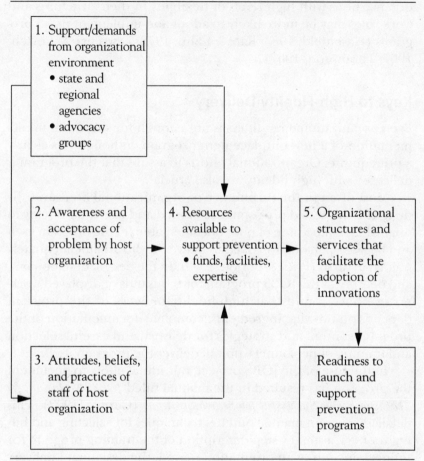

Source: Adapted from Price and Lorion, 1989.

resource staff, for example, feel that the problem of job search and reemployment is not part of their roles and responsibilities, the likelihood of successful implementation is much lower.

In some cases, as the model suggests, there are organizational structures and services already in place in most organizations that can facilitate adoption of interventions such as the JOBS program (Galbraith, 1982; Van de Ven, 1986). For example, organizations that already allow staff to support effective job transitions within the organization using available internal labor markets will also be more likely to adopt an outplacement program such as JOBS. Also, organizations with high levels of flexibility in their structures and work roles may be more likely to adopt and implement novel programs (Hasenfeld, 1983; Katz & Kahn, 1978; Lawrence & Lorsch, 1967; Thompson, 1967).

Keys to High-Fidelity Delivery

Even organizational readiness is not enough for successful implementation of a new outplacement program, although it is clearly a prerequisite. Organizational efforts to assure that the program is delivered with high fidelity are also crucial.

Most often in the turbulence of organizational life, carefully designed and tested programs are eroded and lose their fidelity to original design because of poor documentation of the program itself and because persons are asked to deliver it who are not adequately trained to do so (Price & Lorion, 1989). In the design, development, and delivery of the JOBS program for thousands of displaced workers, we have found that high-fidelity delivery of the program depends on two vital ingredients: complete documentation of the program content and strategies for delivery, and careful selection and training of personnel who will deliver the program itself.

In the case of the JOBS project, our initial effort to document the program has resulted in the manual titled *JOBS: A Manual for Teaching People Successful Job Search Strategies* (Curran, 1992). This detailed program manual outlines techniques for selecting and hiring trainers, a step-by-step description of the training program for trainers, including an orientation period, the design and delivery of a mock intervention seminar, a trainer's forum for fine tuning the intervention, and final rehearsal periods. The manual also contains detailed information for the five-session program itself as well as appendices providing administrative details for the actual design of the training site and observation forms that can be used for quality control in the delivery of the intervention.

A critical ingredient ensuring the strength and integrity (Yeaton & Sechrest, 1981) of an effectively delivered program is the careful selection and training of the trainers who actually deliver the program. The selection process used in delivering the JOBS program involves screening all candidates to assess their ability to meet job requirements and also to assess important personal characteristics including flexibility, empathy, sensitivity, self-confidence, and positive outlook. In addition to these personal characteristics, group trainers are selected based on their speaking and listening skills, talent in giving feedback, skill in facilitating group processes, and ability to manage conflict constructively.

To achieve these selection goals, the JOBS project uses preliminary screening through an inspection of resumes and through personal interviews with two independent staff members, who then identify a subset of the most qualified candidates. These candidates are then called in for an audition in which each finalist plays the role of group trainer, presenting material and facilitating activities for a group of staff members playing the role of participants.

After the trainers are selected, they are formed into two-person teams, one man and one woman, representing the best balance of complementary skills and traits. Once trainers with requisite skills and complementary qualities are selected, they are given seven weeks of intensive training. The training includes a three-day orientation to the entire intervention, one week in which trainers are taken through the entire intervention seminar, a one-week trainers forum, and a four-week rehearsal period.

While adequate training is essential, procedures must be developed to ensure that the trainers will implement the program as intended in their training, that is, with integrity and fidelity. To achieve this purpose, the JOBS program used observers from the staff. They attended 40 percent of the sessions on a regular basis, and recorded the trainers' delivery of the intervention on specially designed observation forms (Curran, 1992). The observation forms included two sections. One section included a rating scale evaluating the quality of delivery with respect to the various specific tasks and activities that are planned for the particular session, such as, "To what extent did each participant role play the information interview?" The second section included rating scales that assess issues common to all sessions; for instance, "To what extent do you [the observers] think that participants understood the material? . . . That the members were actively seeking information, evaluations and comments from one another?"

Further, to ensure continued uniformity in the delivery of the program, the trainers were also required to observe their peers and record their observations on the program rating forms. This provided a corrective feedback loop regarding their own performance as well. In addition, trainers had a bimonthly meeting to share, discuss, and address problems that surfaced in their sessions or that they observed in others. These meetings also served as the main social support structure for the trainers to handle their emotional aspect of their experiences, thereby preventing burnout and maintaining high morale while supporting the norm that quality control is a key to the success of the JOBS program.

Conclusion

Human resources innovations are seldom designed to make optimal use of what we know from social and organizational psychology about maximizing human motivation, providing optimal learning circumstances, and protecting individuals against the threat of failure and rejection. Our development of the Michigan JOBS program attempted to reverse this trend. It attempts to draw on what is known from motivation theory, stress and coping theory, and recent developments on theory and research on self-efficacy and social support to produce a program to support people facing job transitions. The result is a theory-driven intervention tested under large-scale randomized field experimental conditions with relatively long periods of follow-up to produce a job transition program with strong evidence of effectiveness.

Like any other carefully designed and tested prototype, however, JOBS's ultimate effectiveness is only as good as the readiness of its host organization to support it and the fidelity with which it is delivered. These issues of organizational readiness and the need for program integrity represent a generic challenge in the next generation of designing human resource strategies for organizational growth.

References

Bandura, A. (1977). Self-efficacy: Toward a unifying theory of behavior change. *Psychological Review, 84,* 191–215.

Caplan, R. D., Vinokur, A. D., Price, R. H., & van Ryn, M. (1989). Job seeking, reemployment, and mental health: A randomized field experiment in coping with job loss. *Journal of Applied Psychology, 74,* 759–769.

Curran, J. (1992). *JOBS: A manual for teaching people successful job search strategies.* Ann Arbor: Michigan Prevention Research Center, Institute for Social Research, University of Michigan.

French, J. R. P., Jr., & Raven, B. (1959). The bases of social power. In D. Cartwright (Ed.), *Studies in social power* (pp. 150–167). Ann Arbor: Institute for Social Research, University of Michigan.

Galbraith, J. R. (1982). Designing the innovating organization. *Organizational Dynamics, 43,* 3–24.

Granovetter, M. (1974). *Getting a job.* Cambridge, MA: Harvard University Press.

Hasenfeld, Y. (1983). *Human service organizations.* Englewood Cliffs, NJ: Prentice Hall.

Heller, K., Price, R. H., & Hogg, J. R. (1990). The role of social support in community and clinical intervention. In B. R. Sarason, I. G. Sarason, & G. R. Pierce (Eds.), *Social support—an interactional view: Issues in social support research* (pp. 482–507). New York: Wiley.

Katz, D., & Kahn, R. L. (1978). *The social psychology of organizations* (2nd ed.). New York: Wiley.

Kessler, R. C., Turner, J. B., & House, J. S. (1987). Intervening processes in the relationship between unemployment and health. *Psychological Medicine, 17,* 949–961.

Kessler, R. C., Turner, J. B., & House, J. S. (1988). The effects of unemployment on health in a community survey: Main, modifying, and mediating effects. *Journal of Social Issues, 44*(4), 69–86.

Kessler, R. C., Turner, J. B., & House, J. S. (1989). Unemployment, reemployment, and emotional functioning in a community sample. *American Sociological Review, 54,* 648–657.

Lawrence, P. R., & Lorsch, J. W. (1967). *Organization and environment.* Boston: Harvard Business School, Division of Research.

Lin, N., & Dumin, M. (1986). Access to occupations through social ties. *Social Networks, 8,* 365–385.

Meichenbaum, D. (1985). *Stress inoculation training: A clinical guidebook.* New York: Pergamon/Elsevier.

Power, D. J., & Aldag, R. J. (1985). Soelberg's job search and choice models: A clarification, review, and critique. *Academy of Management Review, 10,* 48–58.

Price, R. H. (1987). Linking intervention research and risk factor research. In J. A. Steinberg & M. M. Silverman (Eds.), *Preventing mental disorders: A research perspective* (DHHS Publication No. ADM 87–1492) (pp. 48–56). Washington, DC: U.S. Government Printing Office.

Price, R. H. (1990). Strategies for managing plant closings and downsizing.

In D. Fishman & C. Cherniss (Eds.), *The human side of corporate competitiveness* (pp. 127–151). Newbury Park, CA: Sage.

Price, R. H. (1992). Psychosocial impact of job loss on individuals and families. *Current Directions in Psychological Science, 1*(1), 9–11.

Price, R. H. (forthcoming). Unemployment. In J. Rappaport & E. Seidman (Eds.), *Handbook of community psychology.* New York: Plenum.

Price, R. H., & D'Aunno, T. (1983). Managing work force reduction. *Human Resource Management, 22,* 413–430.

Price, R. H., & Lorion, R. P. (1989). Prevention programming as organizational reinvention: From research to implementation. In D. Shaffer, I. Phillips, & N. B. Enzer (Eds.), *Prevention of mental disorders, alcohol and drug use in children and adolescents* (pp. 97–123). Rockville, MD: Office of Substance Abuse Prevention/American Academy of Child and Adolescent Psychiatry.

Price, R. H., van Ryn, M., & Vinokur, A. D. (1992). Impact of preventive job search intervention on the likelihood of depression among the unemployed. *Journal of Health and Social Behavior, 33,* 158–167.

Reich, R. B. (1991). *The work of nations: Preparing ourselves for 21st century capitalism.* New York: Knopf.

Soelberg, P. O. (1967). Unprogrammed decision making. *Industrial Management Review, 8,* 19–29.

Thompson, J. D. (1967). *Organizations in action.* New York: McGraw-Hill.

Van de Ven, A. H. (1986). Central problems in the management of innovation. *Management Science, 32,* 590–608.

Vinokur, A., & Caplan, R. D. (1987). Attitudes and social support: Determinants of job-seeking behavior and well-being among the unemployed. *Journal of Applied Social Psychology, 17,* 1007–1024.

Vinokur, A. D., Caplan, R. D., & Williams, C. C. (1987). Effects of recent and past stresses on mental health: Coping with unemployment among Vietnam veterans and nonveterans. *Journal of Applied Social Psychology, 17,* 710–730.

Vinokur, A. D., Price, R. H., & Schul, Y. (1994). *Impact of the JOBS intervention on unemployed workers varying in risk for depression.* Ann Arbor: Institute for Social Research, University of Michigan.

Vinokur, A., Schul, Y., & Caplan R. D. (1987). Determinants of perceived social support: Interpersonal transactions, personal outlook, and transient affective states. *Journal of Personality and Social Psychology, 53,* 1137–1145.

Vinokur, A. D., van Ryn, M., Gramlich, E. M., & Price, R. H. (1991). Long-term follow-up and benefit-cost analysis of the JOBS program: A preventive intervention for the unemployed. *Journal of Applied Psychology, 76,* 213–219.

Yeaton, W. H., & Sechrest, L. (1981). Critical dimensions in the choice and maintenance of successful treatments: Strength, integrity, and effectiveness. *Journal of Consulting and Clinical Psychology, 49,* 156–157.

Zimmerman, B. J., & Bonner, S. (forthcoming). A social cognitive view of strategic learning. In C. E. Weinstein & B. L. McCombs (Eds.), *Strategic learning: Skill, will, and self-regulation.* Hillsdale, NJ: Erlbaum.

CHAPTER 10

Creating Opportunities for Displaced Workers
Center for Commercial Competitiveness

Larry R. Last
Robert W. E. Peterson
Jack Rappaport
Carin A. Webb

The Center for Commercial Competitiveness was established to create jobs within the southern tier of New York. The premise underlying the center's existence is that employment in the region will be generated in substantial numbers only by creating new products and services that leverage regional strengths, by reaching new markets, and by making businesses fiercely competitive. Whether the new products, services, and markets enhance the performance of existing businesses or lead to the formation of new ones does not matter; the effect is nominally the same.

The corollary to the above premise is that the more than eleven thousand regional jobs lost as a result of defense cutbacks and the attendant corporate restructurings, downsizings, and right-sizings will not return even when the national economy rebounds. A combination of technology, new ways of doing business, and the region's traditional dependence on defense work will, in general, keep hiring to a minimum as expansion occurs. In the best of foreseeable conditions, regional economic rebound will be inadequate to absorb the existing dislocated workforce without radically innovative job-creation endeavors.

While there is a profound need to train dislocated workers (as well as many currently employed workers), and particularly those who have been in the workforce for some years, it is viewed as insufficient to merely upgrade their skills and attempt to connect them with potential employers. Upgrading the skills of dislocated workers in this environment is a zero-sum game in which one individual obtains employment only at the expense of another. While marginal net productivity improvements can result from hiring people who are more skilled or better trained, these are typically second-order effects and are insufficient to discernibly affect the regional economy in a positive way. The center is designed to use training as a foundation for first-order job-creation effects.

In November 1992 the New York State and U.S. Departments of Labor awarded grants to the center to provide training for defense displaced workers. The program objectives for the first phase are to:

- Train displaced workers in the theory and practice of working in self-directed teams.
- Train displaced workers in the process of developing markets and products for commercial industry.
- Develop a commercial mindset in defense displaced workers.
- Implement the Center for Commercial Competitiveness as an innovative partnership between industry, academia, and government in the region.
- Utilize displaced workers in conjunction with regional industries to identify new commercial markets and products for participating regional industries and for potential joint ventures among those industries.
- Provide a bridge for defense industries into commercial markets.
- Make teams of displaced workers available to industry for work beyond the first phase.
- Define joint-venture agreements and teaming arrangements for synergistic enterprises to be implemented in subsequent phases.

Model and Operational Structure

The fundamental premise of the program is that dislocated workers, if supplemented with the proper training and linked to regional industries, can apply that training and their combined skills and energy to successfully develop new product and market opportunities that result in employment for themselves. A successful new product or market implies the existence of a competitive advantage. The program is structured to surface and analyze the core competencies of the region's industries and leverage these into distinct competitive advantages in the global marketplace.

The operational model and process elements used in the program are shown in Figure 10.1. The primary success path in this model is as follows: dislocated workers lead to team projects, which lead to business proposals, which lead to employment. This path is fed by training, regional industries, and a competitiveness database.

Projects are the heart of the program. Candidate projects may be industry sponsored or self-generated by the participants. Project proposals, accordingly, may be made by participants to candidate-supporting industries or by industries to the class of participants. When a candidate opportunity is determined to be viable and the required mutual interests, skills, and resources are present, a self-directed team forms and the project is launched.

From a market perspective there are two types of projects: "push" and "pull." "Push" projects start with an existing product or service and focus on developing expanded market share and market size. "Pull" projects start with an existing market demand and focus on using the core competencies of the region to develop the product or service that matches the demand. Both types rely heavily on the availability of correct, accurate information regarding the global marketplace, competitive product factors, and commercial best practices.

In general there are more push opportunities than pull since push projects start with existing products and services. Pull project opportunities—especially those where the core competencies of several companies can be synergistically combined and leveraged for competitive advantage—are important to regional economic development since they result in new products and services and represent true growth potential.

Figure 10.1. The Center for Commercial Competitiveness Model.

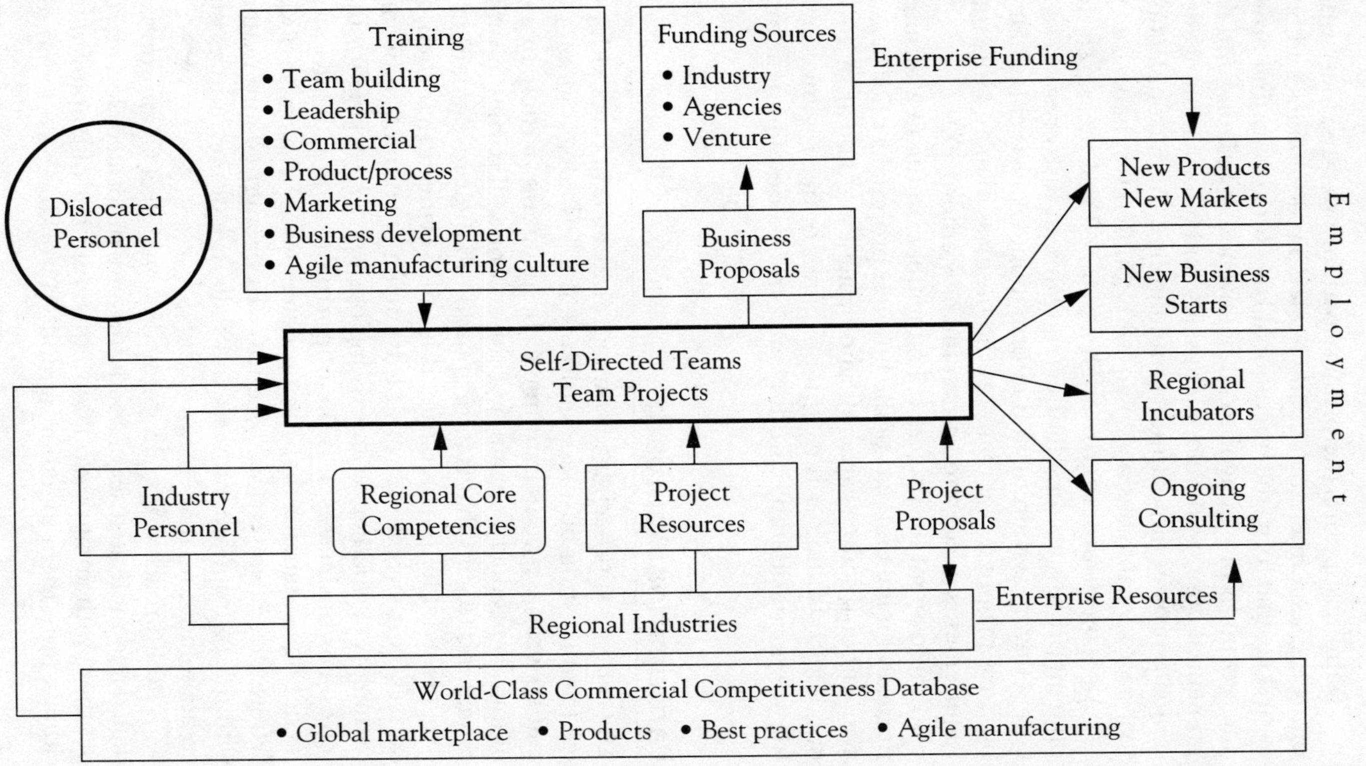

Employment

New Products
New Markets

New Business
Starts

Regional Incubators

Ongoing
Consulting

Enterprise Funding

Enterprise Resources

Funding Sources

- Industry
- Agencies
- Venture

Business
Proposals

Project
Proposals

Self-Directed Teams
Team Projects

Training

- Team building
- Leadership
- Commercial
- Product/process
- Marketing
- Business development
- Agile manufacturing culture

Project
Resources

Regional Core
Competencies

Regional Industries

Dislocated
Personnel

Industry
Personnel

World-Class Commercial Competitiveness Database

- Global marketplace
- Products
- Best practices
- Agile manufacturing

Training supports the primary path in two ways: first by developing the self-directed team and leadership disciplines and behavioral skills that form the operational basis for conducting projects, and second by providing the competitiveness, marketing and entrepreneurial business development skills, and information needed to evaluate project opportunities and develop them from a conceptual stage to viable business plans with sound investment strategies.

All projects progress through a planned and measured development process, using self-directed teams, industry resources, and competitiveness training and information. Projects culminate in a business proposal that contains the business plan and investment requirements needed to launch the new enterprise.

Employment for project team members in the new business is normally an integral part of the business proposal, either in a management or resource capacity. Employment may also arise through ongoing consulting as the center expands or in a regional incubator where considerable product and process development time is required.

Participation Approach

The center's approach is to connect dislocated workers with workers from existing businesses and use the businesses' momentum and systems as a vehicle to make the program participants economically productive again. For this to work, all parties must have something to gain that is in proportion to their investment in the process. For the participants, it is fairly evident that their gain derives from becoming (or at least being positioned to become) reemployed, whether by an existing business or working for themselves. For businesses, it is the opportunity to pursue product or service developments that circumstances would otherwise obviate. Where these two sets of objectives can be aligned and matched with the appropriate interests and skills, the opportunity exists to create something new.

The approach originally defined was to select an appropriately skilled and motivated set of about forty-five dislocated workers, couple them with an approximately equal number of employed individuals, train them together in modern workforce skills and team dynamics culture, and initiate projects around which new products or services would be built. Ideas for the products and services were to originate with the businesses and the program participants. Participant/employee teams would form around particular projects based on skill requirements coupled with interests. The result would be new products for regional business that would employ key participants and others or new business enterprises established by participants with the project business partner as a built-in client.

As the program was beginning to unfold in early 1993, it became apparent that regional businesses were having great difficulty stabilizing themselves in a chaotic business environment. As a result, they were unable to make the major time commitment for full-time support of the program, thus jeopardizing the industry-participation component. The risk of proceeding unmindful of the potential impact of this condition was that either industry people would not appear at the opening session, or they would disappear shortly thereafter or at some critical future point. The effect would have been totally destructive to the program, in that dislocated-worker participants would have interpreted these events as businesses' retreat from program support.

The center restructured the program with a constructive method to minimize the impact of the situation. Projects would continue to be obtained from the two sources—businesses and participants—but businesses would participate in one of three ways:

1. The businesses could propose a project for consideration and, if accepted, designate a key point of contact from within the company to work with the center's participants.
2. Businesses could support a project with the intent of becoming a partner in bringing the project to market. To do this, they would provide a person or persons to work with the center. In return, they might become an owner of the project and also become positioned for access to other projects.
3. A third way to participate would be to provide capital in some form—space, material, equipment, and so forth—in return for which the business would receive teaming help and become a project partner candidate.

Outreach, Screening, and Selection

The outreach, screening and, selection process was conducted during a three-month period in early 1993. The entire process was designed and implemented by a screening and selection council with members from several agencies and industries. The objective was to enroll forty-five dislocated participants who had strong technical, entrepreneurial, creative, and team skills. The process consisted of broad outreach, application, application evaluation, and interviews. Fifty-five initial participants were enrolled, and eleven were added later to make up for early dropouts.

The screening/selection council played a major role in designing an application process that defined the key participant characteristics, attributes, and skills that were most needed for success and most closely matched the center's objective. Primary characteristics considered most important for participation were creativity, entrepreneurial goals and drive, team orientation, technical/product development experience, and innovation/motivation. An application package was developed: a descriptive brochure on the center's project and a three-part application that sought to measure key characteristics. The education and work experience section of the application was designed to obtain specific experience applicable to the center's program, not simply to list recent jobs. The application also required applicants to answer essay questions designed to measure the key characteristics, their understanding of the center's program, and personal motivation factors. Questions asked applicants to provide examples of their creativity, entrepreneurism, and team/leadership skills as well as their working style and personality.

One hundred and four applications were evaluated by a screening team of six individuals using the form in Exhibit 10.1. Unemployment, education, and work experience data for the applicant group are shown in Table 10.1.

Evaluations were weighted and tabulated. Where recommendations to interview did not cluster well, a consensus was reached via a discussion involving the entire evaluation group. Seventy-seven applicants were invited to interview. Two separate one-on-one thirty-minute interviews were conducted. In general interviewers consisted of one member from a business group and one member from a human resource group. Consensus on whether to extend

Exhibit 10.1. Screening Evaluation Form.

Screening Evaluation

Candidate Name _____   Date of Interview _____

		Met	
Basic Criteria	*Benchmark*	*Yes*	*No*
Education	Tech School	____	____
	Bachelor's (minimum)	____	____
Experience	5 years (minimum)	____	____

Check areas of experience

____ Engineering	____ New Product Development
____ Finance	____ Program Management
____ Manufacturing Process	____ Quality Control
____ Marketing	____ Other _____

Desired Basic Characteristics	*Strong Evidence*	*Some Evidence*	*Can't Tell*
Creativity	____	____	____
Enthusiastically embraces change			
Enjoys conceiving new ideas			
Expresses intellectual curiosity			
Entrepreneurial Spirit	____	____	____
Looks for better ways to get things done			
Concentrates on major improvements			
Finds ways to better manage his/her time			
Team Orientation	____	____	____
Can work as either leader *or* team member			
Places the accomplishments of the team above his/her own personal feelings			
Demonstrates flexibility and tolerance of other points of view			
High Performance/Goal Orientation	____	____	____
Is motivated by challenge			
Sets clearly defined, measurable, realistic stretch goals			
Meets goals that he/she sets for self			
Initiative/Motivation	____	____	____
Self-starter			
Has demonstrated an ability to operate without close supervision			
Reaches out for ever-increasing responsibility			

Exhibit 10.1. Screening Evaluation Form, (continued).

Desired Basic Characteristics	Strong Evidence	Some Evidence	Can't Tell
Decision Making	___	___	___
Reviews all data necessary to make an informed decision			
Demonstrates willingness to "stand up" for his/her decision			
Leadership	___	___	___
Demonstrated ability to build a productive team			
Able to plan and organize			
Knows how to delegate effectively			
Puts goals of team above personal goals			
Demonstrates sensitivity to feelings of others			
Effective Communication	___	___	___
Is clear and concise in written and oral communications			
Is honest and open in expressing thoughts and ideas			
Shows good listening skills, is willing to hear all sides			
Maturity	___	___	___
Learns from admitting mistakes			
Has learned to accept limitations and live with them			
Demonstrates strong belief in his/her ability to solve problems			

Comments

_____

_____

_____

_____

Recommendations for Interview

____ Highly Recommend   ____ Recommend   ____ Don't Know

____ Do Not Interview   ____ Wish to Discuss with Group

If interviewed, I'd like the following questions/concerns addressed:

_____

_____

_____

Screened by: _____   Signature: _____
(please print)

Table 10.1. Applicant Data: Employment, Education, and Work Experience.

Unemployment

		Receiving Unemployment Compensation	
Receiving unemployment	50	0–10 weeks	14
Exhausted unemployment	17	11–20	6
		21–30	11
Unemployed > 15 weeks	85	31–40	12
Unemployed > 1 year	29	41–50	1
		51–60	1
Older worker (>55)	32	61–70	0
Retired	30	71–80	1
Early retiree	25	81–90	1

Education

Highest Education Completed

High school	8
Some technical training	11
Technical degree	15
Some college	5
Undergraduate degree	29
Some graduate work	13
Graduate degree	23

Undergraduate Degrees	64	*Graduate Degrees*	23
Engineering	35		
Electrical	14	MSEE	2
Mechanical	9	MSME	2
Chemical	5	MSCE	2
Aerospace	2		
Industrial	2		
Ceramics	1	MS Ceramics	1
General	1		
Civil	1		
BS	14		
Physics	4	MS Physics	3
Computer science	2	MS Computer science	1
Math	2	MS Math	1
Industrial management	2		
Information processing	1		
Systems	1	MS Systems	3
Applied science	1		
Management	1		

**Table 10.1. Applicant Data: Employment,
Education, and Work Experience, (continued).**

Business Administration	6	MBA	6
BA	9		
Economics	2		
Psychology	2		
Business	1		
Social science	1	MA Social science	1
History	1		
Political science	1	MA Political science	1
Library science	1		

Work Experience

Design engineering	17
Product development engineering	10
Project engineering program management	5
Field service/logistics engineering	3
Process engineering	11
Industrial engineering	4
Manufacturing engineering	9
Quality control engineering	6
Manufacturing planning	4
Manufacturing management/administration	9
Manufacturing purchasing	3
Contract management	3
Sales/Marketing	5
Finance	2
Human resources personnel	1
Manufacturing, technician/inspector	7
Teaching	1
Private business	2

an offer for program participation was reached by a comparative review between the two interviewers and the center's project director using forms very similar to those shown in Exhibit 10.1.

Characteristics such as motivation, creativity, entrepreneurism, and team orientation are difficult to assess from written essays and to a lesser extent from oral interviews. Frequently interviewers challenged potential participants regarding their personal assessments of these attributes. All applicants were questioned about their business idea and thoughts about team participation. Interviewers then completed an evaluation form with a recommendation for program participation. Comparisons of recommendations resulted in an 86 percent reliability rating among interviewers. Sixty-nine applicants were invited to participate in the program.

Training Phase

While participant outreach and evaluation were being conducted, the training program was being designed. As the concept for the center was being developed, the industry/agency/university architects recognized that agility (a concept developed by the Agile Manufacturing Enterprise Forum of the Iacocca Institute at Lehigh University) was an important foundational concept from the standpoint of both the dislocated workers and participating industries. Accordingly, agility training components and ongoing Agile Manufacturing Enterprise Forum (AMEF) participation elements were designed into the center's program and coordinated with AMEF. Early in the design of the training program, joint meetings were held with AMEF to establish agility training and awareness elements and identify mutually beneficial ongoing activities.

Five Curriculum Modules

The mission statement for the training program was: "To create a team training program that embodies world-class product development and competitiveness strategies empowering displaced and employed professionals to create jobs and new enterprise opportunities." The center's education subcommittee had developed a list of components for the training program; the training team reviewed these recommendations and grouped the components into five categories, which represented courses, and divided the courses into modules.

The Team-Building Course

The goal of this course is to develop participants' skills in oral, written, and electronic communication, problem solving, solution finding, leadership, decision making, and implementation of decisions so they can actively and effectively participate as members of self-directed work teams in an agile manufacturing environment. The course is divided into the following modules: communication, problem solving, solution finding/decision making, goal setting/implementation, and leadership.

The Business Process Development Course

The goal is to develop awareness and application skills in the organizational, financial, and operational aspects of agile commercial enterprises. The intent is to provide an overview of commercial best practices and detailed training in the elements that are necessary to create and operate an enterprise. The course applies team-oriented exercises to address organizational vision, strategic planning, and management practices. The course is divided into the following modules: general strategic planning, organization and management, business/enterprise formation, financial planning and feasibility analysis, elements of corporate agility, and analysis and measurement of corporate core competencies.

The Commercial Competitiveness Course

The goal is to develop participants' skills in writing an effective business plan. Participants determine the product or service's viability and added value in the marketplace by developing a business plan. The course is divided into the following modules: market surveys, competitor analysis, viability assessment, financial aspects/price-led costing, marketing strategies, and the business plan.

The Systems and Manufacturing Course

The goal is to develop participants' understanding of the strategic importance of information as the foundation for joining all the functional activities of a business into an integrated, agile unit that is focused on the needs of the marketplace. Course emphasis is on facilitating rapid response to changes in the marketplace through implementation of ideas contained in the course modules of: information resource management, manufacturing processes, project management techniques, concurrent engineering/design for manufacture/design for assembly, continuous improvement, and manufacturing procedures.

The Culture Course

The goal is to explore the personal relationships and values of corporate and workforce communities to develop in participants a mastery level of agility and change in today's quickly changing world markets. At the conclusion of this course each team develops a vision and mission statement. The course is divided into the following modules: dynamics of change and risk, creative corporate culture, conflict resolution, agility, continuous improvement, global markets, and professional development.

An Interactive Process

Principles of adult learning theory were incorporated into the curriculum development. Course modules were designed to be interrelated, interdependent, and sequenced to reinforce earlier learning. The training team agreed upon a methodology that provided lecture presentations for awareness, immediately followed by group exercises for application so that participants would learn by doing. Activities were designed to provide for hands-on applications, interaction among participants, and practice of team-building skills. Concepts such as agile manufacturing, core competency, virtual corporations, and continuous improvement were repeated frequently as part of activities. The training team adopted the philosophy that much of the training would be "just in time" in response to requests of participants. Every module was developed to provide meaningful experiences that would prepare participants for the enterprise development phase of the program.

Group activities were attended by a trainer to ensure that the material presented was understood by participants and applied correctly in the exercises. Each exercise was designed to include time for each group to report its outcome to the remainder of the class. Cross-examination by the class was encouraged as part of a philosophy of continuous improvement. Trainers agreed to assume the role of facilitator for exercises. Initially, trainers would assume a leadership role within the group to model behavior, but would quickly assume an inactive role, reverting only when the group did not understand the material presented or the purpose of the exercise, or was unable to function as a team without intervention from a trainer.

During the development of the curriculum, the training team was mindful of its customers. Trainers had the advantage of reviewing applicant applications. Although the specific needs of participants were unknown, a general profile was constructed: a person with at least a bachelor's degree who had enjoyed a stable work history with a major corporation involved in defense contracts and had been out of work for longer than twelve weeks. This profile also included several assumptions about the psychological makeup of the participant group: anger, hurt, and disbelief about what had happened to them after years of service with one company, depression over the lack of job prospects, frustration about the failure of job searches, and conflict about making the right decisions. To address these dynamics, every effort was made to ensure that the orientation period and the training program would be a positive learning experience for participants.

The resources of the community were also taken into account. Although each trainer "owned" a course, it was agreed no individual could cover all the components of each course and that the training program should take advantage of subject-matter experts. The resources of several universities, community colleges, and industry training departments were explored for potential incorporation into the center's training program. Trainers also arranged for participant visits to colleges and industries to demonstrate practical applications for concepts.

Project Phase

At the conclusion of the formal training period, participant teams began the project phase. Project candidates were originated by businesses and the center's participants. Initial contacts with businesses were documented in the form of a briefing sheet outlining the proposition and providing pertinent information. These candidates were screened by the participants against various criteria to determine suitability for further consideration: needed participant skills/availability, uniqueness/competitive situation, market potential and required approach, time to market, producibility, capital/funding requirements, and so on. The result of this initial evaluation was presented to the group at large, along with a recommendation to pursue or not. The participant group could accept the recommendation, overturn it, or open it up for further study.

Projects that survived the initial screen were staffed by forming a team of interested participants, and an abstract was generated. Where needed skills were lacking on the team, participants with those skills were requested to provide support. If the project was initiated with the center, the team would seek an appropriate business connection and call on prospects that showed an enthusiasm about the possibilities. Following this staffing process, projects were worked by the teams under the nominal direction of a team leader and facilitated by a member of the staff.

Projects that led to a contract between the center and a business were submitted to the center's board of directors for its approval before any contractual action. This was a way of introducing an independent evaluation of the basic proposition and ensuring that it was consistent with the center's mission.

Many candidate projects were considered and evaluated. More than half of them were rejected for a variety of viability reasons, the most common being market uncertainty and high-risk product development. Of the many projects considered and evaluated, those actively pursued as representing viable new business opportunities are listed in Table 10.2 along with their general product or service categories.

Outcomes, Recommendations, and Conclusions

The first demonstration run of the center's dislocated worker program produced many interesting and useful results and a considerable amount of information on ways to improve the program. In general, the program was considered to be successful, and a continuation program entitled Worker Enterprise Development (WED) has been funded and launched. The WED program will incorporate the successful outcomes and needed changes described below.

Programmatic Outcomes

The program goals of the center can be summarized as follows:

- Providing assistance to workers dislocated as a result of reduced defense spending, who are in need of commercial business skills development and an appropriate vehicle to launch new careers.

Table 10.2. Final Projects.

Emergency Vehicle Driving Simulator	A
Low-Cost Medical Imaging System	A
Natural Gas Vehicle Compressor	A
Ceramic Candle	B
Dyslexia Exercise Machine	B
Hydroponic Garden Kits	B
Canvas Products	C
Hansmann's Mills Products	C
Polymeric Environmental Lumber	C
Printed Circuit Board Cleaning System	C
Amatech Products	D
Business Information Systems	D
Training/Simulation Specifications	D

Project Categories

A – New products developed and sponsored in conjunction with regional companies

B – New products developed independently by class participation

C – New markets, distributorships, and exporting of products of regional companies

D – Technical and business information services

- Providing regional businesses with assistance that can enhance their commercial competitiveness and thus offer the potential for expansion and increased employment.
- Providing a forum and focal point for contacts between dislocated worker participants, participants, and businesses, and between existing businesses, thereby enhancing the competitiveness of all parties.

The Center for Commercial Competitiveness has developed and delivered an innovative, customized, modern business-oriented curriculum to fifty-five dislocated workers. This curriculum has been documented to facilitate replication for future groups, businesses, and other regions. In addition, its staff members are working with the Agile Manufacturing Enterprise Forum (AMEF) work groups to develop competitiveness enhancement training.

Self-directed teams and individuals are working on projects with existing businesses, working to establish new businesses, or both. Several of these teams are industry sponsored, performing a task under the direct guidance of a business. Some teams are industry affiliated and pursuing a project in conjunction with a potential business partner. Other teams are developing new businesses with the objective of supplying products or services to specific markets.

Core competency assessments were conducted with four businesses in the region to establish and refine the process and methodology. As a result of favorable responses by these companies, this activity will be continued as part of the information services project with businesses. Finally, through multiple avenues, the center is effectively fulfilling its mission to serve as a forum for information exchange and communication between industry, academia, and government in ways that enhance the public-private partnership.

Participant Outcomes

Overall, the first-run results reveal that 86 percent of the fifty-eight credited entrants in the program are now economically productive to varying degrees, albeit a few are working in low-income situations. Thirty-four people are credited with having completed the program, including two who left shortly before the end because of an opportunity that would not wait. Of these, twenty are operating in a teamed or autonomous venture. Fourteen are pursuing initiatives of their own, either in addition to a center project or as their sole venture. These range from specific projects to consulting services. Twenty-four of those who began the program did not complete it. Eighteen dropped out because they found employment or needed to concentrate full time on finding employment for economic reasons. A few dropped out because they did not fit into the team approach that the program tried to foster or were otherwise incompatible with the program's objectives.

Stipend Policy Outcomes

The stipend policy is important to discuss, in part because of the way it was administered and in part because of the effect it had on the program. Overall, stipends are viewed in retrospect as a well-intentioned but poor idea. The intent is obvious: to allow program participants who are no longer receiving unemployment compensation to be in the program and focus on its objectives. But there are two significant concerns with stipend payments, as there are with state-provided training dollars that flow to those in the program. The first is that some number of people will come into the program purely because of the ability to tap these funds and will leave as soon as they are no longer provided. In other words, they are there for the support money, not for the program. The second concern is that sooner or later, these payments will stop and when they do, those who have become dependent on them will drop out of the program.

The center paid stipends from funds contributed by industry primarily for sponsored project work. Stipends were paid to people who met the criteria established by the participants. The control that drove reasonable criteria was that the amount of money was stipulated and limited. In order to stay away from the thorny issue of evaluating individuals' contributions to the progress of the work, payments were strictly on a needs-related and attendance basis.

Overall, while they may have had a momentary positive effect on the participation of a few, stipends are seen as a detriment to true progress and are not being carried into the next program run. As a part of the entrance process, individuals will be required to reveal in some detail how they intend to sustain themselves while they are in the program and for long enough to attain their early objectives.

Screening and Selection Outcomes

The program has clearly demonstrated that the makeup of the center's class—the participants' skills, expectations, and motivations—are keys to a successful program, of equal importance to the program content itself. The program has also demonstrated that there are two clear objectives of the outreach, screening, and selection process:

1. To obtain a high-quality starting group of dislocated workers with the intrinsic skills, experience, and personal characteristics needed to effectively participate and solidly contribute to achieving the program objectives.
2. To be absolutely sure at the outset that the expectations, motivations, goals, and staying power of participants match and are fully compatible with the approach, plan, and demands of the long program.

The first objective was generally met, with a few exceptions: the participant group was too homogeneous and more emphasis is needed on finding participants with strong marketing and front-end-of-the-business skills. The second objective was not met for some participants because of a complex combination of perceptions and expectation coupled with an underestimation of the level of personal and family stress that arises after long periods of unemployment, especially when unemployment benefits have been exhausted. Basically, all dislocated workers have a common goal and pressing need: to receive financial compensation at a high enough level to attain a reasonable comfort level. Outreach and selection effectiveness can be improved by increasing emphasis on exploring, measuring, and discussing these aspects throughout the process and focusing on attracting and selecting those dislocated workers who:

- Want to achieve their goals by starting their own enterprise or being part of a start-up enterprise.
- Realize that, in the center's approach, their financial goals will not be reached in a short period of time.
- Have resources and overall staying power for this entrepreneurial process of developing a new business.

It is probably unrealistic, although desirable, to expect that participants, once in the program, will discontinue their search for outside employment. It is, however, very appropriate and important that during the selection process, candidates be informed that they are expected to spend a much higher level of energy on the program than on finding an immediate job. Reemployment, however, will always be an attrition factor; unfortunately, it is often the very best and most qualified participants who are most likely to receive offers.

Participant Characteristics and Program Barriers

Certain aspects of participants' work experience adversely affected the motivational and behavioral aspects of the group:

- Many participants had a narrow technical, manufacturing, process based background.
- Many had a highly specialized, narrowly focused career.
- Many were not accustomed to making decisions and had been told exactly what to do for most of their careers.

For many, the experience was also affected by the personal impact of unemployment:

- Many were personally hurt and severely damaged as a result of being laid off from productive, high-paying jobs through no fault of their own.
- Self-esteem and confidence levels were low.
- Many had major financial responsibilities that demanded a near-term return to comfortable income levels.
- Some were wary and distrustful of others.
- Sharing of ideas was difficult for some, the perception being that a possible employment opportunity might be lost to someone else.

Some of these, mainly the work experience characteristics, were recognized and, to some extent, can be improved during the selection process. The impact of unemployment, although somewhat anticipated, was not fully known until the dynamics of team behavior and projects were experienced. These concerns must be considered normal for a dislocated worker group and realistically addressed from the outset.

The original participant group was so homogeneous that

needed skills were not adequately represented. Most of the participants were engineers supporting defense manufacturing. There were few individuals with a marketing, finance, or management background. As the development phase unfolded, it became apparent that many teams did not know what to do when it came to these critical areas. Staff frequently offered suggestions, but the territory was so unfamiliar that team members failed to complete actions, thus jeopardizing the entire project. The center will try to ensure a more heterogeneous participant group through outreach and selection targeting for a more even distribution of skill sets.

The work experience of the participant group was so narrowly defined within a large corporation that frequently participants had no idea about the big picture of business processes. The concept of risk was also perceived differently when participants began to realize that they might be required to use some of their own resources to bring their concept to reality. As the concept of risk became more personal, many participant teams became incapable of making decisions, again jeopardizing the project. The center will attempt to personalize the risk concept during the selection process, especially in the interviewing stage during the next round.

A discussion of the concept of risk leads to the question of the level of commitment on the part of individual participants. Commitment was addressed in each interview through questions relating to the applicants' desire to start their own business. All applicants who were invited to participate convincingly demonstrated a strong level of commitment to becoming new business owners. However, the perception of participants changed during the course of the program as people discovered all the general skills they would need to develop to start and maintain a business. One participant verbalized this change of perception by stating that the program had demonstrated for him that starting a business was the wrong thing for him to do. The center will attempt to control this variable through the application process by asking precise questions about an applicant's idea for a business and the steps the applicant has taken to bring this idea to reality.

Outside pressures had a particularly destructive impact on participants' ability to focus on enterprise development. Many participants were at the end of their financial rope and received daily pressure from family members to do something to generate income. Several participants left the course early to accept job offers because of this pressure. Other participants were forced to take low-paying second-shift jobs to accommodate bread-and-butter issues. Some participants stayed in the training program only as long as stipends were paid. The center has developed several methods to attempt to control for this variable: direct questioning during the interview process regarding an applicant's ability to participate in the program without financial assistance; interviews involving the applicant's key family members, focusing on expectations; frequent open houses for family members to demonstrate project progress.

The original training program was designed to result in self-directed teams of participant groups. The center realizes that this is an unrealistic goal because the training program does not provide the time or the specific focus that enables self-directed teams to form. There are also personal dynamics that impact the success of a team-oriented program: the individual participant's experience and comfort with making decisions, accepting leadership roles, level of self-esteem, and ability to trust others. The next training program will focus on entrepreneurial training with the possibility of participant teams, but there will be much more direction and reporting to administration than in the original program.

The outcome of the formal training program will be a written business plan. The center is currently assembling a group of venture capitalists, industry representatives, and more traditional funding agencies who will review the business plans. This new process element should provide viable financial underpinnings for several projects.

Conclusions

The Department of Labor demonstration program has validated the concept that a designed integration of dislocated workers, entrepreneurial competitiveness training, and regional industries will create jobs for the participants and provide a viable model and mechanism for defense conversion and regional economic development. New business enterprises with a broad range of maturity have developed, and positive progress has been made toward achieving the center's goals. Hard programmatic factors and many softer aspects, mainly centering on the motivational and behavioral nature of dislocated worker teams, have surfaced during the program along with identified improvements and recommended changes. These will be incorporated in the second program, Worker Enterprise Development, which will allow a sharpened focus on the methods for job creation through facilitated entrepreneurism.

Additional Readings

Davidow, W., & Malone, M. (1992.) *The virtual corporation.* New York: HarperCollins.

Iacocca Institute. (1992). *21st century manufacturing enterprise strategy* (2 vols.). Lehigh, PA: Lehigh University.

Katzenbach, J., & Smith, D. (1993). *The wisdom of teams.* Boston: Harvard Business School Press.

Prahalad, C., & Hamel, G. (1990, May-June). The core competence of the corporation. *Harvard Business Review.*

Stalk, G., Evans, P., & Shulman, L. (1992, March-April). Competing on capabilities: The new rules of corporate strategy. *Harvard Business Review.*

CHAPTER 11

Engaging Displaced Employees in Retraining and Job Creation

Gerrit Wolf
Joseph M. Pufahl
Jeff Casey
Manuel London

This chapter describes the JOBS project ideas and implementation over two semesters. The project was designed to meet two pressing needs: to help displaced defense industry engineers become managers of new technologies, and to orient high-technology firms, both old ones from the defense industry and new ones in growing industries, become productive and competitive in the global marketplace. Because the JOBS project has no precedent, descriptive details are presented to guide future work, but quantitative results are provided for both semesters to assess what worked.

The project was planned in the spring of 1992, when we discussed the problems that Long Island businesses had in adjusting to the changing defense economy and the opportunity this meant for the Harriman School for Management and Policy at the State University of New York, Stony Brook. At the time, the first author had ideas about building an executive management center, and the second author had sold his business to seek new directions for his career. Wolf is an organizational psychologist and human resource specialist with extensive knowledge of business disciplines and considerable academic administrative experience, helpful for designing and implementing the academic part of the program. Pufahl had business connections as an entrepreneur useful for developing internships and government connections helpful for funding the project.

Both had similar views on Long Island businesses and the university. First, businesses needed to become quality driven to satisfy the customer in a competitive, nondefense marketplace. Second, the university had methods and technologies to improve products and processes, but the bridge between the university and the Long Island business community needed to be built. Third, the relationship had to be developed one business at a time as the university helped solve major problems each business was facing.

These views led to the cooperation of four groups for mutual benefit. Displaced engineers from the Grumman and AIL corporations and their subcontractors needed to get back into the workforce. High-tech firms on Long Island needed to become more competitive in the commercial market because of a downturn in the defense industry. The labor departments from Suffolk County and the town of Oyster Bay needed to spend federally allocated Job Training Partnership Act money in a training program for them. The Harriman School for Management and Policy, a relatively young professional school with undergraduate and graduate programs, needed to grow in reputation and support through additional services to the business community. The JOBS project was the result of a strategic alliance among these four groups.

The Plan

The traditional employment model separates and misreads the needs of the unemployed, university, firm, and government. The linkages are left to the initiative of each player to search and negotiate with each other. The unemployed get help from outplacement services in terms of career counseling and government for unemployment insurance. Universities recruit and place students through job banks and offer consulting to business. Businesses recruit potential employees and hire universities to consult. Government provides unemployment insurance and training for the less skilled. This model works when the economy is growing; it breaks down when the economy contracts, businesses downsize, and markets change.

The traditional employment model focuses on developing and matching technical skills of the (engineering) employee with the requirements for technical skills by the firm. Potential employees are expected to be able to adjust and adapt easily to different industrial markets and cultures. Moving from a defense culture to a competitive market culture is not a problem, according to the traditional model. The unemployed need only technical updating, and this need has been applied only to the high school graduate or dropout in this model. Growing the firm is the job of management, not the technical employee.

The JOBS project is innovative. It integrates the players through technical retraining and managerial culture change required of businesses and employees. It shifts the focus for:

- *Unemployed engineers,* from job search to job creation.
- *University,* from technical retraining to technology management.
- *Business,* from high dependence on government funding to productive independence in the competitive markets.
- *Government,* from funding the retraining of high school dropouts to funding the reeducation of college graduates.

To make these shifts requires the integration of graduate education and career counseling, technical and managerial training, education and placement, and it calls for coordinating separate government programs for unemployment insurance and retraining.

Education and counseling can be integrated through a course that addresses the emotional needs of the students and focuses on career and culture change in the new workplace. Also, professional and career counseling must be available or integrated into the course itself.

Technical and managerial education can be integrated with instruction made to look and feel like transition employment. Because displaced engineers had worked nine to five, the JOBS project was designed with a full educational day from nine to five. Three of the hours were in the classroom with a faculty member, and five hours were with a graduate student mentor or lab supervisor. Homework was done during the lab hours in the library or computer room. This nine-to-five day, five days a week, created full-immersion education, simulated the workday, and fostered managerial behavior. It also satisfied government's requirement to track time; the engineers signed in and out each day.

Education and placement can be merged to implement the idea of job creation through value-added behavior. Four days a week engineers would take classes; on the fifth day they participated in a practicum or internship seminar. Businesses with a major problem came to the university to meet in seminar with a group of engineers; the engineers contracted or interned at the firm to solve the problem.

A major business problem was defined as worth $200,000 to the firm in terms of increased market effectiveness (share, revenue), decreased cost, or increased quality. The firm presented the problem as a live case, to be discussed, analyzed, worked on, and solved by the engineers. The solution demonstrated to the engineers and the business the value-added process. The engineers had the opportunity to convert value-added behavior into a job. These jobs would be worth $40,000 to $50,000, often less than the engineers had earned when employed by a defense industry firm. This figure was chosen as a target because it showed the magnitude of value added: a $200,000 problem solved by a $50,000 investment.

Government and the university came into partnership to adapt a funding program for high school technicians to funding graduate education. The government had to learn about academics offering complete education, different than instructors offering auto or TV repair. The university had to learn to live with paperwork documenting time spent by students and to have funding dependent on the employment of graduates.

First-Semester Implementation

Admissions Process

Prospects for the JOBS project were recruited in a variety of ways. First, a marketing firm was hired to help with brochure design, ads in newspapers and on radio, and media promotion. Then, the county departments of labor mailed information to all qualified applicants in their databases. Also, the two major defense companies, Grumman and AIL, mailed information to all the engineers laid off in the last six months. Last, the engineering professional societies promoted the project through mailings and newsletters.

All of these methods were used because the project had a short lead time. On July 1, 1992, Suffolk County endorsed the plan's concept but without an enrollment commitment. After negotiation and lobbying, confirmation on the support of forty engineers by Suffolk County and twenty engineers by Oyster Bay was received on July 15. The project was scheduled to start on August 10 with the orientation/communication course. Time was of the essence.

Admissions seminars were conducted for groups of ten to twenty applicants. During the two hours, the plan for the project was outlined and discussed. Applications were filled out and connections to support from the labor departments were made. The seminar stressed the focus on job creation through the practicum process, the development of technical and managerial skills in graduate courses, and the innovative orientation and placement processes.

Suffolk County and the town of Oyster Bay, acting on behalf of Nassau County, funded applicants to the program, at an expected cost of $7,560 per student (based on a student spending forty hours a week for nineteen weeks at $10 an hour reimbursement to the university.) After applicants were qualified academically, based on engineering degrees and experience, the counties needed to qualify each applicant for funding. This process was easier for those referred by the counties. Others faced the red tape of getting qualified. While applicants' cost of the program was paid by the county, living expenses were the responsibility of the engineers, and came from unemployment insurance payments, savings, and spousal support. Applicants found this to be a problem if sources of funds would run out before the end of the semester long program.

Of the 150 applicants, 93 did not qualify for funding because of prior funding or because their firm was not a subcontractor of Grumman or AIL, or because they did not have the resources to live on for a semester. The 57 admittees had a range of characteristics (see Table 11.1).

Selection issues for the program included concerns about age discrimination, managerial potential, and computer literacy. As

Table 11.1. Characteristics of First-Semester Participants.

Age	26-39: 39	40-66: 28		
Race	White: 50	Black: 3	Asian: 3	Hispanic: 1
Gender	Male: 51	Female: 6		
Months Unemployed	Three: 4	Six: 18	Nine: 22	Twelve/or more: 13
Advanced Degree	None: 50	M.S.: 3	M.B.A: 3	P.h.D.: 1

Table 11.1 suggests, the average age of applicants was forty-eight. There were concerns about whether participants with twenty years or more of experience (about one third of the group) could adapt to the entrepreneurial job-creation focus of the program. Half had managerial experience but in a bureaucratic setting of extensive rules, few cost constraints, and demands driven by a single customer, rather than a market. While three quarters reported computer experience, it was not hands-on experience. Most did not know how to use a PC and were rigid about learning how to use it.

Career Counseling

After participants were selected, questionnaire data were collected about their career interests, managerial styles, and biographical history. Then before the semester started, all participants took an intensive three-week orientation/communication course. In this course they planned their careers and wrote resumes, played the role of a manager in business games and group problem-solving exercises, and learned for the first time or increased skills in the use of business software in the computer lab.

Most participants experienced phases of anger, denial, and learning during the program. One purpose of the orientation course was to address these emotional processes.

- *The first two hours* each day for fifteen days addressed emotions through case discussion, role plays, and career assessment and planning. Many engineers described themselves by the projects they had worked on rather than the skills they had. They saw the world in closed loops with little room for uncertainty, rather than in terms of new opportunities. They tended to demand that jobs like their old ones be found during this program. During this time career planning exercises were used and the tracks described by faculty teaching in the track. After counseling, the engineers chose their tracks, with the result of twelve to sixteen engineers in a track.

• *The second two hours* were spent in the computer lab learning business software by doing problems. For most, they had less experience than reported on their application, and they felt uncomfortable with doing the work. Many did not like the inductive approach to teaching and showed little ability to problem solve. Those with more knowledge were encouraged to help those less skilled. Some cooperated but many did not.

• *The third two hours,* immediately after lunch, focused on cases and role playing using the group's problem-solving skills. Their typical approach was assertive and nonlistening, reflecting experience in the bureaucratic defense industry. Cooperative problem solving did not come naturally. In addition, their assertive behavior produced defensive communication of a win-lose style, rather than win-win.

• *The last two hours* teams worked on a business game. The first ten days, most teams bankrupted their simulated firms. The engineers did not understand how a market economy worked. We taught them microeconomics and how price, advertising, production, and sales related to each other. Most succeeded in playing the game profitably by the end of the three weeks. All wrote a business plan for playing the game.

Frustration often led to anger in the classroom; five engineers left the program during the orientation course and were replaced with others. After the semester started, three or four people had deep emotional problems that needed professional help. In contrast, there were half a dozen who became team leaders, reaching out to pull fellow students along.

At the end of the course the engineers selected one of the four tracks. This selection involved counseling and consideration of technical, managerial, computing, and job opportunity interests and skills. Some chose the area closest to their present expertise, and others chose an area that they always had wanted to study.

Education

Four alternative tracks were offered, based on discussions with Long Island businesses and academics across the University. The criteria for defining the tracks were the need for the skills in industry and the availability of course offerings in the university. Four tracks were selected for the program:

1. *Manufacturing Track:* quality improvement, operations management, computer integrated manufacturing, and management of information system principles (substitute business strategy for MIS in the spring).
2. *Management Information Systems:* systems design, expert systems, principles of management information systems, and finance.
3. *Environment and Waste Management:* environmental issues, principles of waste management, legalities of environmental policy, hydrology.
4. *Materials Analysis:* electron microscope, operations management, quality improvement, and finance.

Courses were selected from a variety of divisions across the university: biology (electron microscope); engineering (environmental issues, quality improvement, and computer integrated manufacturing systems); the Harriman School (communications, operations management, management information systems principles, expert systems, systems design, finance, and business strategy); marine sciences (principles of waste management and legalities of environmental policy); and physical sciences (hydrology). This was necessary in order to offer the engineers the best in technology and management knowledge. While courses came from across the university, they were offered in a single location to create an identity for the program.

All classes were located in Harriman Hall of the management

school. One classroom was dedicated solely for use by the program for teaching and study. Two other classrooms were used substantially by the project but shared with courses in the school. The electron microscope and computer integrated manufacturing labs in engineering were used three hours a week each. The computer lab in Harriman was expanded and shared with Harriman students.

Most courses used cases. Case analysis did not come easily and naturally to the engineers, who felt they lacked sufficient information to find the solution. Case analysis worked better using small-group discussion with feedback from the instructor. It worked less well when the engineer was required to work individually and write up the analysis. Many had trouble crossing the bridge from engineering, where specifications constrain the problem, to management, in which the constraints are fewer and vague, yet a decision is required.

Trade-offs were demanded when practica and site visits conflicted with regular course meetings. Many did not like to make the decision between class and the desired field experience. The field experiences were not exploited fully through preparation of questions and background information. The engineers failed to grasp that the field situation provided the opportunity to impress a potential employer. Showing a potential employer how one's knowledge and skills applied seemed like salesmanship, a technique that most shied from.

Assessment of faculty and meetings of faculty were held periodically throughout the term. Systematic student feedback showed that students liked faculty and situations that were highly structured, provided a small activity that allowed for positive feedback, and encouraged the engineer to have some control of the situation. Situations that fell into this category were the quality and MIS courses and the orientation/communication course. Faculty who provided little or negative feedback about ill-structured cases made the engineers feel out of control and unable to learn. Situations that fell into this category were term projects, cases requiring work individually, and practica.

Of the fifty-seven entering engineers, five dropped out to accept jobs, and nine withdrew for personal reasons. The remaining forty-three received certificates in technology management for completing the academic work.

Placement Processes

Traditional placement assumes there are jobs for the applicant to choose. The function focuses on helping the applicants portray their skills and experience in the most effective fashion for the employer. In the JOBS program this function was added to in significant ways because of few jobs.

First was the use of practica in which firms presented problems to the engineers, who then were engaged by the firm as an intern to solve the problem. A firm would take an hour to present a case problem to a small group of engineers. The engineers were expected to respond in writing how they would approach the problem. Then consulting contracts were encouraged to have the engineer work only on a specific project. These steps provided a basis for the firm and the engineer to get to know each other at low cost.

More than twenty firms were recruited through personal visits to participate, and over half of these presented one or more problems to a group of engineers. The firms ranged in size from five employees to four thousand, with a median of fifty. They are categorized by industry and presenting problem as follows:

Industry

Light manufacturing	5
Aircraft	4
Electronics	4
Environment	4
Biomedical instruments	3
Computing	3
Systems design	3
Consumer products	2
Health care	2

Problem

Manufacturing efficiency	9
Strategy and growth	8
Handling of chlorofluorocarbons	4
Unknown	9

Among the problems brought by these firms to the practica for the engineers to work on, along with engineers' responses, were the following:

1. A medium-size manufacturing firm showed the need for engineering and development of a device to analyze for and prevent gaps in adhesive coatings. Three engineers developed a device, tested it, and may market the device to the industry via a joint venture.
2. A unique application of bar coding for process control of materials, quality, and system utilization in real time was demonstrated by the same firm. Engineers suggested the most recent software designs for improving efficiency and have taken on a new project at a large firm that saw the presentation.
3. An MIS engineer with a marketing and bar code background joined with another bar code consultant, who made a presentation on opportunities in using bar codes, to market asset management software and is developing a business plan.
4. A firm presented a problem in developing the plan for cells or group manufacturing. The engineers did the analysis as a field project for the firm, which was predicted to result in a 100 percent increase in output. An engineer in the spring class will intern with the firm to expand the cellular concept to short-run jobs.
5. The firm also presented a problem of choosing a new CIMS system to manage its manufacturing. The engineers did a field analysis and made a proposal that included a screen modeling of the new system and a demo using the Harriman computer lab. The company is considering seriously the proposal, which may be used by the engineers as a springboard for the development of a consulting firm to other small manufacturers.
6. The firm also presented a problem of cracking with ABS injection-molded products it made. The engineers designed an experiment using the electron microscope to test for contamination in reused plastic that is mixed with new plastic. The company created a production control manager's job for one of the engineers from the JOBS project.
7. A firm manufacturing small pumps demonstrated a ferrous magnetic noncontact pump for aquariums and ponds. It chal-

lenged the engineers to develop this pump design for larger pumps and markets. No engineering response.

8. This company also presented the problem of developing an MIS and cost system to help it develop as a cost-driven firm. A group of engineers met with the company and were eventually unsuccessful in their efforts to design an MIS system.

9. A company that designs restraint systems for military aircraft wanted to meet the requirement of the Israeli Air Force for a lightweight, five-point restraint system and an electronically interfaced inertial system. The company, with the assistance from other engineers, submitted a proposal for the system. The engineers are in the proposal as subcontractors for alternative approaches to the system. The proposal is pending.

10. A research and testing firm discussed a contract it had won from the Air Force to find a replacement for chlorofluorocarbon (CFC) propellant cleaner. Several engineers interviewed for the position of lead researcher on the project, and one engineer submitted a paper on a test methodology he developed as part of a term project in an environmental course.

11. Three other firms presented to practica the need for replacing the CFCs. This led to the design of a regional workshop on the replacement of CFCs in printed circuit board manufacturing, organized by the engineers and jointly sponsored by the Harriman School for Management and Policy and the university's College of Engineering. More than twenty-five firms attended.

12. A firm presented a shop floor and systems design problem in the use of a replacement for the CFCs used for decreasing aircraft gas actuator systems. The engineers through a project designed the system.

13. The world's leader in frequency oscillators and time standards presented five problems to the engineers as part of a tour of the plant. The problems included replacing CFCs, low product yield in final manufacturing, the development of surface mount technology, aluminum welding problems, and conformal coatings for encapsulation. The company pursued some of these problems with the engineering college and several other firms that have similar problems and offered an internship for a JOBS engineer for the spring to work on a database and documentation for ISO 9000 standards.

14. A company had a CFC problem and participated in the spring conference. It was also put in touch with the BETA project on medical devices in the medical school. The company is seriously considering going into the device business.

15. A company presented a problem in getting desired reliability in wave soldering. Engineers suggested various experimental research designs and variables to locate the cause of the unreliability.

16. A computer manufacturing firm discussed its just-in-time system and sought help in developing an expert scheduling system for daily manpower. One engineer is pursuing a proposal with the company.

17. An automobile steering wheel manufacturing company now makes 25 percent of the steering wheels in the country and plans to double in size in the next five years. It presented MIS problems in tracking and scheduling. Engineers toured the plant and one was hired who supervised a group of interns on the project in the spring.

18. A small engineering consulting firm in the environmental field had growth issues. One engineer was hired for a part-time position but has actually been working full time.

19. A facility tour of a local town's landfill operations by the engineers in the environmental track led to a job offer because of questions one participant asked on the tour.

20. The region's major utility had a program initiative in research that led two engineers to propose original research on preventive gas maintenance. The proposed research was combined with a proposal for complementary research to be conducted at the Long Island Lighting Company by Harriman faculty members. The project was funded within a month.

21. A small firm that monitors indoor air quality developed a range of air sensors for contaminants. The firm needed technical writers, programmers, and mechanical engineering help. Several engineers expressed interest in developing a relationship, but never delivered on promised work. Harriman faculty continue to give advice on the development of its distribution system.

22. Eight of the engineers from the environmental track were

allowed to take the environmental engineering civil service exams after several requests by a program director and faculty member. Three eventually got jobs because of passing the exam.

Practica were held every Friday starting in the middle of the semester. While there were written guidelines for a practicum, they were rarely followed, for several reasons. For one thing, engineers view them as taking up valuable study time, and they did not know how to tackle the ambiguous problems brought by business. The engineer would see the problem as uninteresting and claim there was no job because the firm did not frame a job. Problems needed research, but were rarely tackled in a systemic fashion, such as through experimental design, field research design, or systematic review of the literature. The process of reaching a contract between the firm and the engineer was unfamiliar and emotionally too difficult for many of the engineers.

A second approach helped the engineers network. Faculty through the courses in the program took engineers on field trips to Brookhaven National Laboratory and introduced them to their collegial networks. Engineers were invited to attend several major conferences at no cost, including the Long Island Environmental Show with 50 companies, the Long Island Quality Conference with 400 firms, and the University Beta Conference on biomedical devices. Guest speakers—Jack Bierwirth, retired CEO of Grumman; Phil Palmedo, CEO of Long Island Research Institute; and Mike Daly, entrepreneur—made presentations about approaches to job creation.

A third approach was instituted at the end of the semester to substitute for the lack of initiative in the practica and to try to build relationships with firms. Career counselors from the university and a professional outplacement firm provided counseling about resumes, job search, presentations, and so on. Interviews were done with thirteen of the forty-three who wanted help with career interests and goals. Guides to the job-creation, value-added approach to firms were offered. All engineers who had not landed a position by the end of the semester were requested to come to the project office twelve hours a week for up to three months for help in networking with business and continued counseling.

Employment

By the time of graduation four participants had created jobs, five had dropped out of the program to take full-time jobs, and nine had dropped out for personal and family reasons, most by the first third of the semester. By six months after graduation, thirteen had created full-time employment. Seven participants retired, nine quit searching, and the remaining eleven were working part time trying to find or create full-time employment. (See Table 11.2.)

Table 11.2. Results for the First Semester.

Students by Track (% of 57 total)	Materials 16 (.28)	Environment 15 (.26)	MIS 14 (.25)	CIMS 12 (.21)
Graduates by Track (% of track total)	Materials 12 (.75)	Environment 14 (.93)	MIS 8 (.57)	MS 9 (.75)
Education Completion (% of 57 total)	Graduated 43 (.75)	**Dropped out** For Job 5 (.09)	Personal 5 (.09)	Family 4 (.07)
Education Performance (% of 43 graduates)	License 5 (.09)	Masters 2 (.04)	High Grades 30 (.56)	Incomplete Course 28 (.53)
Job Creation (% of 57 total)	Interned 13 (.23)	Consulted 13 (.23)	Networked 12 (.21)	Entrepreneured 8 (.14)
Career Orientation (% of 57 total)	Nonresistant 30 (.53)	Active 21 (.37)	Computer Literacy 32 (.57)	Career Plan 34 (.60)
Employment Outcome (% of 57 total)	Full Time 22 (.39)	Part Time/ Temporary 11 (.19)	Quit Search 8 (.14)	Retired 7 (.12)
Quality of Employment (% of 57 total)	Salary 20 (.35)	Timely 19 (.32)	Underemployed 9 (.16)	
Employment by Track (% of track totals)	Materials 4 (.25)	Environment 6 (.40)	MIS 6 (.43)	CIMS 6 (.50)

Second-Semester Implementation

The second semester changed based on what we learned from the first semester. We took in fewer students, focused on personal change aided by professionals, formed a single track of education, and immersed students in a facilitated internship with potential employers.

Admission

The second semester was scheduled to start the end of January, one month after the finish of the fall semester, with a second set of engineers. The county and town were reluctant to continue to commit to fund the program because most of the engineers from the first semester were not reemployed. Suffolk County eventually agreed to fund a group of twenty engineers for the second semester. With less than a week to go before the start of the semester, fifteen displaced engineers were recruited with only a few referred by the county. All were white males.

Career Counseling

Career counseling was divided into three parts over the semester, in contrast to three intensive weeks before the fall semester. The change was made for practical reasons, and also because the first semester indicated the engineers needed continual professional support throughout the semester.

In the first seven weeks, an hour and a half a week were allocated to group counseling conducted by a professional social worker. In this setting, the engineers dealt with their anger and depression from the layoff and frustrations with the process of changing careers. The remaining seven weeks, an hour and a half a week were allocated to career counseling including insight, development, and planning, conducted by an outplacement professional. These two parts directly and more effectively dealt with personal change problems, as reported by the engineers.

Training in the use of business software on PCs was given for two hours each week for four weeks, and then individual help was provided the rest of the semester. This counseling focused the engineers on business information systems.

Group problem-solving material, which had been part of the fall communication course, was moved for the spring semester to the business strategy course and integrated with the facilitated internship. This change was key to making the internship effective.

Education

A single track of manufacturing management included courses in operations management, computer integrated manufacturing systems, total quality management, and business strategy (in place of management of information systems.) Business strategy became the vehicle for the facilitated internship. Each course met once a week for three hours, and students studied together for the remaining hours each day, forming a nine-to-five day.

Total quality was the most well-received course the second semester, because the instructor had industry experience and had taught the course previously. Computer integrated manufacturing systems used a laboratory in engineering and was taught by a practitioner. The engineers liked the technical nature of the course, but the use of the laboratory conflicted with uses of the lab by the engineering school. The operations management course was taught by an outstanding engineering student from the first semester, who had made the emotional and cultural shift but turned out to have trouble helping her fellow students make the shift.

The strategy course focused on the businesses for which the students interned. Each business was a case with a student bringing fresh information about the business to each class. Students were exposed to guest experts in strategy and discussed common strategic problems across their live cases. These included resource assessment within a firm and in the market, analysis of objectives of firms in the market, and negotiation of alternative deals.

Placement

The facilitated internship replaced the practicum from the first semester. Firms from the first semester practica were recruited to take on interns. After two weeks of the semester, students had been exposed to internship possibilities and were required to select one firm or problem to work on the rest of the semester. By the third week, eleven students were spending two days each week working on a firm's $200,000 problem; ten different firms were represented. Four students had left the program by this point to take a certified engineering network course that was shorter, less demanding, and with a high probability of employment. Those that stayed in the program showed increased motivation because of the internship.

Finding solutions to the problems on which each worked was only part of the learning. As important was learning the culture of the firm, making connections with employees, and ultimately negotiating a job with the firm. Each of these steps took coaching from each other and the instructor, resulting in a change of attitude from their experience in the defense industry.

Employment

Three more students dropped out during the semester because they found jobs. The remaining eight students completed the coursework and spent three weeks after the semester ended working full time on the internship. Six of the eight turned the internships into full-time positions.

Analysis of Results

Employment results for both semesters are reported in Table 11.3. Three facts stand out. First, 40 percent became reemployed whether the program was completed or not. Second, the percentage rose to almost 50 percent in the first semester for those who entered an internship. Third, the percentage reached 75 percent the second semester for those who completed the facilitated internship.

To understand the effect of career actions, job-creation behaviors, and educational activity on employment results, a scale was defined to measure each of these factors. A checklist of twenty-two behaviors was used as items for the scales. Each item was judged present or absent for each engineer by the program administrators, using attendance, psychological, biographical, and class performance information available in the students' file.

The employment results scale (alpha = .64) consisted of the sum of the items measuring the presence or absence of full-time

Table 11.3. Comparison of First- and Second-Semester Results.

	Semester 1	Semester 2	Total
Students	57	15	72
Program Dropouts	14	7	21
Quit/retired	9 (.62)	4 (.57)	13 (.60)
Full-time work	5 (.38)	3 (.43)	8 (.40)
Graduating	43	8	51
Quit/retired	15 (.35)	1 (.125)	16 (.31)
Part-time	11 (.26)	1 (.125)	12 (.25)
Full-time	17 (.39)	6 (.75)	23 (.44)
Without interning	30	0	30
Quit/retired	13 (.43)	0	13 (.43)
Part-time	6 (.20)	0	6 (.20)
Full-time	11 (.37)	0	11 (.37)
With Interning	13	8	21
Quit/retired	2 (.16)	1 (.125)	3 (.14)
Part-time	5 (.38)	1 (.125)	6 (.29)
Full-time	6 (.46)	6 (.75)	12 (.57)

employment, part-time employment, timeliness of job acquisition, salary adequacy, minus the presence or absence of dropout status, underemployment, quitting search, and retirement. The job-creation scale (alpha = .69) summed the presence or absence of interning, consulting, entrepreneuring, and networking. The career behavior scale (alpha = .66) added the presence or absence of nonresistance, career proactivity, computer literacy, and career plan interviewing. The education scale (alpha = .63) was defined as the sum of the presence or absence of certificate completion, high grades, enrollment in further education, and licensing exam enrollment, less the presence or absence of not completing a course.

Means, standard deviations, and correlations among behavioral scales and six attitude scales collected at the program's beginning are reported in Table 11.4. The attitude scales included locus of control, self-esteem, anger, career insight, personal resilience, and career identity. The behavioral scales tended to correlate with each other, while the attitudinal scales tended to correlate weakly with each other and with the behavioral scales.

Table 11.4. Scales of Behavior and Attitudes.

Means, Standard Deviations, and Correlations of Behaviors and Attitudes

		Mean	S.D.	(1)	(2)	(3)	(4)	(5)	(6)	(7)	(8)	(9)	(10)
Results behaviors	(1)	.60	2.33		22	43	52	13	08	15	-07	-11	-05
Educational behavior	(2)	2.02	1.26		100	44	49	04	10	-04	-09	-16	-16
Job-creation behavior	(3)	1.21	1.22			100	52	00	08	-02	-08	04	00
Career behaviors	(4)	1.58	1.28				100	02	08	08	-22	-15	01
Locus of control	(5)	4.36	.76					100	40	18	-12	-08	-44
Self-esteem	(6)	5.53	.95						100	45	18	24	-71
Resilience	(7)	3.71	.54							100	23	40	02
Identity	(8)	2.99	.88								100`	59	08
Insight	(9)	3.18	.79									100	10
Anger	(10)	2.30	.52										100

Table 11.5 reports regression analysis tests of predictors of employment results, predicted positively by job creation and career behavior scales. Also, resilience, only one of several attitudinal variables, and age were significant in predicting the employment results scale. The more resilient and the younger the engineer, the better the employment results. There were no differences in effects between semesters, and no effects of the education scale directly on the results scale.

Job-creation behavior and career activity scales were regressed on the education activity scale and six attitudinal variables. Edu-

Table 11.5. Regression Tests of the New Employment Model.

Results = - 2.09 - .60(Age) + .36(Career Behavior) + .31 (Job Creation)

$(SE = 1.06)$ $(SE = .31)$ $(SE = .12)$ $(SE = .13)$

$(t = -1.97)^*$ $(t = 1.90)^*$ $(t = 3.07)^*$ $(t = 2.33)^*$

- .06(Education) + .48(Resilience)

$(SE = .18)$ $(SE = .28)$

$(t = -.35)$ $(t = 1.69)^*$

	SS	df	MS	F	p	R^2 adj
Model	56.2	5	12.2	7.5	.001	.31
Residual	99.4	66	1.5			

Career Behavior = 2.38 - .47(Age) + .85(Semester) + .84(Education)

$(SE = .43)$ $(SE = .35)$ $(SE = .41)$ $(SE = .17)$

$(t = 5.60)^*$ $(t = -1.35)$ $(t = 2.07)^*$ $(t = 5.01)^*$

	SS	df	MS	F	p	R^2 adj
Model	50.7	3	16.9	9.22	.0001	.26
Residual	124.6	68	1.8			

Job Creation Behavior = .09 + .22(Age) + .45(Semester) + .57(Education)

$(SE = .38)$ $(SE = .31)$ $(SE = .37)$ $(SE = .15)$

$(t = .24)$ $(t = .69)$ $(t = 1.22)$ $(= 3.80)^*$

	SS	df	MS	F	p	R^2 adj
Model	27.3	3	9.1	6.10	.001	.18
Residual	101.4	68	1.5			

$^*p = .01$

cation activity was the only predictor of job-creation scale, and along with semester the only predictor of career behavior scale. None of the attitudinal variables was significant in predicting education, career, or job-creation behavior scales.

In summary, employment results were determined by career and job-creation behaviors, and these in turn were determined by educational activity. Age and psychological resilience in addition predicted employment results but none of the behaviors. The indirect effect of education on results through job-creation and career behavior shows two conclusions: students were as successful at employment by dropping out for jobs as at creating jobs at the end, and job creation and career behavior were determined by the integration of education, job creation, and career behavior in the project.

Discussion

The human resource (HR) practitioner and industrial psychologist have roles to play in each part of a JOBS project: career assessment and educational choice, job-creation design and business recruitment, the design and implementation of technology management education, or the development of funding of projects. The HR specialist could be effective in the firm doing the layoffs, the university offering the program, the firm with a business problem, or the policy planning unit of the funding agency of government.

The pain of unemployment for educated people differs little from the experiences of blue-collar workers. Unemployed workers from the rust belt in the early 1980s found that change was traumatic. It is just as traumatic for white-collar as for blue-collar employees. Personal and career counseling are required, and can be done for academic credit within the university, by the firm planning the layoff, or by an outplacement firm. If a firm decides not to handle the process internally, the firm's HR person should refer displaced employees to universities or outplacement firms with programs to handle the stress and opportunity of career transition.

Dealing with the pain is a complementary, not a substitute, activity for job-creation activity to achieve reemployment. Teaching educated people to be entrepreneurial and create a job is difficult because the change required—learning how to create value—is emotional and cultural, not just technical. The facilitated internship addresses the cultural and technical complexities of successful change in order to create value. Job creation, not job search, is needed in order to achieve employment when business downsizes. The facilitated internship can be managed as a new line of business for the outplacement firm, a new activity called inplacement of the human resource department within a firm facing downsizing, or by a university. There may be more credibility for the program if done by the university with companion reeducation, and the university gets the opportunity to get closer to its customers and donors.

Management education brings together job creation and career activities. The educational process ties new technical knowledge to new ways of managing and creating business development. The human resource faculty person in the university needs to integrate courses from across departments and then provide the support services to give an identity to the courses for the students. Education without job creation or career behavior does not have an impact on employment results. Job creation and career activities without university education can produce employment results, limited by the existing skills of the applicant, and passing up the opportunity for technological transfer from the university to the business.

Businesses adapt when approached about the mutual benefits to the university and the business of working together. This relationship needs to be developed at the personal level by someone who understands business and the university. Job creation by the engineer needs to be seen as directly creating value for the firm. The university needs to be seen as providing technical and managerial knowledge to the engineer and the firm. The human resource practitioner in industry needs to have a relationship with universities. Knowing what the university is offering or is able to tailor can help with referrals to the university during the outplacement process or with internships during the recruitment process.

Government can respond to a new situation but worries too much about downside risks, rather than upside opportunities: Job Training Partnership Act (JPTA) funding for retraining turned out to be inappropriate for reeducation and repositioning represented by the JOBS program and for women and single parents, who had to drop out for financial reasons.

The JTPA funds paid $10 an hour per student, with 20 percent of the funds withheld until employment. The county human resource practitioner audited attendance figures, disallowing field trips, sick days, personal time, and some internship time, undercutting the central trust of and income to support the program. The training practitioner had nothing to do with unemployment insurance. Students had to go to the unemployment office to get paid, and this time was deducted from the university's reimbursement.

Funding for training and unemployment need to be coordinated and administered through a job shop that offers vouchers to the unemployed to be spent on education and stipends for living expenses. A human resource person overseeing policy and its implementation needs to see the whole process and make the parts work together.

Conclusion

How well did the engineers do? Of the 150 applicants the first semester, 57 started the program and 43 finished the educational work to get a certificate. Of these, 4 had jobs as of January 5, and 10 had consulting projects. A total of 17 of 43 graduates had full-time employment and 11 had part-time employment by July 1. Of the 20 applicants the second semester, 15 entered the program, 8 finished the coursework, and 6 had created jobs for themselves.

How well did government do? It got a program that it did not have before, but it wanted to see results of employment before expressing praise publicly. One county was willing to continue funding for the spring, at $150,000, half the support of the fall.

How well did the business community do? More than fifteen firms got advice on problems, and the majority reported the experience was worthwhile. Many wished to continue with interns for the spring. All were very happy with the new hires.

How well did the university do? It made contact and friends with executives from over thirty firms. The groundwork was laid for further work with these firms to solve their problems and to gain support for the university. The opportunity emerged to start the executive management center with full-time programming.

CHAPTER 12

Developing Computerized Outplacement Counseling Programs
The Philadelphia Naval Shipyard and Base

Robert J. Vance
David V. Day

The need for reduction of the U.S. military became apparent with the end of the cold-war era in the early 1990s. In addition to the lessened external threat, the enormous expense of the defense budget (estimated at up to 50 cents of every tax dollar), coupled with increasing federal deficits, makes defense downsizing imperative. The 1990 Base Closure and Realignment Act established a process for downsizing. The Commission for Base Realignment and Closure was established, with the mission of recommending military bases and defense establishments for closure to Congress

---

Note: The authors contributed equally to this article. The project was a team effort. Other team members were Frank Landy, Mary Kay Cote, Roger Garthwaite, Tonia Heffner, and Charlotte Gerstner.

This chapter was written in July and August 1994, shortly after completing work on the Philadelphia Naval Shipyard and Base project. Because the PNSB will continue to downsize during 1995 and 1996, tenses used throughout the chapter vary from past to future so as accurately to describe events that have occurred or are expected to occur. When necessary, we note when data are current as of the time of writing.

and the president. The act requires that Congress and the president either accept or reject the entire list of recommended closures—the list could not otherwise be altered. The intention of Congress was to shield closure decisions from the usual partisan politics.

The Philadelphia Naval Shipyard and Base (PNSB) is the site of the oldest shipbuilding facility in the United States, with origins dating back to colonial times. It opened as a defense facility in 1801, and it appeared on the first closure list, released by the commission in 1991. (A second larger list was released in 1993.) Slated for final closure in 1996, the PNSB has been gradually downsizing since the mid–1980s. It had a post–World War II employment peak of about 14,000 workers. By mid–1994, the complement was approximately 7,500 workers. Reductions were achieved through retirements, attrition, transfers, and outplacement. In May 1994 the first reduction in force (RIF), or involuntary separation, was announced. The bulk of the remaining workers will be displaced by September 1995, with only a small contingent remaining until final closing in 1996.

In response to the 1990 act, the U.S. Department of Labor (DOL), together with the Department of Defense (DOD), began searching for innovative solutions to transitioning defense workers. In December 1992 the Commonwealth of Pennsylvania Department of Labor and Industry, the Private Industry Council (PIC) of Philadelphia, and the Pennsylvania State University were awarded a demonstration grant from the DOL, Employment and Training Administration. This eighteen-month project was to develop an employee skills inventory, occupational assessment, and comprehensive training plan for PNSB workers.

To help achieve these broad objectives, a Penn State research team based at the Center for Applied Behavioral Sciences developed the Skills Training and Employment Program for Upgrading Personnel, or STEP-UP. This relational database system brings together information concerning knowledge, skill, ability, and task requirements of PNSB jobs, training histories of individual workers, and information on job openings in the Philadelphia region as well as attribute requirements of those jobs. STEP-UP was designed for use by counselors as a tool for advising PNSB workers of training needs and employment potential. STEP-UP was grounded in the Minnesota theory of work adjustment, which defines work adjustment as "the continuous and dynamic process by which the individual seeks to achieve and maintain correspondence with the work environment" (Dawis & Lofquist, 1984, p. 55). According to this theory, the key components to successful work adjustment are the satisfaction of the individual with the work environment and the satisfaction of the work environment with the individual (also termed *satisfactoriness*). STEP-UP was designed to identify areas of correspondence between an employee's knowledge, skills, and abilities (KSAs) and the KSA requirements of work environments in similar labor market positions. This information was used to determine the number of available labor market positions and the level of fit or satisfactoriness with the employee's present capabilities. A primary role of the counselors was to assist employees in evaluating the desirability of these positions, as well as the amount and type of retraining that would be needed as a prerequisite to successful work adjustment. Counselors were deemed to be instrumental to the overall STEP-UP system in helping to ensure the satisfaction component to work adjustment for PNSB employees.

Design, development, logic, and use of STEP-UP will be described in this chapter. Design choices and project achievements must be understood in the context of the complex and often turbulent Philadelphia political scene. Before relating the details of STEP-UP's development, therefore, we will provide an overview of the players and politics forming the backdrop of our project.

Political and Economic Contexts

Closing the PNSB will have a potentially devastating effect on the economy of the Philadelphia region, which includes parts of southern New Jersey and Delaware, collectively known as the Delaware Valley area. A 1993 report by Coopers & Lybrand, an accounting firm hired to study the economic impact of closing the PNSB, estimated that $471.2 million will be lost in direct income, $47 million annually in state taxes, and $66 million annually in local taxes. Up to 36,000 civilians will lose their jobs, including PNSB workers and those of area employers economically dependent on the PNSB. A study by the U.S. Navy estimated that this will cause a 25 percent increase in local unemployment. With the demise of the PNSB,

Philadelphia will lose its largest manufacturing employer and its last center of heavy manufacturing.

In the face of such dire economic consequences, it is not surprising that the fate of the PNSB and its workers appeared at the top of the priority lists of a host of local, state, and national politicians and bureaucrats. There have been nearly as many proposed plans and possible solutions as players in the scramble to do something constructive. However, these initiatives would require scarce resources, and their proponents were often locked in intense and often acrimonious competition. To give a sense of this contentious climate, we provide a few critical incidents.

The Commerce Department of Philadelphia, through its Office of Defense Conversion, released a fifty-page conversion initiative report in December, 1993. Based largely on the Coopers & Lybrand study, it claimed not to be a plan but "a strategy that is constantly evolving." This constantly evolving strategy reflected the inherently political nature of trying to build a consensus among the many affected constituents. The report argued that the best solution would be to attract a variety of businesses to occupy the PNSB site and to convert it to an industrial park. The city could use some of the $50 million conversion money set aside by Congress to attract companies through tax abatements, upgrading of facilities, and so on.

Upon release of the city's conversion initiative, Sen. Arlen Specter (R., Pa.) called a news conference to blast the report as a "doomsday scenario." He saw it as counter to his own attempts to secure additional work from the Navy to keep the PNSB in business. Specter's approach to finding government contract work was the traditional response of politicians to rectify unemployment in one's home district. In a related initiative, Sen. Specter, together with U.S. Reps. Curt Weldon (R., Pa.), Robert E. Andrews (D., N.J.), and local union officials, filed a lawsuit challenging the decision-making process for closures. They contended that the Navy rigged the process by suppressing its own experts' evidence that the PNSB should be kept open. The case was argued unsuccessfully by Sen. Specter before the U.S. Supreme Court in February 1994. The Court's unanimous ruling concluded that Congress did not grant judges the authority to second-guess the president's decision to close military bases (*Dalton* v. *Specter,* 1994).

Other initiatives included a plan for a National Maritime Industrial Center, proposed by Coopers & Lybrand and supported by Sen. Specter, Rep. Andrews, Rep. Thomas M. Foglietta (D., Pa.), and the Joint Committee for Yard Development, an internal PNSB organization. It would provide state-of-the-art shipbuilding technology and would cost about $300 million annually. Peace Action Delaware Valley, a local action group, produced a report titled "Alternative Uses of the Philadelphia Naval Shipyard." This group argued that the skills of the PNSB workforce and the technology available should be employed in refurbishing the massive and aging infrastructure of the city. Peter D. Linneman, a real estate expert from the Wharton Business School, University of Pennsylvania, made a case that the site should simply be abandoned, left to future generations to use as needed.

What is the likelihood for success of any of these proposals? The fundamental problem is that no one really knows how best to cope with conversion of a defense facility of this magnitude. The idea to turn the facility into an industrial park, for instance, must be examined in the context of a city that is full of abandoned industrial sites. According to a 1990 study of industrial land use by the city's planning office, between 1975 and 1985 there was a 343 percent increase in acreage of vacant buildings in Philadelphia's thirteen industrial districts. A recent estimate is that 20 percent of that land—about 4,400 acres—is not being used at all. Of the 1,425 PNSB acres, the Navy will turn over 900 to the city and keep 500 for its own use, including the most valuable assets. The Navy will retain the waterfront property, with three of the largest drydocks on the East Coast, and the bulk of the technological and manufacturing facilities. The city will get land (much of it likely to be contaminated with industrial wastes such as PCBs, petroleum, asbestos, and various metals), office buildings, warehouses, dormitories, and so on.

The National Maritime Center idea should also be considered in light of the virtually complete demise of the U.S. commercial shipbuilding industry in the mid–1980s. Most shipbuilding now occurs overseas, where wages are much lower and environmental and other regulations are lax. The likelihood of additional Navy work should be evaluated within the context of today's environment of military downsizing on a national scale. It is estimated that several hundred defense installations will be closed in the next few years, with as many as 200,000 workers losing their jobs. These facilities compete for whatever work remains. Jobs for one location mean lost work elsewhere, particularly in communities without employer-enticing defense conversion funds.

Except for the Peace Action Delaware Valley group, these initiatives address conversion of the land and physical plant, and only indirectly address employment of the current workforce. From the workers' viewpoint, the problem is one of timing. Even if one or all initiatives eventually succeed, PNSB workers are being outplaced at an ever-increasing rate. Nearly all will be displaced by late in 1995. There is no guarantee that businesses that occupy the site will hire former PNSB workers. Thus, remedies being pursued are by and large remedies for the economic woes of the Delaware Valley region, not of the PNSB workforce. As noted by Barbara Smith, executive director of Jobs With Peace, another Philadelphia grassroots community activist organization, "I don't think any of their ideas are going to be in place in time to save even one worker's job at the yard" (Quinn, 1994, p. 17).

It is within this tumultuous environment that we developed the STEP-UP system for outplacement counseling of displaced defense workers. This environment shaped our efforts and the product we produced, and it will no doubt influence the ultimate effectiveness of STEP-UP. Our goal was to design a worker-oriented reemployment counseling tool, responsive to the increasingly urgent needs of the PNSB population for individual guidance on their job and career options.

STEP-UP: Skills Training and Employment Program for Upgrading Personnel

STEP-UP was developed under a subcontract with the Philadelphia Private Industry Council (PIC). Funding for the project originated with the DOL through the Job Training Partnership Act, funds targeted for retraining of displaced workers. The PIC's mission as stated in the contract was to establish a Transition Assistance Center that would provide services to employees before layoff and to continue delivery of services after layoffs occurred. Many of the services to be provided by the PIC were directed at the individual employee, such as career counseling, stress management, job search assistance, and interviewing techniques.

The PIC then contracted with Penn State for three tasks: conduct a large-scale evaluation of the skills of the PNSB workforce (approximately 7,500 employees when the contract was signed early in 1993); conduct an employment opportunity analysis identifying occupational areas with the greatest projected growth and job availability in the Delaware Valley region; and identify matches between specific PNSB jobs and available labor market positions, as well as to identify gaps in these matches indicating retraining needs. The overarching goal of this multipartner effort was to provide a user-friendly system for use by PIC counselors in individual sessions with employees.

As stated, the project appears straightforward. Complicating matters, however, were the various constituencies involved, most of whom claimed some degree of ownership of the project, and all of whom had expectations about what we would accomplish. Constituents included PNSB employees; PIC and PNSB managers and counselors; PNSB union and employee representatives; U.S. DOD and DOL, State Department of Labor and Industry, and city officials; state and local politicians; and various task forces and committees in the Delaware Valley area. Part of our challenge was managing their often conflicting expectations at various points during the project. For example, the term *assessment* was interpreted by some as interviewing and testing all 7,500 workers. Neither time nor budget allowed for this, but once this notion was in place it was difficult to change.

Another issue that became an immediate concern was the projected RIF timetable. Even before signing the formal eighteen-month contract in early 1993, we were informed that if we waited until the end of the contract period to deliver a product, it would be of little use—RIFs were to commence within weeks of the contract signing, reaching a peak sometime in late 1994 or early 1995. As it turned out, no RIF occurred until more than one year after the beginning of the contract, but the pressure was there to develop a working system as soon as possible. To accommodate this, PNSB managers identified those positions most at risk for a RIF. We first developed a system tailored to those jobs, then added to it as more positions were identified. Unfortunately, this created the expectation that the initial versions of STEP-UP would be as good as the final version, despite cautions that this would not be the case.

System Design and Development

In addition to career and outplacement counseling services provided by the PIC, PNSB also provides similar services through its Career Transition Center. A survey of the workforce revealed that most employees preferred to remain in federal employment. For most, this was an unrealistic hope. Most also indicated that they wished to remain in the Delaware Valley area. We determined early on that employment counseling should incorporate information on actual and anticipated job openings in the Philadelphia area, to accommodate both the needs of the PNSB workforce for jobs and their desire to remain in the area. We expected that PNSB employees, performing jobs often unique to shipbuilding, would require retraining to be eligible for private-sector employment. It was therefore important that decisions made by employees regarding investments in time and money for retraining have a likely payoff in job availability upon training completion.

STEP-UP was built around concrete information about job openings, which could be used to guide career, retraining, and job-search strategies. It is a skills matching program that compares KSAs of a PNSB employee (a "client") with requirements of available and anticipated job openings. Gaps in client qualifications for a desired position indicate training needs. Development of STEP-UP required construction of databases containing the relevant information, as well as an algorithm to match clients to job openings. Figure 12.1 shows the sources of information used in the databases. Each of these important aspects of system design and development is discussed separately below.

Internal Skills Assessment

Because of contract length and budget, it was a logistically insurmountable task to conduct a traditional job analysis on all PNSB jobs, as this would entail developing lists of duties, tasks, and KSAs through observations, interviews, and questionnaires. This was also unnecessary, as position descriptions (PDs) existed for all jobs,

Figure 12.1. Sources of Information Used to Develop STEP-UP.

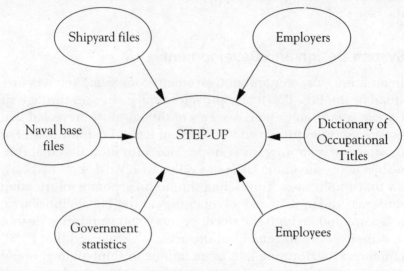

most of which were up-to-date. Our approach was to code KSAs and key tasks from PDs. A total of 642 PDs were obtained from base and shipyard files and analyzed, beginning with those identified as most at risk for an early RIF. Between 30 and 50 KSAs and tasks (KSATs) described the typical PD. Ultimately, approximately 2,400 unique KSATs were coded into the PD database. An example of a partial KSAT listing produced by STEP-UP for a shipwright job is shown in Exhibit 12.1. PDs coded into STEP-UP represented approximately 95 percent of the PNSB workforce.

Training Databases

Assessment of a match between a client's qualifications and a potential job opening depended in part on relevance of the client's previous training to the requirements of the job. The PNSB maintained extensive records of the training provided to each employee. These employee records were uploaded into training history databases within STEP-UP. An example of a training record for an individual client, identified by badge number, is shown in Exhibit 12.2.

Exhibit 12.1. Partial KSAT Listing for the Shipwright Job.

Occupational Code	PD Number	Job Title	KSA Type	KSA Code	KSA Description
WG-5220	38230	Shipwright	A	1108	Lifts/carries moderate items (20–100 lbs.)
			A	631	Ability to work in potentially threatening/dangerous environs.
			A	651	Ability to work in uncomfortable conditions/positions
			A	1095	Dexterous use of arms and legs
			A	3003	Ability to work in extreme temperature areas
			A	3002	Ability to work in high noise level area
			A	1085	Ability to work in confined areas
			K	1981	Knowledge of building materials
			K	3655	Knowledge of construction standards, methods
			K	164	Knowledge of mathematics
			K	634	Knowledge of requisitioning procedures (materials and services)
			K	412	Knowledge of shipwright trade
			S	1966	Skill in structural woodwork construction and repair
			S	1758	Skill in creating diagrams/sketches
			S	3725	Skill in performing basic mathematical calculations
			S	141	Skill in blueprint interpretation
			T	1980	Reviews sketches, drawings
			T	416	Uses basic measuring tools

Exhibit 12.2. Training Record for an Individual Client.

Badge Number	SAID	Course Title	Start Date	Finish Date	Duty Hours
49295	49150	QUALITY IMPROVEMENT	09/29/89	12/21/89	0004
	50000	01943 RESPIRATOR PNS	06/06/88	09/30/88	0002
	50000	01943 RESPIRATOR TRN	09/30/88	12/31/88	0002
	50000	GAS-FREE ENG PNSY	02/20/91	09/30/91	0001
	50000	HAZ WASTE MINIMIZ	02/02/93	02/02/93	0001
	50000	HAZARDOUS COMMUNICAT	01/30/91	08/16/91	0004
	50000	HEARING CONSERVATION	11/19/90	11/19/90	0001
	50000	HEARING CONSERVATION	04/04/91	04/04/91	0001
	50000	PQP FOLLOW ON TRNG	02/18/92	02/18/92	0004
	50000	RESPIRATORY PROTECTI	07/17/91	09/04/91	0002
	58000	HEARING CONSERV PNSY	09/18/89	09/22/89	0001
	83SXP	PREV SEXUAL HARASS	08/26/92	08/26/92	0004

External Labor Market Analysis

A defining feature of the STEP-UP skills-matching system is that it includes information concerning available jobs from the area labor market. For the skills-matching algorithm to work, we first had to identify job openings and then code them for their requisite KSATs. Discussions with federal, state, and local labor and employment officials indicated that we would have to develop our own process of uncovering this information. Although state job services compile and disseminate information about job openings, typically fewer than 10 percent of area employers list with these services. Therefore, a process was designed (see Figure 12.2 for a summary) to identify job openings in the Delaware Valley area and to code these jobs for KSATs.

We began by using occupational information system software supplied by the states of Pennsylvania, New Jersey, and Delaware to identify growth occupations. We targeted those occupations most likely to employ large numbers of people and to show growth during the 1990s, according to government economic forecasts for the Delaware Valley region. This software permitted searches of its databases according to various growth projections, such as the highest number employed, highest annual average job openings, and fastest employment percent growth. It produced lists of occupations that met the search criteria and names of companies employing people in these occupations. Next, addresses and telephone numbers for targeted companies were obtained from sources such as the Harris Directory (a listing of all employers), local and state business directories, area telephone directories, or PhoneDisc, a CD-ROM directory of employer information. For inclusion on our list of employers to contact, a company must have employed twenty-five or more people.

Next, companies were contacted by mail, with an introductory letter from the project director explaining the purpose of the project and stating that within two weeks a staff member would telephone to obtain information about current and anticipated job openings. Two letters endorsing the project and urging cooperation were also enclosed. One was signed jointly by the mayor of Philadelphia and the commander of the Philadelphia Naval Shipyard. The other was signed by the chief operating officer of PIC, the director of the Greater Philadelphia Chamber of Commerce,

Figure 12.2. Summary of Steps in the Labor Market Analysis.

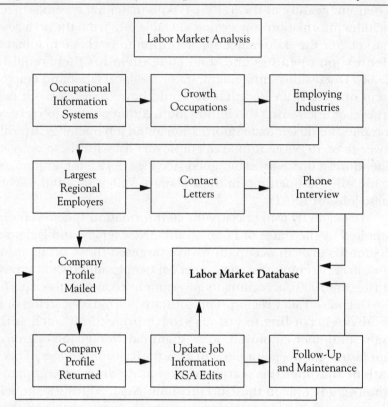

the executive director of the Technology Council of Greater Philadelphia, and the executive director of the Greater Philadelphia Economic Development Coalition.

A telephone interview protocol was developed in consultation with PIC and PNSB officials. It required ten to fifteen minutes of the respondent's time, and inquired primarily about current and anticipated (within the next twelve months) job openings. Of the 828 initial contact letters sent out during the eighteen-month project, 570 (69 percent) were followed by successful telephone interviews, 37 (4 percent) companies refused to participate, and 221 (27 percent) companies could not be reached after five or six attempts and were abandoned.

Once current and anticipated job openings were identified,

Dictionary of Occupational Title (DOT) code numbers were assigned based on job titles and descriptions of work provided by employers. KSAT requirements for these jobs were then identified using job descriptions provided in the DOT, and coded into STEP-UP labor market databases in a manner parallel to that of the PNSB PD coding described above. The dictionary of some 2,400 KSATs developed for PD coding was used. Because of the need to keep job opening information up to date, we periodically sent a report to each employer in STEP-UP's databases asking them to verify, update, and supplement information gathered during the initial telephone contact. In addition to updates concerning available and anticipated job openings, we asked respondents to review the KSATs that had been coded for their positions, to rate each on a four-point scale from "essential" to "does not apply," and to add and rate any KSATs missing from the list. Our overall response rate to follow-up employer contacts was 27 percent.

Employers were generally receptive to being contacted. We believe this is largely attributable to the initial letter explaining the nature and importance of the project. Even after repeated contacts, very few employers ($n = 3$) asked to be dropped from the project. There are areas that can be improved, however, for future efforts of this type. The return rate for the follow-up questionnaires was low, probably due to its length and the sensitivity of information requested. Future efforts would also benefit from an organized consortium of interested parties, so that employers would be approached only once with requests for employment information. Nonetheless, employer reactions were much more positive than expected.

Skills-Matching Program

The hinge to the system's success was a software system to match KSAs of PNSB positions with external labor market openings. A relational database management system (Microsoft Access) was selected as the operating system for STEP-UP. Working in a Windows environment, this software was adopted because it provided a user-friendly, point-and-click (mouse-driven) interface. This made it comparatively easy to train users. The fully relational database architecture permitted flexibility in system design, allowing us to produce successive versions after having obtained input and suggestions from users.

Figure 12.3 is a flow diagram illustrating a typical counseling session. A session can take less than fifteen minutes of system interface time. An actual session generally takes longer, to permit discussion with the client. As used at PNSB, activities described below occur over several counseling sessions.

Working from STEP-UP's main switchboard, the first step is to select a client's job title from a list provided by the program. When a job title is selected, a list of KSAs and tasks associated with that position appears. This list typically needs to be tailored to the specific client, which can be done by checking boxes to the right of KSAs to indicate those that represent the client's strong points or those on which the client wishes to capitalize in searching for a job. An assumption in the design of STEP-UP was that requirements of a job describe capabilities of the individual who performs it. This assumption was verified through counselor-client discussion of capabilities, which produced the client-tailored KSAT list.

The tailored list can be saved in an individual client file, printed, or sent to the job-matching algorithm. The matching algorithm compares KSATs in the client's file with KSATs associated with jobs in the labor market databases. Matches appear as an ordered list of job titles for available and anticipated job openings in the Delaware Valley area, from best to worst matches. This matrix can be printed or reviewed on screen. Users can set the minimum KSAT match criterion, with only those jobs with KSAT matches equal to or greater than the criterion appearing on the list.

The counselor and client can discuss jobs appearing on the match list, evaluating the goodness of fit to the client's capabilities and interests. For jobs of interest, information on companies with actual or anticipated openings can be requested. From this list further information about specific companies can be obtained by checking off the company name, as shown in Figure 12.3. This produces a printout of company information, including name, address, and telephone number of a contact person and the numbers of current and anticipated job openings.

Goodness of fit can be assessed further by requesting a list of KSATs for a labor market job. An example is shown in Exhibit 12.3 for the job of mechanic. The KSATs that constitute the match between this job and the client are indicated by asterisks. The counselor can discuss KSATs on the list *not* possessed by the client

Figure 12.3. Matching PNSB Employees with Job Prospects.

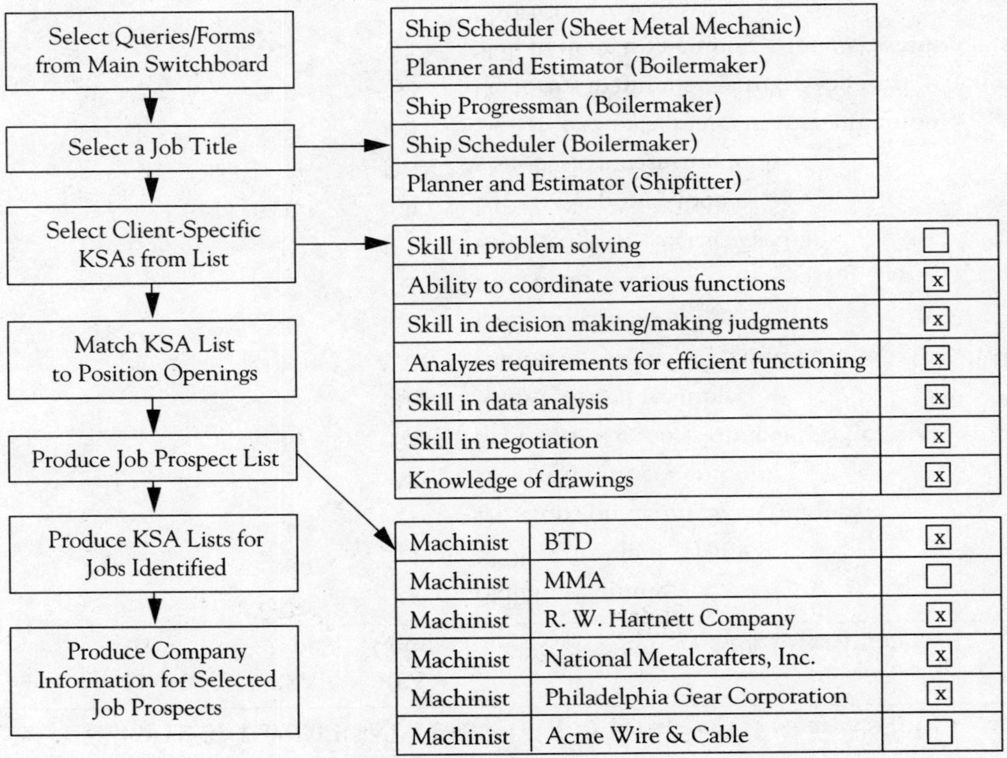

Process flow:

Select Queries/Forms from Main Switchboard → Select a Job Title → Select Client-Specific KSAs from List → Match KSA List to Position Openings → Produce Job Prospect List → Produce KSA Lists for Jobs Identified → Produce Company Information for Selected Job Prospects

Job Titles:

- Ship Scheduler (Sheet Metal Mechanic)
- Planner and Estimator (Boilermaker)
- Ship Progressman (Boilermaker)
- Ship Scheduler (Boilermaker)
- Planner and Estimator (Shipfitter)

KSAs:

KSA	Selected
Skill in problem solving	☐
Ability to coordinate various functions	☒
Skill in decision making/making judgments	☒
Analyzes requirements for efficient functioning	☒
Skill in data analysis	☒
Skill in negotiation	☒
Knowledge of drawings	☒

Job Prospects:

Title	Company	Selected
Machinist	BTD	☒
Machinist	MMA	☐
Machinist	R. W. Hartnett Company	☒
Machinist	National Metalcrafters, Inc.	☒
Machinist	Philadelphia Gear Corporation	☒
Machinist	Acme Wire & Cable	☐

Exhibit 12.3. Partial KSAT Listing for Job Prospect (Mechanic's Job).

Job Title	Match (*)	KSA Type	KSA Code	KSA Description
Mechanic		S	1	Skill in planning
	*	S	14	Skill in problem solving
		T	21	Develops procedures/techniques
		T	58	Interacts with general public
	*	S	65	Skill in oral expression/comprehension
	*	K	116	Knowledge of welding
		K	126	Knowledge of weight handling equip. (e.g. hydraulic jack, hoist)
	*	T	178	Uses basic hand tools
		T	185	Uses drills
	*	K	401	Knowledge of electrical systems
		T	409	Uses basic power tools
	*	T	416	Uses basic measuring tools
		S	438	Skill in technical material interpretation
		T	582	Performs maintenance following work schedule/manual
		S	584	Skill in detecting equipment deterioration by listening
		T	585	Lubricates machinery
		S	588	Skill in truck driving (capacity > 3 tons)

and their implications for additional training before applying for that job. If training is indicated, the counselor can further discuss, for example, likely time and money investment in training, the likelihood that a suitable job will be available upon completion, and likely competition for each available opening. In essence, a discussion of the risk parameters associated with a career option and the client's tolerance for risk would be considered. The list of matches can also elicit discussion of job possibilities that the client had not previously considered. It can thus serve as an adjunct to traditional career counseling for individuals who may desire a radical change in career.

STEP-UP has a variety of other capabilities in addition to those outlined above. KSATs for a client can be accessed by entering the individual's ID number rather than job title. An individual client file can be created from a composite of KSATs for all jobs held by the client at PNSB. The client's training history can be printed. The system will batch process client information, so that KSAT lists can be printed in advance for clients scheduled for sessions, rather than having the client and counselor work with STEP-UP in real time. Each of these options was added to the system in response to user requests. Six successive versions of STEP-UP were installed during the project, each with greater capabilities than its predecessor.

Formal evaluation of STEP-UP has not been performed, at least by the system's developers. A primary reason for this apparent oversight is that the DOL contracted with an independent agency to conduct periodic program evaluations. However, if we were to conduct such an evaluation, three primary criteria would be recommended. The most proximal criterion would be the reactions of the counselors. Our experience suggests that if counselors do not find a system to be useful and user-friendly, it will not be used. Any counseling support system is in competition with numerous other databases and information sources for a counselor's attention. This is especially true when the amount of interaction time is limited, as was the case here.

Relevant intermediate criteria would be the number of employee users of the system, as well as their reactions regarding the usefulness of the information provided by STEP-UP. For example, were satisfactory KSAT matches made? Did the number of jobs identified meet employee expectations? Were job matches made that would be seriously pursued? Did any matches indicate potential employment opportunities that had not been previously considered? The most distal—and ultimate—criterion would be the number of successful job placements, either immediately or following retraining.

Our discussions with transition center counselors, both in focus groups and informally, indicated an increasing acceptance of STEP-UP. Thus, it appears that we were at least somewhat successful in fulfilling the most proximal criterion. Before large numbers of employees can be placed, however, they need to use the system. It is at this intermediate step that certain issues have arisen to reduce the number of employee users.

Issues Surrounding the Use of STEP-UP

Use of STEP-UP by counselors has been affected by the number of qualified clients. As of this writing, the number of prospective clients has been diminished by the delay in the RIF schedule, as described above. Because the ultimate closure date has not changed, however, one implication is that the demand for transition services will increase dramatically during the remaining interval. In the meantime, other programs that have encouraged separations from PNSB have circumvented Transition Center and PIC counseling services.

In 1993, DOD authorized separation incentive pay (SIP) to encourage PNSB workers to voluntarily resign or retire—up to $25,000, depending on an employee's severance pay entitlement. This offer was extended only until January 31, 1994, and by that time 820 employees had taken advantage of the offer. This effort is worth noting because it highlights that DOD is using incentives for separation and early retirement similar to those used in the private sector. One consequence of this action, however, was that those employees with the most transferable skills, and thus most easily placed in the private sector, were most likely to accept the SIP offer. The remaining employees will generally have a more difficult time finding suitable private-sector employment without considerable retraining.

Another consideration in evaluating the potential success of STEP-UP is that many employees are closer to retirement than to their date of hire, and thus would prefer to remain in federal service. The DOD has recognized this concern and has instituted a priority placement program. This program is usually available to an employee only when receiving a notice of separation. The PNSB received permission, however, to allow its employees to register for placement beginning in September 1993 if they wished. Since that time, approximately two hundred employees have been placed at other DOD facilities. Another similar program is the Defense Outplacement Referral System, a cooperative effort between DOD and the U.S. Office of Personnel Management to provide placement opportunities within DOD, non–DOD federal agencies, and the public sector including state and local governments. These programs are seen by civilian defense workers as their most promising means of securing continued government employment.

These programs indicate that if the proper financial incentives or perceived opportunities are present, a significant number of employees will voluntarily separate. It appears that managing contingencies to make private-sector employment more attractive to civilian defense workers and reducing obstacles to their effective transition are the keys to effective defense conversion from a human resources standpoint. Although STEP-UP was developed to facilitate the latter objective, as it stands there is little reason for PNSB workers to look toward private-sector employment as anything but a last resort.

Implications for Human Resource Strategies and Defense Conversion

As of this writing, our contract with the PIC has expired and the last version of STEP-UP has been installed at the Transition Assistance Center. Use of STEP-UP is increasing as greater numbers of PNSB workers are exploring their job placement and career options. In this section, we will discuss several issues surrounding STEP-UP as a human resource initiative for defense conversion as well as broader issues concerning national defense downsizing.

STEP-UP and Employee Outplacement Counseling

As noted at the outset of this chapter, development of STEP-UP must be viewed in the context of multiple constituents at all levels, from PNSB employees to officials at the highest levels of the federal government. Each constituent viewed the project from its unique perspective. The DOL, in awarding funds for the project as a demonstration grant, sought to promote an innovative response to dislocations resulting from base closures and defense expenditure reductions. If successful, the project could be used as a model at other defense conversion and base closure sites. City of Philadelphia officials, together with other state and local officials, wished to keep unemployment as low as possible and to have a system that would successfully (and quickly) place PNSB workers in other gainful employment. The PIC, on the other hand, primarily provides job-search and job-training services to individuals. They have found STEP-UP most useful as a tool to identify retraining needs of the PNSB population and to recommend particular programs to meet those needs. Although intended to satisfy each of these diverse objectives to some degree, in all probability no constituent would evaluate the project as completely satisfactory.

Ironically, most PNSB employees continue to resist the idea that their jobs are in peril. Rather than becoming proactive in preparing for their imminent career transitions, they hold out hope for another job with the federal government, preferably in the Delaware Valley region. A special challenge in providing transition counseling services is convincing the intended recipients that they need assistance.

History is on the side of the workers. Employees report that rumors of downsizing and closing have been a daily fact of life since at least the 1950s. It has been more than twenty years since the last sizable PNSB layoffs near the end of the Vietnam War. PNSB workers "find reassurance in the fact that over the last two decades the shipyard has been on more hit lists than Saddam Hussein; yet, it has always survived" (Hollman, 1993). The faulty logic of the physician's reassurance to the dying man, "Don't worry, you'll get better; after all, you always have," strikes a chord here. The *Philadelphia Inquirer* quoted one PNSB manager as saying, "We are still a shipyard in denial" (Holcomb, 1994).

The predominant view of the PNSB workers, together with the economic outlook for the Delaware Valley region, complicate the career counseling mission of the PIC. It is difficult to find private-sector employment that can match the pay, benefits, and job security offered (until recently) by federal government employment.

This is especially true for traditional blue-collar trades jobs. Occupations showing most rapid decline in the Philadelphia area, according to PIC projections, are machine tool operators (14 to 30 percent decline by 1995), tool and die makers (14.7 percent decline), electromechanical equipment assemblers (10.7 percent decline), and machinists (10.5 percent decline). A large proportion of the PNSB workforce have principal skills in these occupations. Thus, consistent with the PIC's perspective on STEP-UP, its most promising aspect may be as a tool to identify retraining needs.

The logic underlying how STEP-UP is used to identify retraining needs (or job placement opportunities) is grounded in an interactionist theory of behavior, and specifically in person-environment congruence (Bowers, 1973; Dawis & Lofquist, 1984; Pervin, 1968). Congruence refers to the degree of fit or match between two sets of variables, which results in positive (or negative) outcomes. For example, Pervin (1968) proposed that a good fit between people and environments results in high performance, high job satisfaction, and low stress.

Most human resource applications are based on *complementary* congruence, whereby characteristics of the individual serve to complement or complete the characteristics of the environment (Muchinsky & Monahan, 1987). The better the fit between an individual's KSAs and the KSA requirements of a prospective job, the greater the predicted success of that individual in that job. Training needs are identified by determining where areas of nonoverlap occur. Jobs identified by STEP-UP as potential matches can be discussed to determine client's interest level, and the amount and type of training needed to improve the match can be identified.

STEP-UP was designed neither as a "self-directed" system for use by clients, nor as a substitute for counselors. Rather, it is used by counseling professionals to assist clients with important career decisions. STEP-UP contributes very useful information to this process, but the role of the counselor is central in helping clients evaluate this information, considering their own personal circumstances.

The counselor can conduct a risk assessment with the client, with risk defined jointly by the gap between the client's qualifications and the requirements of a potential job, the investment in time and money in training needed to narrow that gap, the likelihood that a suitable position would be available upon completion of training, and the client's personal circumstances and interests that might affect the feasibility of various alternatives. For example, a thirty-year-old client with no dependents may be willing to invest time in training in pursuit of a change in career direction, whereas a fifty-year-old client with two children approaching college age may need to pursue currently available positions. It would be difficult to incorporate such personal factors into a STEP-UP-like system other than via counselors.

As Dawis (1991) and others have noted, a well-known proposition in applied psychology holds that performance is a function of ability and motivation. STEP-UP was designed to match workers to job opportunities based on abilities (and knowledge and skills). Individual motives, however, including interests, values, and preferences, are equally important to complementary congruence and therefore to job success and adjustment. A job placement system such as STEP-UP depends on collaboration between industrial/organizational psychologists *and* vocational counselors to be effective. We encourage close collaboration between these disciplines in future defense conversion and organizational downsizing endeavors.

In addition to use by counselors in outplacing PNSB workers, STEP-UP's databases are also used extensively by PIC managers to summarize labor market information, to profile the PNSB workforce, and to track individual clients as they progress through the counseling process. These applications are feasible because of the extensive databases encompassed by STEP-UP, including worker, PNSB job, and external labor market files, and because of the flexibility of the underlying relational database software that permits virtually any combination of variables to be accessed, summarized, and reported. For example, a report was designed at the request of PIC managers to provide a list of job openings in the Delaware Valley region, organized by area (defined by zip code), providing job titles and numbers of current and anticipated openings, rank ordered from most to least in number. This report can be printed as needed, each time summarizing the most current information. The report-generating capabilities of STEP-UP enhance its value to those responsible for managing the human resource aspects of downsizing and outplacement activities.

System Maintenance and Technology

STEP-UP must be maintained if it is to be useful. This is most apparent with the external labor market database, which has an estimated half-life of only several weeks. Information on current and anticipated job openings must be continually updated. The system also requires routine maintenance, with monitoring to ensure proper operation of hardware and software and database management to delete former employees and labor market positions no longer available. Just as the system was continually enhanced throughout the project, with modifications and desired features added as suggested by users, continued use of the system will undoubtedly lead to more suggestions for improvements and expanded capabilities.

Indeed, system databases contain numerous variables on which data were gathered but are not currently accessible via STEP-UP. These data can be made available if desired by counselors or clients. We have trained PIC staff members on procedures necessary to accomplish system maintenance and development. However, it will be a real challenge for PIC staff to maintain the system as they become increasingly busy delivering client services. Further development by users is even less likely. It remains to be seen whether complex human resource systems such as STEP-UP can function effectively without continued assistance of system designers and support staff.

A more general issue concerns the adequacy of the supporting relational database software for this application. The system is powerful in that it brings together vast amounts of information and places it at the disposal of counselors and clients. The price of this user-friendly system, however, comes at the expense of computational hardware requirements and user time. The system databases and supporting software require more than 60 megabytes of hard disk space on a PC. Other minimum hardware requirements include a 486 CPU and 12 megabytes of RAM. As installed at the PIC Center, STEP-UP operates from a server computer through a local area network to counselor computers, thus supporting multiple users.

In spite of these state-of-the-art capabilities, the system is reported by counselors to be too slow to use in real time with clients. Instead, they prepare for counseling sessions by printing needed materials in advance. This is done to optimally use client contact hours. Each client has a set number of duty hours for job and career counseling, and both parties feel that they cannot spend time waiting for STEP-UP to produce printouts or job-match matrices.

Other software exists around which a STEP-UP-like system could be designed. Alternatives that offer faster processing speed have less sophisticated screen graphics capabilities and would be less user-friendly. Thus, technology forces trade-offs in system design. Future advances in computer hardware and software will permit movement along the continuum from satisficing to optimizing design parameters, but the needs and demands of users will probably always tax available technology. Applications that could be designed for job analysis, job matching, career development, outplacement counseling, and so on, are "information intensive," and thus will challenge the limits of available technology for the foreseeable future.

Examples of further developments of STEP-UP that would increase both system complexity and utility include:

- A job competency structure overlaid on the present KSAT structure to describe work performed and individual capabilities in broader terms than the more elemental KSATs. This would add to the flexibility of the system, for example, permitting hierarchical searches of job matches first using competencies and then deeper processing of a competency-matched subset using KSATs.
- A third dimension of the system in the form of a training program database that would describe the competencies and KSATs learned in various training programs. This would parallel the present labor market position database by which clients are matched with potential jobs; recommendations for training would be produced by comparing competencies, KSATs, and training histories to training programs oriented toward particular career progressions.
- Automatic updating of the system, whereby job availability and training program files are compared to client files and coun-

selors are informed of new potential matches and opportunities for clients. This takes advantage of the continually changing contents of the databases.

Future Developments and Applications to Defense Downsizing

Defense facility closures will proceed throughout much of the remainder of this decade. With a third base-closure list slated for release in 1995, a need for defense worker transition services coordinated at the national level becomes increasingly apparent. Based on our experiences working with the multiple players and constituents in the Delaware Valley region, we offer several suggestions for creating an effective STEP-UP-like system for use throughout the country.

As described above, a base closure occurs in a politically charged arena, with many players independently pursuing often conflicting initiatives. Each works according to the usual framework—politicians grandstand, bureaucrats form committees, and researchers conduct surveys and process data. There is a tendency for clients and customers to get lost in the shuffle. In our view, the customers who should be served in a base closure are, first, the workers being displaced and, second, employers in the surrounding community who account for its economic vitality.

The first and perhaps most critical step in developing a career counseling and job placement process is to identify clients and customers and to define their needs. This requires working closely with them from the earliest project stages. As a corollary, other constituents, some of whom claim to represent clients, should be consulted and perhaps even brought into the project-planning loop, but their priorities should be considered as secondary to the needs of the clients and customers. The reality is that whatever transition support system is developed, it will not satisfy all constituents who claim an interest in it. It is therefore essential to design a system according to the needs of the primary constituents.

The amount of information that must be assembled in constructing a responsive system, the variety of sources of information, and the need for timely information complicate the development process. Our experience with STEP-UP suggests several avenues to follow to increase efficiency. Because much of the needed information resides outside the boundaries of the downsizing organization, employers and educational institutions should be included as transition partners from the beginning. They have a vested interest in the economic vitality of their community and should therefore assume a proactive role. With partners included early, the project could proceed with minimal time spent in establishing and maintaining contacts. Information about job openings, requirements of available positions, availability of and prerequisites for training classes, and so on, could be transmitted at the initiative of partners instead of having to be procured by project researchers. Cutting-edge technologies such as touch-tone telephone survey technology and electronic mail could be used by partners, at their initiative, to periodically review and update the information they provide. The burden of system maintenance would be shared by all users and constituents.

To better meet the needs of clients, a next generation STEP-UP could be designed as a two-tier system. At the first tier, clients could work directly with the system, assisted by a built-in intelligent tutor, help menus, and so on. They could review their training histories and competencies and KSAs associated with past jobs, and respond to a vocational interest survey. They could explore various career and job options, requesting competencies and KSAs associated with jobs and occupations, review econometric forecasts for job openings, projections of the available labor supply for occupations, and so on. The system could guide them in conducting their own risk appraisals and in thinking about realistic options.

Clients could then move to a second-tier application of the system, during which they would confer with a counselor about possible career direction and job-search strategies. The role of the counselor would be to assist the client in the self-assessment process, and to interpret career, occupation, and job information available through the system. The counselor would guide the client in making choices about training and job-search options.

The philosophy behind such a two-tier system would depart from that underlying STEP-UP, which placed the counselor in the key service role and permitted no direct access to databases by the client. The advantages of a two-tier system would come in more efficient use of counselor's time, reserving counselor-client contact for a later stage of the outplacement process, and in greater flexibility and control by the client in outplacement services accessed.

This decentralized approach to transition counseling system design, with substantial input from employers, educators, and clients, as well as from system designers, poses the challenge of making the system foolproof, user-friendly to the point that data input errors are very unlikely and easily corrected. This would provide the advantage to designers of removing some of their burden for ensuring the comprehensiveness and timeliness of the databases, a very time-consuming process in STEP-UP's case.

The next generation STEP-UP-like system should be designed as an "intelligent" system, with expert and perhaps artificial intelligence capabilities. Such a system could anticipate the needs of clients, and make informed judgments about how best to assist them. It might, for example, alert individual clients to new employment or training opportunities as these arise, using individual client profiles previously stored to identify matches between clients and new opportunities.

It could also assist designers by reducing the arduous data entry task. For example, as employers announce job openings, they could be presented with a dictionary of perhaps a hundred competency areas (see above). They would indicate the competencies associated with the job opening (typically five to ten). The program would then automatically assign KSATs to the job, based on its structure of work assumptions. These would be presented to the employer for review of relevance and comprehensiveness. This approach would greatly circumvent the several thousand hours of KSAT coding that went into the development of STEP-UP. (A working prototype demonstrating the feasibility of this approach was included in the last version of STEP-UP delivered to the PNSB). To be maximally useful, the system could be networked to career transition centers nationwide.

If we examine the potential contribution of human resource initiatives in the rapidly changing economy of the 1990s, the implications of several trends are apparent. As organizations "right-size" and "reengineer," investing in human capital is an important means by which employers acquire and maintain competitive advantage. A highly trained and flexible workforce is essential to leading-edge products and technologies. The flip side of this coin is that individuals must assume greater responsibility for managing their careers and maintaining their value on the job market. These trends imply need for greater flexibility and responsiveness in human resource services as well. STEP-UP represents a merging of traditional job analysis, individual assessment, and career counseling. This interdisciplinary approach to human resource technology is likely to increase in importance with time.

References

Bowers, K. S. (1973). Situationism in psychology: An analysis and critique. *Psychological Review, 80,* 307–336.

Coopers & Lybrand. (1993). *Diversification plan for the Philadelphia Naval Shipyard.* Philadelphia: Coopers & Lybrand.

Dalton v. Specter. 114 S. Ct. 1719 (1994).

Dawis, R. V. (1991). Vocational interests, values, and preferences. In M. D. Dunnette & L. M. Hough (Eds.), *Handbook of industrial and organizational psychology* (2nd ed., vol. 2, pp. 833–871). Palo Alto, CA: Consulting Psychologists Press.

Dawis, R. V., & Lofquist, L. H. (1984). *A psychological theory of work adjustment.* Minneapolis: University of Minnesota Press.

Holcomb, H. J. (1994, March 21). Plotting a course for Navy shipyard. *Philadelphia Inquirer,* pp. D1, D2.

Hollman, L. (1993, January 31). Facing a nightmare, the shipyard has a dream. *Philadelphia Inquirer,* pp. C1, C9.

Muchinsky, P. M., & Monahan, C. J. (1987). What is person-environment congruence? Supplementary versus complementary models of fit. *Journal of Vocational Behavior, 31,* 268–277.

Pervin, L. A. (1968). Performance and satisfaction as a function of individual-environment fit. *Psychological Bulletin, 69,* 56–68.

Quinn, J. (1994, January 7). Anchors away. *Philadelphia City Paper,* pp. 14–18.

CHAPTER 13

Coping with Job Loss
The Collective Activism of Community-Based Job Creation and Retention Strategies

Carrie R. Leana
Daniel C. Feldman

The topic of job loss has received considerable attention by researchers over the past decade. Most of the studies have concentrated on the effects of unemployment on individuals' psychological and physical health, and strongly suggest that job loss can have powerful negative effects on individuals (Kessler, Turner, & House, 1989; Leana & Feldman, 1990; Payne & Hartley, 1987).

Because of these negative effects, many researchers have focused their attention on factors that might predict or assist laid-off workers in finding reemployment. This research has generally been of two types. First, there are studies that have examined the effects of corporate- and government-sponsored training and outplacement programs aimed at assisting the unemployed in finding new jobs (such as Caplan, Vinokur, Price, & van Ryn, 1989). A second set of studies has examined the effects of personal and demographic characteristics such as age (Shapiro & Sandell, 1985), gender (Rosen, 1987), and personal expectations (Kanfer & Hulin, 1985) on the ability of individuals to find new employment.

Although there is great variety in the methods and samples used in this research, the studies share a common focus on individual job-search strategies and reemployment efforts. This chapter takes a somewhat different focus. We examine laid-off employees who engage in collective activities to create new jobs in their communities and to prevent further layoffs. Particularly in communities hard-hit by business downsizing and plant closings, individuals have joined together in various activities aimed at stopping plant closings and attracting new employment to an area.

This chapter focuses on collective activism as a mechanism for individuals to cope with job loss. First, we describe collective activism and provide examples from a geographic area that has been hard hit by plant closings. Second, we discuss this form of coping from the individual's perspective, using Lazarus and Folkman's (1984) stress-coping framework. Third, we present empirical data from two studies that highlight the predictors and outcomes of individuals' involvement in collective activism. Finally, we discuss the implications of our findings for the research on both individual and institutional coping with job loss.

Collective Activism as a Response to Plant Closings

The past two decades have been marked by economic uncertainty for much of the American workforce. The 1980s saw a drastic reduction in blue-collar employment in basic industries such as steel and automobile manufacturing. The 1990s are shaping up to be the decade of white-collar job cuts as professional staff and managers at all levels are facing the same sort of downsizing that blue-collar workers experienced in the 1980s.

When large-scale layoffs are concentrated in specific geographic areas, the negative effects reverberate beyond the laid-off individuals and their families. Many communities that have experienced the closing or significant downsizing of large-scale facilities have been economically devastated. The departure of major corporate taxpayers and the resultant depletion of municipal revenues, when coupled with the increased demands placed on public services by the growing ranks of the unemployed, severely strain the weakened resources of these communities. While federal and state-funded programs are often available to assist such communities, the level and type of support often fall short of community needs. Consequently, it is not unusual for new organizations to spring up whose mission is to address the problems. They are typically grass-roots organizations and have as their base the individuals who have lost their jobs as a result of the plant closing or downsizing.

The nature of such organizations, and the involvement of individuals in collective activism, can be understood by focusing on community activism efforts within a specific geographic region. The Monongahela Valley, located just outside Pittsburgh, Pennsylvania, was hard hit by the decline in the manufacturing sector in the 1980s. The dominant industry in the region was steel production; nearly one hundred thousand manufacturing jobs, many of them in the steel industry, were lost in the region during the 1980s. In response to the problems created by this drastic decline in employment, several grass-roots community groups were formed.

One of the first organizations to get actively involved in challenging plant closings in the region was the Tri-State Conference on Steel (Leana & Feldman, 1992). The Tri-State Conference describes itself as a labor-religious-community coalition made up of activists from all three domains. Although its current agenda encompasses a wide range of issues and projects involving economic justice and community control, its initial focus was on plant closings, specifically trying to prevent corporations from moving or closing steel facilities in the region (McCollister & Stout, 1990). Perhaps its most widely known activity was the campaign to save the "Dorothy Six" blast furnace at a U.S. Steel facility—a campaign that consisted not only of rallies and plant-gate vigils but also the mobilization of union, governmental, and community action group support for economic feasibility studies.

While the campaign to save Dorothy Six ultimately failed, the Tri-State Conference did spur the subsequent creation of the Steel Valley Authority, a state-chartered industrial jobs authority vested with the state's power of eminent domain. The Steel Valley Authority has overseen the completion of numerous feasibility studies for ESOP-financed restarts of local steel facilities. Other recent projects have included the start-up of an employee-owned commercial bakery in place of a closed facility and the implementation of an "Early Warnings Network" to anticipate plant closings well before the sixty-day notification period required by the federal Workers' Adjustment and Retraining Notification (WARN) Act.

Still other agencies, such as the Rainbow Kitchen and Homestead Unemployed Center, organized laid-off workers to provide direct services to the unemployed in the form of financial and psychological counseling, health care, and groceries and hot lunches for their children (Serrin, 1992). These activities, along with the political tactics of groups such as the Tri-State Conference, are usually described in terms of their aggregate effects on social and economic conditions. They can also be conceptualized from a psychological perspective, however, as a way for individuals to cope with the stress of job loss.

Collective Activism from the Individual's Perspective

Coping refers to active attempts by individuals to establish new routines after they have experienced a stressful event. In the case of those who have lost their jobs, coping behaviors are attempts to gain reemployment or to regain some semblance of psychological well-being after the job loss (Leana & Feldman, 1992). Lazarus and Folkman (1984) have described two broad classes of coping behavior: problem-focused coping and symptom-focused coping.

Problem-focused coping is aimed at controlling or eliminating the stress itself; in the context of job loss, this type of activity would be geared toward finding a new job and thus correcting the state of unemployment. Symptom-focused coping refers to activities aimed at alleviating the negative consequences of a stressful event. Examples of symptom-focused coping are engaging in social interaction to reduce feelings of isolation and depression commonly associated with job loss or applying for government financial assistance to relieve the economic distress. Such activities do not directly address the source of the problem but rather concentrate on alleviating its symptoms. In the context of job loss, the individual's employment situation may not change as a result of symptom-focused coping behavior but psychological well-being may be enhanced.

In previous research, we have described collective activism as a form of symptom-focused coping (Leana & Feldman, 1990; 1992). The reasons for this are twofold. First, although collective activism such as that promoted by the Tri-State Conference in Pittsburgh may, in the end, result in job creation or retention, these potential benefits are typically realized only over the very long term, if at all. Moreover, any jobs that might be created will not necessarily be obtained by those individuals most involved in such activities.

Second, it is reasonable to assume that many people who become involved in collective job-creation efforts do so at least in part, and perhaps primarily, as a way to address the symptoms of stress that accompany job loss. Social isolation, anger, depression, and a loss of direction and routine are commonly reported in studies of the effects of job loss. Engaging in group activities such as rallies and lobbying can not only restore people's feelings of control and dignity, but can also provide social interaction and a sense of purpose to people who have traditionally relied upon their jobs for such experiences. As Jahoda (1982) has suggested, work provides not only "manifest" functions for individuals in the form of financial compensation but also what she terms "latent" functions such as providing structure, routine, and opportunities for social interaction. Collective activism, ranging from lobbying government officials to protesting the closing of facilities, will not provide the manifest (financial) benefits of work but may substitute for it in fulfilling many of work's latent functions.

A question that is of great practical interest to grass-roots organizers concerns why individuals choose to become involved in collective activism. Such a question is also of interest to researchers who examine individual coping behavior in response to job loss. We have conducted two studies that address this question. These studies were carried out at different times and with different samples, but both examine the predictors and consequences of individual involvement in community activism efforts. Both studies were conducted in the Pittsburgh region, a geographic area that has not only experienced a large number of plant closings and downsizings but has also seen a good deal of collective activism in reaction to job loss. Several findings from these studies are pertinent to our discussion of collective activism as a way for individuals to cope with job loss.

Predictors of Collective Activism by Individuals

In two surveys administered to different groups of laid-off steelworkers in the Pittsburgh region, we examined predictors of how individuals coped with job loss. Collective activism was measured by individuals' responses to such items as: "Since my layoff, I have become active in community efforts to aid the unemployed in the area" and "Since my layoff, I have become active in efforts to stop further plant closings in the area."

In the first study, we surveyed two hundred steelworkers from U.S. Steel's Homestead plant. They had lost their jobs over a twelve-month period. They were the last to be let go before the plant closing and had thus enjoyed substantial seniority and job stability. All were members of the United Steelworkers of America union. On average, they had spent twenty-five years working full time, twenty-three of those years with U.S. Steel (now USX). At the time of our study, the Homestead group had been out of work an average of nine months; only 12 percent had found new jobs. This study was cross-sectional in nature.

The second study was longitudinal in nature; the predictors were measured nine months before the assessment of collective activism. In this study, the participants were sixty-two steelworkers who were laid off when a smaller steel plant was closed. As in the Homestead study, nearly all of the participants were male (98 percent), Caucasian (93 percent), long-term residents of the region (average residency of thirty-four years), high school graduates (84 percent), and married (78 percent). (Complete information on the sample, study design, measures, and statistical analyses for the cross-sectional study is provided in Leana & Feldman [1990, 1992], and for the longitudinal study in Leana & Feldman [1994] and Tan, Leana, & Feldman [1994]).

In both studies we examined individual differences and situational factors as possible predictors of collective activism. Some predictors were examined in both studies while others appeared in just one of the two studies.

The individual differences examined were demographic factors (such as age, education, and the number of dependents); career variables (such as job tenure and reported attachment to the profession); and psychological adjustment, as defined by Lazarus and Folkman (1984) as efforts to adapt to stress cognitively through such processes as redefining the problem or avoiding thinking about it. Here we used items from Folkman, Lazarus, Dunkel-Schetter, De Longis, and Gruen's (1986) revised Ways of

Coping questionnaire, which assessed seeking social support ("In reacting to my layoff, I accepted sympathy and understanding from someone"), planful problem solving ("In reacting to my layoff, I drew up a plan of action"), positive reappraisal of the situation ("In reacting to my layoff, I have rediscovered what is important in life"), psychological distancing ("In reacting to my layoff, I have made light of the situation—tried not to get too serious about it"), and escapism ("In reacting to my layoff, I have tried to forget the whole thing").

The situational characteristics examined were: the level of severance pay and benefits received by the individual, and the level of disruption the individual reported in four areas: livelihood, career, family relations, and daily routines.

Table 13.1 shows the correlations between collective activism and the predictors measured in each study. As shown in the table, the cross-sectional study found collective activism to be negatively correlated with age and job tenure, and positively correlated with educational level and severance pay. A larger number of predictors were measured in the longitudinal study; moreover, the predictors were measured nine months before the assessment of collective activism so the results should be relatively free of percept-percept bias. In this study, support of relatives, attachment to profession, and psychological adjustment (specifically, through social support, planful problem solving, and positive reappraisal) were significantly correlated with collective activism. Perceived disruption to daily routines was also a significant predictor.

In a regression analysis of all predictors in the longitudinal study (Table 13.2), the adjusted R square was .39; age, psychological adjustment through social support and distancing, and perceived disruption to daily routines each explained a significant portion of the variance in collective activism.

These results suggest that the demographic profile of a person likely to get involved in collective activism is that of a younger, more educated individual with less job tenure yet some cushion in the form of severance pay and benefits. The longitudinal study further suggests that activists are those who initially adjust to job loss through seeking social support, planful problem solving, and positive reappraisal of their situations. They may also be less likely to engage in avoidance in the form of distancing and escapism.

Table 13.1. Predictors of Community Activism.

	Longitudinal Study	Cross-Sectional Study
I. Individual Differences		
A. Demographics		
1. Age	-.07	-.27**
2. Education	.20	.27**
3. Number of children	.08	
4. Support other relatives	.28*	
B. Career		
1. Job tenure	-.16	-.33**
2. Attachment to profession	.29*	-.11
C. Psychological Adjustment		
1. Social support	.38**	
2. Planful problem solving	.29*	
3. Positive reappraisal	.38**	
4. Distancing	-.17	
5. Escapism	-.10	
II. Situational Characteristics		
A. Extended pay and benefits	.18	.20**
B. Level of disruption		
1. Livelihood	.07	
2. Career	.13	
3. Family	.14	
4. Routines	.28*	

*$p < .05$

**$p < .01$

Finally, someone who feels a good deal of disruption to personal routine on account of job loss also seems to be more likely to cope through collective activism.

Outcomes of Collective Activism for Individuals

Table 13.3 shows the correlations between collective activism and several psychological and attitudinal measures. As shown in the table, in the cross-sectional study collective activism was significantly correlated with self-esteem, physiological distress, and perceived job prospects. In the longitudinal study, collective activism

Table 13.2. Multiple Regression Results of Predictors of Community Activism (Longitudinal Study).

Predictor	Beta	ΔR^2
I. Individual Differences		
A. Demographic and career variables		
1. Age	-.25	.03
2. Education	.06	.00
3. Number of dependents	.16	.02
4. Tenure	-.24	.04
5. Attachment to profession	.16	.02
B. Psychological adjustment		
1. Social support	.34	.05
2. Planful problem solving	.14	.01
3. Positive reappraisal	.20	.14
4. Distancing	-.32	.04
5. Escapism	-.10	.00
II. Situational Characteristics		.14
A. Extended pay	-.03	.00
B. Level of disruption		
1. Livelihood	-.07	.00
2. Career	-.09	.02
3. Family	-.20	.02
4. Daily routine	.56	.10
R^2		.49
Adjusted R^2		.39
$F(10,61)$	3.39**	

**$p < .01$

was strongly correlated with enhanced feelings of control, self-esteem, and optimism. These results suggest that involvement in collective activism can have quite positive effects on the mood and outlook of job losers.

The only negative finding—the positive correlation between activism and physiological distress in the cross-sectional study—was quite weak and not supported in the longitudinal study. Thus, the studies show that collective activism can be quite beneficial to individuals' esteem, optimism, and feelings of control. These factors

Table 13.3. Outcomes of Community Activism.

	Longitudinal Study	Cross-Sectional Study
1. Depression	-.10	.11
2. Anxiety	-.03	
3. Feelings of control	.71**	
4. Self-esteem	.46**	.13*
5. Optimism	.72**	
6. Psychological distress	-.10	.08
7. Physiological distress	.05	.13*
8. Perceived job prospects	.08	.22**
9. Life satisfaction	.08	-.08

*$p < .05$
**$p < .01$

are potentially important not only for dealing with job loss but also for people's ability to engage in problem-focused behaviors, such as job search, which often require a great deal of psychological stamina (Leana & Feldman, 1992).

Discussion

For researchers interested in individual adjustment to job loss, the results regarding outcomes associated with collective activism are most interesting. In the studies, individual coping through collective activism was strongly correlated with feelings of control, self-esteem, and general optimism. In addition, the cross-sectional study found that activists tended to have much more optimistic assessments of their future job prospects. These findings suggest that collective activism may be as helpful to individual esteem building and confidence as are more traditional methods such as individually focused training in job skills, job-search methods, and so on. To the extent that these feelings of optimism, control, and esteem carry over to other aspects of laid-off workers' lives, they may help people maintain their confidence and direction through difficult financial circumstances and often lengthy and discouraging job-search efforts. In these regards, the spillover benefits of collective activism may be quite substantial and warrant closer investigation.

These findings may also be interesting to organizers attempting to attract individuals to collective job-creation and retention efforts. For organizers, the profile of a potential activist is a job loser who is relatively educated, low in seniority in the previous job, and with some financial cushion in the form of extended pay and benefits. This person is also rather concerned about no longer having a daily routine as a result of job loss, and focuses initial adjustment on social support, problem solving, and positive reappraisal of the situation. This person does not try to avoid problems through distancing and escapism.

This research also has some implications for human resource (HR) professionals although these are much less direct. In many ways and for many reasons, HR professionals have largely been tangential to community activism efforts. As representatives of the organizations engaging in layoffs, they may not be readily accepted as trustworthy or likable experts by displaced workers themselves. Moreover, because they are employees of the organizations engaging in layoffs, anything they do to help organize efforts to stop plant closings or erect exit barriers may be seen as disloyal or disrespectful. Thus, by default and by design, many HR professionals have not been directly involved in community activism efforts.

There are some more indirect ways, however, in which they may be able to become involved in job-creation strategies and community activism. As part of the outplacement process, HR professionals may be able to steer displaced workers to local community support groups that would benefit them. Also, many HR professionals are closely networked to other HR professionals in their home communities. Thus, they may be in a unique position of having insider information on which companies are hiring and what types of positions are currently available. Another way in which HR professionals can contribute is volunteering to help displaced workers in community support groups with concrete assistance in job hunting, resume preparation, and interviewing skills; these activities do not represent any conflict of interest with their current employers. In addition, HR professionals can be advocates within their own companies to sponsor retraining programs through local community colleges or vocational training programs and to organize job fairs. Finally, HR professionals can be advocates within their own companies of making charitable contributions to community groups that provide social support and financial aid services to displaced workers.

Future Research

Our research findings on collective activism suggest some interesting directions for future research. Much of the research to date on coping with job loss and reemployment focuses only on individual job-creation efforts, ranging from established approaches such as training in resume writing, job-search strategies, and esteem-building programs, as well as through more recent efforts such as pursuing internships and temporary employment in hopes of creating permanent jobs. This research has provided a substantial and important body of knowledge on assisting the unemployed to find reemployment.

The examination of coping with job loss through collective activism that is reported here complements our already considerable knowledge of coping through individual reemployment strategies. It suggests that such activism, in addition to its direct benefits if jobs are created or maintained through the collective political strategies, may also indirectly help people in their personal job-search efforts by helping them to maintain the confidence and esteem that are so necessary to finding successful reemployment.

References

Caplan, R. D., Vinokur, A. D., Price, R. H., & van Ryn, M. (1989). Job seeking, reemployment, and mental health: A randomized field experiment in coping with job loss. *Journal of Applied Psychology, 74,* 759–769.

Folkman, S., Lazarus, R. S., Dunkel-Schetter, C., De Longis, A., & Gruen, R. (1986). The dynamics of a stressful encounter: Cognitive appraisal, coping, and encounter outcomes. *Journal of Personality and Social Psychology, 50,* 992–1003.

Jahoda, M. (1982). *Employment and unemployment.* London: Cambridge University Press.

Kanfer, R., & Hulin, C. (1985). Objective and subjective underemployment relationships to job satisfaction. *Journal of Business Research, 22,* 211–218.

Kessler, R. C., Turner, J. B., & House, J. S. (1989). Unemployment, reemployment, and emotional functioning in a community sample. *American Sociological Review, 54,* 648–657.

Lazarus, R. S., & Folkman, S. (1984). *Stress, appraisal and coping.* New York: Springer.

Leana, C. R., & Feldman, D. C. (1990). Individual responses to job loss: Empirical findings from two field studies. *Human Relations, 43,* 1155–1181.

Leana, C. R., & Feldman, D. C. (1992). *Coping with job loss: How individuals, organizations and communities respond to layoffs.* New York: Lexington.

Leana, C. R., & Feldman, D. C. (1994). Finding new jobs after a plant closing: Predictors and outcomes of the occurrence and quality of reemployment. Unpublished manuscript.

McCollister, C., & Stout, M. (1990). Tri-State Conference on Steel: Ten years of labor-community alliances. In J. Brecker & T. Costello (Eds.), *Building bridges: The emerging grassroots coalition of labor and community* (pp. 106–112). New York: Monthly Review Press.

Payne, R., & Hartley, J. (1987). A test of a model for explaining the affective experience of unemployed men. *Journal of Occupational Psychology, 60,* 31–47.

Rosen, E. (1987). *Bitter choices: Blue-collar women in and out of work.* Chicago: University of Chicago Press.

Serrin, W. (1992). *Homestead: The glory and tragedy of an American steel town.* New York: Times Books.

Shapiro, D., & Sandell, S. (1985). Age discrimination in wages and displaced older men. *Southern Economic Journal, 52,* 90–102.

Tan, G., Leana, C. R., & Feldman, D. C. (1994). A longitudinal study of predictors of job loss coping strategies. *Academy of Management Best Paper Proceedings.*

Name Index

Subject Index

A

Academy of Management, 62

Activism. *See* Collective activism

Advanced Research Projects Agency, 112, 119

Aetna, and introspection, 65

Age: and contingent workforce, 136–137; and discrimination issues, 23; and job search skills, 200, 201; and retraining, 111

Agile Manufacturing Enterprise Forum (AMEF), 221, 227

AIL, displaced engineers from, 235, 238

American Management Association, 53, 108, 109, 119

Arizona Public Service (APS), and work-life balance, 62–63

Asia, joint ventures in, 19–20

AT&T: Alliance Learning Center (ALC) of, 63–64; contingent workforce at, 144–163; dilemma at, 144–146; and divestiture, 51; extended compensation option (ECO) at, 161–162; and introspection training, 65; and job creation, 188; programs at, 145–146; Resource Link at, 146–164; resource management center (RMC) at, 144

Attribution theory: and employee responsibility, 64; and entrepreneurs, 175

B

Babson College, entrepreneurship classes at, 181

Baby boom generation: and career development, 57–58; and obsolescence, 108

Base Closure and Realignment Act of 1990, 258–259

Benefits: and contingent employees, 123, 130–131; extent of, 12

Brookhaven National Laboratory, and retraining, 247

Burdine's, contingent workers at, 135

Burger King, contingent workers at, 135

C

Career counseling, in retraining, 239–241, 247, 249–250

Career development; aspects of, 27–101; background on, 27–30; changing paradigm for, 56–59; content-based activities for, 60–63; for contingent workforce, 137–138; in downsizing organizations, 49–70; human resource development for, 71–101; innovations in, 59–68; and level of control, 61–62; position changes for, 60–61; process-based activities for, 63–66; and promotion rates in growing organizations, 31–48; resources for, 67; as self-affirmation, 56–59; and work environment, 66–68